M000190236

Panagiotis Dimitrakis specialises in Cold War and intelligence history and obtained his PhD in War Studies at King's College London. He is the author of *Greece and the English: British Diplomacy and the Kings of Greece* (2009); *Military Intelligence in Cyprus: From the Great War to Middle East Crises* (2010); *Greek Military Intelligence and the Crescent: Estimating the Turkish Threat – Crises, Leadership and Strategic Analyses, 1974–1996* (2010); *Failed Alliances of the Cold War: Britain's Strategy and Ambitions in Asia and the Middle East* (2012).

THE SECRET WAR IN AFGHANISTAN

The Soviet Union, China and the Role of
Anglo-American Intelligence

PANAGIOTIS DIMITRAKIS

I.B. TAURIS

LONDON • NEW YORK • OXFORD • NEW DELHI • SYDNEY

I.B. TAURIS
Bloomsbury Publishing Plc
50 Bedford Square, London, WC1B 3DP, UK
1385 Broadway, New York, NY 10018, USA
29 Earlsfort Terrace, Dublin 2, Ireland

BLOOMSBURY, I.B. TAURIS and the I.B. Tauris logo
are trademarks of Bloomsbury Publishing Plc

First published in Great Britain 2013
This paperback edition published 2022

For legal purposes the Acknowledgements on p. viii constitute an
extension of this copyright page.
The assistance of the Iran Heritage Foundation is gratefully acknowledged.

ISBN: HB: 978-1-7807-6419-1
PB: 978-0-7556-4953-2
ePDF: 978-0-8577-2243-0
eBook: 978-0-8577-3377-1

Series: Library of Middle Eastern History, vol. 39

Typest by Newgen Publishers, Chennai

CONTENTS

LIST OF ABBREVIATIONS

ASEAN	Association of Southeast Asian Nations
AGSA	Department of Defence of the Interests of Afghanistan (pre-1979)
CENTCOM	Central Command (US)
CIA	Central Intelligence Agency
CWIHP	Cold War International History Project
DIA	Defense Intelligence Agency (US)
DShK	Heavy Machine Gun (Soviet Union)
FCO	Foreign and Commonwealth Office
FCD	First Chief Directorate (KGB)
FRG	Federal Republic of Germany
GDR	German Democratic Republic
GID	General Intelligence Directorate (Saudi Arabia)
GRU	Soviet Military Intelligence
INF	Intermediate-Range Nuclear Forces Treaty (1987)
ISI	Inter-Services Intelligence Directorate (Pakistan)
JIC	Joint Intelligence Committee (UK)
KGB	Committee of State Security
KHAD	Afghan Government Intelligence Agency (after 1979)
MI6/SIS	Secret Intelligence Service (UK)
NATO	North Atlantic Treaty Organisation
NSA	National Security Agency
NSC	National Security Council (US)

PCC	Politburo Central Committee (Soviet Union)
PDPA	People's-Democratic Party of Afghanistan
RPG	Rocket Propelled Grenade (Soviet Union)
SAS	Special Air Service (UK)
SALT II	Strategic Arms Limitation Treaty II
SEZs	Special Economic Zones (China)
Spetsnaz	Soviet Special Forces
Stasi	East German Secret Service
USSR	Union of Socialist Soviet Republics

ACKNOWLEDGMENTS

Special thanks go to Rosalie Spire for her research aid as well as to Joe Maiolo, Professor of International History at King's College London for helping me with key sources. The staff at the National Archives, Kew deserves a special mention as well as Olympia Wood, John Wood and Peter Barnes for their help in copy-editing. I would like also to thank my editor Tomasz Hoskins at I.B.Tauris for believing in this monograph and working towards its publication. Finally, I owe a great debt to my family for their support.

PREFACE

Afghanistan has been and remains a country to which foreign armies have always seemed to return, from the time of Alexander the Great to today's NATO counter-insurgency operations in support of the Afghan government. This far-distant country of inhospitable mountains and desert plains has never enjoyed strategic resources such as oil, and was deemed valuable only in connection with the 'Great Game' – the Anglo-Russian rivalry in the nineteenth and early twentieth centuries. Throughout the centuries the different tribes and ethnic groups inhabiting Afghanistan – fragmented, and undisciplined by central authority – could not readily understand why foreign peoples were so much interested in their poor lands. Eventually, however, they would turn guerrilla warfare from an art into a science – having grasped its elements only too well.

The Cold War affected Afghanistan's importance vis-à-vis the superpowers and their allies. To what extent, however, this country – seemingly a member of the non-aligned movement, but by the late 1970s in reality a protégé of the Soviet Union – was of genuine strategic value to the West remains debatable, for historians and scholars of international relations alike. Indeed, recently declassified UK and US archives show that, in the eyes of British and American planners, Afghanistan's strategic value was limited. Yet the Soviet incursion there in 1979 – which was seen by the West as following the pattern of two earlier such invasions, Hungary in 1956 and Czechoslovakia in 1968 – induced Western diplomacy and intelligence services to take an active interest in helping the Islamic guerrillas to oust the Soviets. In an irony of history, the unintended consequence was the rise of Osama bin Laden and al-Qaida. The Arab (and Chinese) proverb 'the enemy of my enemy is my friend' may be the most deceptive and dangerous assumption for strategists keen to take advantage of a conflict.

Afghanistan put a mark (or a stain) on leaders' tenures: Leonid Brezhnev, the USSR's chairman, crippled by illness and now frustrated with dealing with Afghan leaders who were fighting and killing each other in successive coups, took the fateful decision to invade in 1979. He died three years later, while Russian troops performed miserably against the then equally badly led Mujahedeen. Yuri Andropov, the first KGB chairman to rise to become head of the USSR, and Konstantin Chernenko, who succeeded him, were too old to change their mentality and opt courageously for a rapid exit from Afghanistan. Andropov himself was obsessed with the possibility of a surprise US nuclear strike. Ironically, while the White House was informed of these paranoid fears, the CIA discounted their impact on Soviet foreign and defence policy. It was left to Mikhail Gorbachev to end the war in Afghanistan, to complete the Soviet withdrawal in February 1989, and two years later to seal the fate of the USSR itself.

President Jimmy Carter, a strong supporter of détente who always sought to bring respect for international law and human rights into US–Soviet relations, was surprised and confused by the events in Afghanistan; the fall of the Shah of Iran in January 1979, and later the taking hostage of the US Embassy staff in Tehran, shattered his profile as a superpower leader. Americans realised that the administration (with the world's largest annual defence and intelligence budget) could do nothing to save the hostages from the hands of the new fundamentalist regime in Iran. This feeling of helplessness led Carter into the desperate decision to give the green light to a catastrophic military rescue mission, costing the lives of eight servicemen and failing to release a single hostage. Predictably, he would lose the presidential election of 1980. Ronald Reagan took over, unleashing – in his second term – the full-scale secret arming of the Mujahedeen's war against the occupiers of Afghanistan, while attempting, in vain, to convince the Islamist groups to view the Americans as allies. Nonetheless, the

Afghan guerrillas and their allies proved themselves sufficiently astute to secure sophisticated Stinger missiles from the US, while continuing to hate their benefactors.

For Margaret Thatcher, having just taken office in May 1979 as the first woman prime minister of Britain and determined to introduce a new style of leadership, the December invasion was her first serious international security crisis. While learning the ropes in diplomacy, defence and intelligence matters, Thatcher provided unquestioning support for US policies and strategies towards the Soviet Union.

As for Deng Xiaoping, the de facto leader of China, and his supporters, the conflict provided a great opportunity to improve relations with America, following the brief Sino-Vietnamese war (17 February–16 March 1979). China joined the arming of the rebels in 1980 (well before a deal was struck for the Americans to buy Chinese-made weapons and turn them over to Pakistan, to be passed on to the Mujahedeen). By 1982 the Chinese, shrewd traders and long-term strategists, had confidently opened the door to a parallel improvement of relations with the USSR. In the meantime, after the euphoria of 1979–80, Sino-American relations cooled in the wake of the American arms sales to Taiwan. Nonetheless, China continued to sell weapons to the Afghan rebels, and to seek commercial and economic deals with the US, including the acquisition of much-needed advanced technology for industry and defence.

This book gives the first detailed, archive-based account of Anglo-American secret intelligence and diplomacy during the invasion and occupation of Afghanistan, narrating and analysing contemporary perceptions and assessing their accuracy, examining the evolving attitudes and policies of London and Washington, and discussing covert operations, espionage and the secret collaboration with China. The author's main task has been the assessment and evaluation of contemporary intelligence reports, cross-referenced with the opponents' reports and views.

Secret intelligence played a major part in decision-making in the top echelons of government, but was notably unsuccessful at the start of the story: another intelligence failure, with operatives writing reports dismissing their own responsibility, and scholars left to mine a rich vein of debate for years to come. In the tumultuous year of 1979, with the Iranian revolution, the hostage-taking at the US Embassy in Tehran and the crisis in Cambodia, Anglo-American intelligence failed to predict the invasion, save a last-minute warning by the NSA which was, anyway, erroneously discounted by the CIA and the Defense Intelligence Agency (DIA). The NSA, meanwhile, predicted a massive Soviet deployment to help the regime defeat the rebels, rather than the overthrow of the communist Afghan president.

However, in 1980 secret intelligence helped to avoid escalation and a nervous response after the initial surprise, while the international media ominously declared the death of détente and the advent of a Soviet thrust into Asia in the 1980s. London soon understood the real proportions of the Soviet bid for Afghanistan, rather than those imagined by some American hawks. In the first post-invasion days, Carter and his cabinet were debating optimum diplomatic strategy against the Soviet Union, but – given the reassuring secret intelligence – discounted any likelihood of the Soviets wanting to upset the regional balance of power by a new invasion of Pakistan or Iran. Nonetheless, the Carter administration failed to calm the nations of the non-aligned bloc, which – almost in a state of panic – tabled a resolution at the General Assembly condemning the invasion. Eventually, in the spring of 1980, NATO members were reassured by Washington that the Soviets would concentrate their efforts in Afghanistan rather than seeking to destabilise the subcontinent by thrusting towards Pakistan or Iran, in a bid to reach the Gulf or the Indian Ocean.

Covert action in Afghanistan was the only means available to Anglo-American intelligence to help the Afghan rebels without escalating the conflict. The KGB responded with a sustained campaign to shake the regime of Pakistani dictator Zia ul-Haq, whose intelligence services supported the Mujahedeen and distributed the arms provided and paid for by the United States, Britain, Saudi Arabia, China, Egypt and other Middle Eastern countries, while Islamabad shrewdly took advantage of the developing US strategy and the gradual involvement of the CIA. The KGB employed elaborate ploys to foment civil war among the Afghan tribes, and on many occasions succeeded. Meanwhile, British intelligence and the SAS remained the hidden junior partners, lacking any considerable financial resources, but keen from early 1980 onwards to undertake dangerous reconnaissance missions and to establish independent channels of communication with Islamist groups.

Today, after the attacks of 11 September 2001 in New York and of 7 July 2005 in London, and the realisation of the global threat of Islamic terrorism (despite the death of Osama bin Laden in the 1 May 2011 Navy Seal raid on his mansion near Islamabad), we see that the Afghan story is full of ironies, erroneous beliefs and inaccurate estimates. If knowledge is power, then Anglo-American and Soviet intelligence services and leadership were powerless, despite the vast resources at their disposal.

Beyond espionage, covert action is a dark art: it is not an academic exercise – ethical and pragmatic expectations do not apply – and almost by definition concentrates on elaborate and frequently over-ambitious plots which authors of fiction would be happy to adopt in their novels, but which parliaments and Congressional hearings would always scrutinise, seeking to make intelligence agencies accountable and to weed out rogue bureaucrats. In the real world, covert action means dealing with some of the most unpleasant and ruthless people an allied government has to offer, employing them as surrogates; such people tend always towards indiscipline, and retain their own secret agenda. It is debatable whether politicians urging covert action are aware of the real characters and intentions of their foreign, secret partners.

For US intelligence officers who had witnessed the humiliation of Vietnam, Afghanistan certainly offered an opportunity to repay Moscow for its arming of Hanoi. In Vietnam, however, their opponents had been driven by ideology and nationalism, whereas in Muslim Afghanistan it was Sharia law that motivated the tribal fighters, driving them even to suicidal charges (a tactic brought in by Arab volunteers).

Ironically, Anglo-American intelligence could have remained un-involved in covert action, rather than resourcing it. In January 1980, Carter and Zbigniew Brzezinski, his National Security Advisor, keen to avenge the invasion, forgot that China, Pakistan and Saudi Arabia, as key long-term contenders with Soviet influence and policy in the region, would certainly have supported the Mujahedeen with arms and money. Islamabad would have complained to US administrations that they did not care about Pakistan's security (a familiar litany all presidents had to experience). In any case, the Pakistani armed forces would have had no other option but to arm the Mujahedeen out of their own resources; this applied also to China. Washington could have provided merely humanitarian aid for refugees, and in parallel increased the pressure for Pakistan to abandon its nuclear programme. But in December 1979 it was Carter who blinked, eagerly agreeing to provide support for Zia ul-Haq's regime. In his turn, Zia was not a man easily frightened; he knew that as long as he continued to apply pressure, Washington would help him without having to make meaningful concessions in return. Eventually, in February 1989, President George Bush decided to exert some pressure himself by suspending military aid to Pakistan from 1990 onwards; it was too late – the Chinese had provided vast amounts of military hardware, and the Pakistanis had nearly completed their nuclear weapon.

Meanwhile, Saudi Arabia (fearing its own growing fundamentalist problem, and exploring ways to rid the country of religious fanatics) eagerly announced the setting-up of committees, as early as January 1980, to support the 'holy war'. The Saudis did not drive a hard bargain with the Americans, and willingly agreed to provide large sums to equal the US resourcing of covert warfare. It was evident that even without US aid the Saudis would have spent millions in financing the Mujahedeen.

The Carter and Reagan administrations' and the Thatcher government's assessment that the Soviet Union had no interest in invading either Pakistan or Iran, and upsetting the balance of power in Southwest Asia, was proving correct. Indeed, the Soviets never reacted too aggressively to Pakistan's support of the Islamists; only occasional bombings of border areas were carried out – leaving aside the KGB's habitual disinformation operations. On the contrary, the alliance of Washington and London with Saudi Arabia, the other Gulf states, Egypt and China for the secret arming of the Mujahedeen turned Afghanistan into a paradise for the Islamists.

Ironically, however, Anglo-American intelligence failed to discover the Kremlin's secret – that as early as 1981 Soviet leaders had started discussing a policy of withdrawing their troops from Afghanistan. Despite top-secret sources at the disposal of the CIA, the agency continued right up until 1988 to discount, any serious intent on the Russian side to negotiate their way out – Western intelligence experts monotonously asserted that Gorbachev was simply interested in tactical ploys and propaganda in his talks on Afghanistan and nuclear-arms reduction. It is evident that the CIA and the Joint Intelligence Committee (JIC) based their assessments on Soviet official statements and propaganda, and on analysing the incremental build-up of forces in Afghanistan. They focused on capabilities rather than on Moscow's evolving policy. Gorbachev, seeking to improve US–Soviet relations to that end, was willing to sacrifice Afghanistan; without insisting that Pakistan and the US stop supporting the rebels, he agreed to a withdrawal; this was concluded in February 1989.

The Mujahedeen won their war, but the Afghan communist regime survived, to the surprise of Anglo-American intelligence. In the Afghan civil war of the 1990s, US and Russian covert-action forces continued their activities (though on a much-reduced scale, almost on auto-pilot) while their political masters were preoccupied with the Tiananmen Square student revolt in Beijing, the destruction of the Berlin Wall, the dissolution of the USSR, the end of communist regimes in Eastern Europe, Iraq's invasion of Kuwait and the subsequent Operation Desert Storm, and the war in Yugoslavia.

1

AFGHAN FEUDS AND SECRET INTELLIGENCE

The political process in Afghanistan was influenced by three long-lasting factors: successive coups, murder and terror. In the catalogue of Afghan rulers during the Cold War, only two died peacefully: Babrak Karmal, the coup leader supported by the Soviet Union in 1979, and King Zahir Shah, who abdicated. All their predecessors and antecedents, either communists or nationalists, together with their close associates, met a grim fate, either dying in a firefight in the palace or executed after a coup. Anglo-American intelligence and diplomacy had to keep track of the evolving hatred among Afghan leaders so as to have a reasonable chance of predicting the events in this lethal political arena. But keeping track of animosities and ambitions among Afghan leaders proved a frustrating business for Washington and London, as indeed for Moscow. The KGB, despite their immense espionage apparatus in Kabul, failed to predict the coups of June 1973, April 1978 and September 1979. Unsurprisingly, these consecutive coups and the invasion of December 1979 also took British and American agencies by surprise, lacking as they did the local resources of the KGB.

Afghanistan had been the first state to recognise the Bolshevik government after the October revolution of 1917. In 1933, the 19-year-old Zahir Shah was crowned king following the assassination of his father, Nadir Shah. In the early days of the Cold War, Afghanistan under

Zahir Shah and his prime minister (a Royal Prince), Sadar Mohammed Daoud, joined the non-aligned movement, but developed strong economic and military ties with Moscow. This leaning towards the Soviets was interpreted by the Americans as Daoud's strategic real-politik – he had witnessed the US arming of Iran and Pakistan, two traditional contenders for influence with his country; meanwhile, there was no strong American interest in arming and aiding Afghanistan. In 1963, Daoud was ousted from the government on the apparent grounds that he provided military backing for Afghan claims over Pashtunistan (a region of Pakistan with a large Afghan-Pashtun minority), but Soviet–Afghan relations continued to develop – by 1973 one-third of the Afghan officer corps had been trained in the USSR. Development projects, the provision of military hardware and an ever-expanding contingent of military advisers showed the extent to which the Soviets considered it was in their strategic interest to influence events in Afghanistan.

Meanwhile, the Afghan communist factions were involved in inter-necine strife. Both called themselves the 'People's Democratic Party of Afghanistan' (PDPA) and adhered to strict Marxist doctrine, but their leaders were power-hungry enough to frustrate the Soviets (who monotonously appealed for union). In the September 1965 parliamen-tary elections, the PDPA under Babrak Karmal (born in 1929) won four seats; the PDPA of journalist Nur Muhammad Taraki (a Pashtun, born in 1917) and his second-in-command Hafizullah Amin (also a Pashtun, born in 1929) failed to win any. Taraki and Karmal had been agents of the KGB since the 1950s.[1] During the last years of Zahir Shah's reign, Taraki accused Karmal of being a 'royal communist', sup-porting the king, and Karmal deplored the 'leftist adventurism' of the Taraki faction. In essence, Karmal (whom the Soviets deemed more obedient to their policy over Afghanistan) sought to take advantage of the new constitution, and one day to take power. In contrast, Taraki was considered by the KGB as 'a complex and contradictory character. He was painfully vain, often took jokes made about him in the wrong way and liked to be given a lot of attention.'[2] Furthermore, he sought the overthrow of the government. Both communist parties were identified by their newspapers, Karmal publishing *Parchman* ('Red Banner') – his supporters thus being known as 'Parchamists' – and Taraki being supported by *Khalq* ('Masses'), thus 'Khalqists'. Each faction accused the other of betraying Marxism, while Daoud planned his own advancement.[3] Taraki suspected Daoud's aspirations, and as early as October 1972 warned the KGB that Daoud was planning a coup. Another Afghan agent, Azhar Abdullah Samad, a Parchamist, gave further warning in May 1973 that Daoud was ready to seize power.[4]

On 17 July 1973, the 65-year-old Daoud toppled King Zahir (who at the time was on holiday in Rome), declaring a republic with himself as president. The king had no choice but to abdicate, which he did on 24 August. The coup was conducted with the support of Soviet-trained Afghan officers who remained strong nationalists, believing that Daoud was the sole leader to promote national interests. US Ambassador Ted Elliot, in his first post-coup telegram to Washington, noted:

> Daoud has executed brilliantly organized takeover of country. Supported primarily by small number of dissident military officers ... coup has been greeted with some visible public jubilation ... new government likely to be authoritarian, highly nationalistic, puritanical and reformist ... Daoud government will undoubtedly seek maintain close and friendly relations with USSR as well as the non-aligned ... relations with the United States most likely will be cordial and correct but beyond that, we will have to wait and see. With luck and delicate handling, new regime need not necessarily present threat to any major US interests.[5]

But soon the ambassador was complaining of problems with intelligence sources. In mid-September 1973 he stated:

> We are operating in an environment which inevitably produces some differences in perspective, depending on the sources from which our reports are taken. Kabul is even more that usual a hotbed of rumor, half truths, and hardly disinterested informants. Access to former sources is being steadily restricted or made less useful as the new regime moves to replace many individuals

formerly in key positions. And the extraordinary centralized nature of decision-making makes it even more difficult to rely on information obtained from middle or upper level contacts. In the mosaic we can only see certain pieces, and they reflect only dimly those which are missing ... all foreign observers [are] cut off from old friends or traditional sources of information and watching unhappily the steady reimposition of a police state atmosphere, largely absent during the past decade while Daoud was out of power.[6]

With reference to the role of the Soviet Union, the embassy concluded:

The Soviet role in these events, both pre and post coup, remains mysterious. Thus far we have no reliable sources of intelligence on which to depend. Logic sides with those who believe the Soviets were at most aware that something was coming and have subsequently moved to exploit the results to the degree possible without risking overt signs of interference ... we believe Daoud is very unlikely to play deliberately into Soviet hands, while undoubtedly [he is] ready to milk the Soviets for all possible economic and political support for his scheme.[7]

The CIA suffered also from the lack of informed sources, a fact which could not be hidden post hoc by officers' reports of political developments after the coup. In August 1973, in Khanabad, the Muslim Brotherhood and other Islamist groups protested against the Parcham communists, but soon turned their anger against Daoud, who ordered the use of the military to crush the protests, while avoiding a confrontation with the leftists. Late the same month, when an ex-deputy called on the people to revolt, the regime immediately dispatched helicopter-borne paratroopers to deal with the demonstrators; the deputy was eventually arrested and imprisoned.[8] On 20 September former Prime Minister Maiwandwal was taken into custody; this, it was announced, was due to his 'anti-regime activities', and on 1 October a broadcast claimed that he had committed suicide by hanging himself in his cell. Agents in the local CIA station, trying to make sense of the regime's attitude, estimated that it would have either to continue the repression or to offer meaningful reform that would appease Maiwandwal's followers – who might have assumed that by dying in prison he would become a martyr in the eyes of his supporters and inspire more protests. According to intelligence reports, Daoud and his brother Naim (also his political advisor) had asked for copies of the constitutions of Algeria, Tunisia and France in an attempt to draft a constitution that would suit them: 'Naim has probably told Daoud that they must think ahead and cannot leave matters to the "Central Committee" [of the revolution] and their ilk. The request for the constitution is an encouraging spot in an otherwise bleak picture.' In mid-October the CIA reported back to Washington that, according to secret intelligence, the former prime minister was beaten to death in the Ministry of the Interior:

> The final fatal beating of Maiwandwal was administered by Engineer Ghausuddin Faid, GOA [Government of Afghanistan] Minister of Public Works. A witness who had seen Maiwandwal's body after his death reported eight of his finger nails had been extracted during the course of interrogations and there was evidence of electric torture [two and a half lines erased] the two other alleged leaders of the counter-coup plot, General Khan Mohammad (former governor of Nangrahar), and General Abdul Razak (former chief of Royal Afghan Air Force) are allegedly being tortured and beaten severely in order to extract confessions. Very recently General Khan Mohammad was, at President Daoud's order, beaten in front of him and then severely reproached by Daoud for accepting his aid in the past and then repaying this with conspiracy ... Among the Afghan populace there is much skepticism regarding Mainwandwal's suicide ... there is a strong feeling that Maiwandwal had been involved in a counter-coup plan, that he had been too hasty in trying to bring this about and that he was in fact in collusion with Government of Pakistan.[9]

Meanwhile, Karmal had already established contact with the army, and, once the coup of Daoud succeeded, found himself in the coalition government, sidelining Taraki and Amin. Parchamists were appointed to the cabinet, as ministers variously of education, the interior, information and culture. Moscow welcomed Daoud's coming to power, while investing in Karmal's aspirations to succeed him. In his turn, the new president signed a new US$600-million economic aid agreement with the Soviets in 1974. But Daoud was not a communist, and explored policies that would expand Afghanistan's international relations (for instance, he signed a military agreement with Egypt to facilitate Afghan military and police training). For Moscow, Sadat's policy of approaching the West and ousting the Russians' mission was anathema; and Daoud had made the mistake (in Soviet eyes) of cultivating relations with him.[10]

Brezhnev agreed to a visit by Daoud in June 1974, praising his leadership. The KGB resident in Kabul was ordered to tell Karmal and Taraki that they should consolidate their forces and work with Daoud (despite the fact that in February and March 1974 Daoud had turned against them by declaring their parties illegal): both communist leaders should understand 'the need to cease internecine fighting, unite both groups in a single party, and concentrate their combined efforts on comprehensive support of the republican regime in the country'.[11] The KGB resident was informed of the very positive results of the Daoud visit to Moscow, and instructed to try to reason with the communist leaders.[12]

Iran and Pakistan considered that, unless something was offered to the nationalist Daoud, Moscow would turn Afghanistan into a base that would facilitate the long-feared advance in the Indian Ocean. In 1974 the Shah readily offered a $40-million credit to Daoud; the Iranian economic aid would escalate, and overshadow even that provided by the Russians. US Secretary of State Henry Kissinger paid a brief visit to Kabul on 1 November 1974, signalling increased American interest in the country. He held a discussion with Mohammed Naim, Daoud's brother and foreign policy adviser; they touched upon the Pashtunistan and Baluchistan questions, the Afghan line being that the new Pakistani constitution should grant equal rights to the tribes there.[13] The US Agency for International Development offered economic and technical aid packages, though Washington felt it could not raise the level of such aid, given the likelihood of protests by Afghanistan's neighbours. Pakistan complained strongly about Afghan claims over Pashtunistan; there was also a revolt in Baluchistan (a region of Pakistan) in 1974, and Iran also had troubles with its Baluch minority. Daoud was presumed to be at least tolerant of the Baluch rebels who had found safe haven in Afghanistan.[14]

Pakistan's reaction came in the form of aiding those tribes who resisted Daoud's secular reforms. As early as May 1978, the Mujahedeen had set up camps in Pakistan with the help of the Inter-Services Intelligence Directorate (ISI),[15] and Iran also provided arms to these groups; there was a 'loose collaboration' with the CIA on this.[16] Soon Saudi Arabia entered the arena with a bid to help the Islamists.[17]

On 30 June 1976, Naim met Kissinger at the latter's office and asked explicitly for the American presence in his country to become 'more apparent', with development projects and economic aid. But he also requested secret intelligence on external and internal threats to his country; Kissinger agreed in principle, but warned that he could not help with intelligence against either Iran or Pakistan. Naim's reply was carefully phrased:

> Intelligence against Pakistan and Iran is not the question. The security of Pakistan, Iran and Afghanistan is interlinked ... we want to be more informed about the intentions of the Soviet Union in Afghanistan. Allow me to tell you from what we feel and see that the Soviet Union has no intention of applying in any way the process of détente toward Afghanistan.[18]

Next day Naim met President Ford. He reminded him that, back in the 1950, Washington had not been interested in supplying arms to Afghanistan, thus turning the country to purchasing from the Soviet Union. He asked for a secret intelligence liaison and the president sounded positive, remarking, 'as for intelligence, I think we can work something worthwhile'.[19] Kissinger flew to Kabul on 8 August to discuss the issue of intelligence with Daoud. The discussion was calm and pleasant, Daoud stating:

> I don't believe aggression from abroad is something that will materialise. We don't have any fear about that. But subversion

internally is something that concerns us. We have good relations with our neighbours and presently we don't fear any aggression from them. But in our policies, domestic and in general, we follow a line that is characteristic of our way of life and special to us. It is an Afghan line, in keeping with our people and our traditions. Therefore this kind of attitude – an independent attitude and independent line – may not be to the liking of the Left or to the liking of the Right. Therefore we are prone to any kind of influence [over] our people, and during the past ten years the situation was such that our country was open to all kinds of influence and all kinds of ideas. Therefore we would be very happy and would appreciate it very much if our American friends, with the worldwide means they have at their disposal, if they feel or see a threat to our security, could inform us as soon as possible.

The conversation then proceeded as follows:

Kissinger: In principle we are prepared to do it, and it concerns both internal and external security, if I understand the President.

Daoud: Yes, external and internal.

Kissinger: And to whom should we give this information?

Daoud: Of course, we would not like you to give us this information in the form of a note or letter, but to an individual whom we are to choose and introduce you to and an individual whom you will designate.

Kissinger: We would prefer that too. Anything on paper in Washington ends up in the *Washington Post* [laughter].[20]

Daoud moved confidently, on several simultaneous fronts. He started getting rid of Parchamists in the government, ousting two ministers in 1974, before his visit to Moscow, and commenced a purge in the security forces to ensure their loyalty. He showed serious interest in discussing the Pashtunistan question with Zulfiqar Ali-Bhutto, the prime minister of Pakistan. He declared that he would not tolerate 'imported ideology' in Afghanistan (meaning communism). By the end of 1975 no Parchamist remained in the cabinet, and the purges in the civil service and the military were intensifying. Parchamists were called upon to dissolve their party and join the National Revolution Party, prescribed to be the sole party under the new draft constitution. Dismissals of Soviet-trained officers aimed to make sure that the military sided with Daoud. In 1977 the new constitution was adopted, outlawing the PDPA. In April, during the Afghan leader's visit to Moscow, Brezhnev tried to instil fear in Daoud (or at least reason with him), claiming that NATO spies operated in Afghanistan, and hinting at a Soviet response. The President, in defiant style, answered that the remarks of the Soviet leader constituted 'unacceptable ... interference' in domestic affairs.[21]

In the Kremlin's view Daoud was playing with fire. He had stepped up military training programmes with Egypt, India and Turkey, and improved relations with Yugoslavia. By early 1978, he had secured $500 million from Saudi Arabia and the US, and was even scheduling a meeting with President Jimmy Carter. The previous year General Zia ul-Haq had overthrown Bhutto, but the new Pakistani leader believed in improving relations with Afghanistan and resolving the Pashtunistan question.[22]

The Soviets could not sit back and contemplate losing Afghanistan to the new foreign policy of the over-confident Daoud. They pressed Taraki and Karmal hard, and the Afghan factions were persuaded to form a unified PDPA, with Taraki as secretary-general and Karmal as first secretary, and the remaining posts divided between Parchamists and Khalqists. But Amin was not elected to the PDPA Politburo, due to the strong rumours that he was a secret agent of the CIA – indeed, he admitted that 'he played with the CIA because he needed money to continue his studies' in the United States.[23]

Meanwhile, Taraki and Amin took advantage of dissatisfaction among the military officers purged by Daoud. This cadre viewed the Parchamists as supporters of the regime, a stance which proved highly convenient for the Khalqists.[24]

In April 1978 came the showdown. On 17 April Mir Akbar Khaibar, a leading Parchamist, was assassinated in Kabul, and the united PDPA turned his funeral into an anti-government riot. Daoud ordered the arrests of Taraki and Karmal on 26 April, but the PDPA and their supporters were sufficiently powerful and unafraid to launch a coup the following day. The coup took the British and American diplomatic missions by surprise – their intelligence agencies had not anticipated such an outcome. In the confusion of the first hours of gunfighting, British diplomats in New Delhi reported to London:

> According to reporting telegrams sent by US embassy in Kabul, more than 50 tanks are in the centre of the city where street fighting is taking place. A building in the palace grounds was reported to be on fire at 12.30 today, local time.[25]

Next day the British Embassy in Kabul informed London:

> All indications are that there has been a successful military coup and that new regime is at least for present firmly in control. Kabul is quiet. Counter-coup by pro-Daoud forces seems unlikely. Daoud and brother Mohd Naim reported dead and this report universally accepted ... radio broadcasts by new regime have been in name of colonel Watan Jar who is said to be in charge of new military council. We know nothing of Jar. Nor do Americans nor Germans. Broadcasts have been made by General Abdul Qadir as head of defence forces. Qadir was chief of staff air force and trained in the USSR. Slogans of new regime are that it will be nationalist, Islamic and democratic.[26]

Daoud was killed in a firefight; many of his family were executed in cold blood. The coup cost the lives of some 2,000 troops, the majority Daoud loyalists besieged in the palace. Two days later a staffer in the office of Cyrus Vance, the US secretary of state, wrote a classified memorandum emphasising that Pakistan and Saudi Arabia had both assumed a Soviet hand in the coup.[27]

In their turn, however, the KGB and the Soviet Embassy in Kabul had also been taken aback by the coup. On 26 April, Ambassador Puzanow expressed his concern in a telegram to the Politburo:

> There is a danger that among the members of the PDPA central committee still at liberty [at that time Taraki and Karmal

were imprisoned] there may be some who will take extreme measures ... they may be incited to do this by provocateurs from the government's [Daoud's] special organs. In our view such extreme action in the present situation could lead to the defeat of the progressive forces in the country.

The KGB centre replied the same day with an utterly improbable allegation:

The possibility cannot be excluded that MOSSAD is wilfully provoking the military organisation of the party to take action against the government in order to deal it a blow.

These reports show that Soviet spies and diplomats had not anticipated that PDPA would take the initiative. Taraki was freed, assumed the chairmanship of the Revolutionary Council, and at 4.30 pm on 28 April one of his trusted delegates appeared at the Soviet Embassy.[28] (Probably the KGB had earlier information that Daoud might have sought the cooperation of MOSSAD for his security apparatus; soon the KGB initiated active measures to get hold of the intelligence files of the Ministry of Internal Affairs, the police and security forces, and military counter-intelligence under Daoud.)[29] The Soviets helped Taraki to establish a new intelligence agency, the 'Organisation for the Defence of Afghan Interests' (AGSA).[30] In August 1978 KGB foreign-intelligence chief Kryuchkov (later KGB chairman and coup plotter) paid a visit to Taraki and his associates in a bid to help them set up their own secret service.[31]

By 30 April 1978, the British Embassy had estimated that, against all odds, the mutineers had succeeded. Daoud loyalists were possibly numerically superior in the armed forces, but they were surprised and confused during the early stages of the coup; in addition the air force backed the rebels. Their confusion and inability to respond in a coor-dinated fashion contributed to the deaths of the minister of defence and the chief of the air force. Nonetheless, divisions within the army would not soon be eradicated. In any case, 'the new regime is likely to be more left of centre than Daoud, but the force of Islam will be a restraining factor on the development of any communist state'[32] (this was a very perceptive remark). Meanwhile, Puzanov protested at the allegation that Moscow was behind the coup.[33]

Both India and Pakistan assumed (wrongly) that the Soviet Union had been directly involved. New Delhi worried about the consequences for the non-aligned movement and the diminishing potential for regional cooperation.[34] The Pakistanis were more emotional: Foreign Secretary Shah Nawaz claimed that the Afghan coup 'had realised Pakistan's worst fears'. 'There was no doubt' of a Soviet hand in the coup, and Moscow's wish to see a puppet government installed, serving its long-term aspiration for the 'domination of South Asia and access to the Indian Ocean ... the consequences for Pakistan were likely to be a renewal of active subversion' and the revival of the Pashtunistan question. Islamabad was angered by India's immediate recognition of the new regime (though London had done the same).[35] As for the Shah, he also struck a pessimistic note, as always fearing the encirclement of Iran. The Iranian Ministry of Foreign Affairs argued that the coup was a 'more serious' development than the 1958 Baghdad coup that had led to the demise of the Iraqi royal family and the coming to power of the Baathists. The Shah repeated his allegations that Pakistan and Turkey remained weak, and that the West lacked the resolve to stand up to Soviet policy. Nonetheless, Tehran's official public comments were restrained, to avoid provoking the USSR.[36] Prime Minister James Callaghan, who read the telegram from Sir Antony Parsons, the UK's ambassador in Tehran, commented laconically: 'The Shah has every cause to be worried.'[37]

In Kabul, British Ambassador Crook had his first interview with Taraki on 6 May 1978. He found someone who spoke good English, and gave 'the appearance of being a moderate man'. Taraki sought to deceive Crook by arguing that Afghanistan would remain in the non-aligned movement, and sounded in favour of the expansion of British educational and development initiatives in his country.[38] Initially, Taraki was named both president and prime minister, while Karmal became his deputy in both posts. Amin was assigned the Ministry of Foreign Affairs, where he showed himself both ruthless and Machiavellian, playing up any threat to the regime. In late summer, he confided to Puzanov that in August a coup plot was discovered – the

US, the Federal Republic of Germany (FRG), Saudi Arabia, Iran and China were all implicated.[39] Neither Puzanov nor the KGB expressed an opinion on Amin's claims.

US intelligence admitted that there was no evidence pointing to a Soviet hand in the 1978 coup. Moscow had been informed of the coup before it was launched, but expected it to take place in August rather than April, and possibly with a substantial input from Karmal's faction. It seems that Amin, who had not been arrested by Daoud, seized the moment of a provocation by the latter (the murder of Khaibar) in launching the coup, sidelining the Parchamists. Moscow was willing to improve relations with Taraki, and a new military-assistance protocol was signed on 31 May 1978; the number of Soviet military advisors soared from 350 (before the coup) to 500. PDPA intrigue led to the manipulation of voting and the dominance of Khalqists over Parchamists; by mid-July, seven leading Parchamists had been sent abroad as ambassadors. Karmal was dispatched to Czechoslovakia – it seems that he had already set up a cell to launch a counter-coup in September, but his plans and fellow conspirators were discovered by Amin in time.[40] Meanwhile, the latter took office as Deputy Chairman of the Revolutionary Council.

US intelligence assumed (wrongly) that the Soviets had agreed to Karmal's exile. This hypothesis was supported by the disclosure that, after his departure, another military-assistance deal (involving some $250 million) had been signed with Moscow, and that the number of Soviet advisors had now reached 700.[41]

Cyrus Vance, the US secretary of state, was unhappy at the developments in Afghanistan, but assumed that moderate American influence could be maintained by continuing with the economic aid programme agreed with Daoud earlier. But Zbigniew Brzezinski, the national security advisor, protested that the 1978 coup revealed a Soviet bid for domination in the region. He favoured covert action against the regime, but Carter (at a time when congressional hearings on CIA abuses had just ended) did not concur. The State Department won the argument about continuing with economic aid to Afghanistan, but soon Adolph Dubs, the new American ambassador, was abducted by anti-regime extremists, and killed in a failed police rescue attempt in

February in Kabul (KGB officers nearby watched this operation, and US intelligence was aware of this). The Afghan government failed to apologise to Washington, and Carter, already shocked at the fall of the Shah a fortnight earlier, decided to suspend all American economic aid to Afghanistan.[42] The KGB's view was that Dubs had been an expert on Middle Eastern and Central Asian affairs, whose appointment revealed Washington's intention of becoming further involved in Afghanistan. The Soviets assumed that 'Dubs was one of the people behind the idea of the Afghanistan–Pakistan–Iran triangle' to contain Soviet influence in the region. Certainly, under his stewardship the US Embassy had ramped up its propaganda over the Soviet deployment of civil and military advisers in Afghanistan.[43]

Meanwhile, Amin was extending his personal reach in the military (where loyalty to Taraki was diminishing) and the secret services, while secularisation and land reforms caused an escalation of the Islamist insurgency. Large areas in north and east Afghanistan were now controlled by the rebels, who were also receiving aid from Pakistani Pashtuns. Taraki flew to Moscow and, on 5 December 1978, signed the 'Treaty of Friendship, Goodneighbourliness and Cooperation', in a bid to get more aid to combat the Islamists. In the text there was a clear reference to the non-aligned policy of Afghanistan, as well as a provision that could facilitate direct Soviet military aid to Afghanistan in the future: the two governments would 'consult with each other and take appropriate measures to ensure the security, independence and territorial integrity' of their states. By early January, the number of military advisors had peaked at some 1,000, and about 2,000 Soviets were working in civil projects.[44] The FCO concluded that

> The treaty obligations assumed by the Soviet Union, while wide-ranging, do not amount to a commitment to go to the rescue of the Taraki government should its existence be threatened whatever the circumstances. The treaty does not include anything which might be construed as a 'Brezhnev doctrine' clause under which the Soviet Army might march in to preserve Afghanistan's 'socialist gains', though this contingency cannot be ruled out: everything would depend on the situation at the time.[45]

When the Soviets signed the treaty they had no intention of overthrowing the Khalq faction, despite not approving of Taraki and Amin's policy of forced reforms, which had incited an Islamist reaction. By February 1979, Ambassador Crook had sensed that the regime was disappointed with the Soviet Union – Taraki had not received all he had asked for from Moscow.

The impression expressed time and again by those in much daily contact with [the] government [is] that disillusionment is beginning to be felt with communist theory, with Russian technology and Russian beneficence; there are indications that economic and commercial policy may become a bit less doctrinaire than at first seemed likely.[46]

In April, Ambassador Crook wrote that Amin (now prime minister)

is a much more urbane man than some of his colleagues. He received me warmly, and his comments, especially about Islam, seemed to me to reflect a more positive attitude that I have detected in the past. His tendency to take a defensive short-term line about Islam was interesting, and his long-term objective clear.[47]

It was evident that Amin, and possibly Taraki, aimed to distance themselves from the Soviet Union in the long term.

After her election on 3 May 1979, Prime Minister Margaret Thatcher was informed of the deteriorating internal-security situation in Afghanistan, with civil war raging between the regime and the Islamists. Afghan refugees were massing in the Pakistani border areas, and Islamabad had been doing all it could to provide relief; there were also reports of Pakistani and Iranian support for the guerrillas. Thatcher understood the gravity of the situation and the potentially explosive effects of any intervention to boost the regime. In the summer of 1979, she informed Lord Avebury that she had warned USSR Chairman Leonid Brezhnev: 'We regard interference by outside powers in unstable situations in the world as contrary to the spirit of détente.'[48]

Meanwhile, during the period April–May in Washington, President Carter was warned by Brzezinski of the gradual increase in the Soviet deployment in Afghanistan, fearing that the Soviets could incite trouble for Pakistan by promoting Afghan claims over Baluchistan and Pashtunistan. A domino effect could be created, with the Soviets gaining access to the Persian Gulf and Indian Ocean, and the 'dismemberment' of Pakistan and Iran. In outlining such scenarios, Brzezinski also referred to Molotov's proposal to Hitler in 1940 that Nazi Germany should recognise Soviet claims over the region south of Batum and Baku.[49] Carter, convinced by Brzezinski's arguments, had 'approved several messages of warning to Brezhnev', to the effect that the Soviets should not intervene in Afghanistan.[50]

On 18 June 1979, in Vienna, Carter and Brezhnev eventually signed SALT II. Moscow did not wish a confrontation over Afghanistan: six days later, Vasily Safronchuk, a senior Russian political counselor in Kabul, told the American chargé d'affaires that there was no intention of dispatching Soviet troops to deal with the Islamist rebels. He stressed that such a move would damage both the freshly signed SALT II and the Soviet Union's prestige in the world.[51]

Nonetheless, 15 days later Carter signed an authorisation for the CIA to support anti-regime groups. The same day, Brzezinski argued in a memorandum to the president that the possible discovery of CIA aid to the Afghan guerrillas would cause the Soviet Union to intervene, and back the regime of Taraki. Thus Moscow would be trapped in a Vietnam-like situation, to the benefit of the West.[52] (The idea of turning Afghanistan into a 'Vietnam quagmire' for the Russians was first aired by Walter Slocombe, a Defense Department official, during a meeting with Brzezinski on 30 March 1979).[53] However, Lawrence Freedman warned that these statements by Brzezinski should not be 'over-interpreted'. He suspected that the former National Security Advisor

> was reclaiming from Reagan and for Carter some of the credit for bringing down the Soviet Union, as the inability to cope with the Afghan insurgency was one factor in draining credibility from Soviet leadership. But in 1979, the United States was at

most a bit player in a local drama with its script written elsewhere ... nothing the United States did that summer [of 1979]
led to the fiasco of Amin's victory over Taraki or to the Soviet
misapprehension that if only they could engineer a takeover by
more politically savvy communists, then everything would be
fine.[54]

The CIA secret aid to Taraki's opponents had now reached $500,000,
but was not of a military nature. Besides, Afghanistan could not
necessarily be turned into a Soviet Vietnam; there were scant simi-
larities between the Afghan guerrillas, who were 'badly organised
and poorly led', and the North Vietnamese. Hanoi enjoyed central
administration and a coherent military structure, as well as vast foreign military aid.[55]

Throughout the summer of 1979, in embassy receptions in Kabul
and in private meetings, Soviet diplomats made it clear to their Western
counterparts that they were unhappy with Taraki and Amin – particularly the latter – and would welcome new leaders to replace them.
The current regime was responsible for inflaming the civil war with
their excessive reforms. In mid-July the ambassador of the German
Democratic Republic (GDR) hinted that the Soviets were willing to
use force if necessary. Secret intelligence sources revealed Soviet consultations over a possible coup, to be organised by Afghan officers dis-
gruntled at Amin's policies. This information hit the headlines in a
New York Times article on 2 August. Meanwhile, the Soviets urged
Amin, the 'zealous revolutionary', to slow down the reforms.[56]

On the tactical level, the Soviets moved in. In May a company
of the elite KGB 'Zenit' group reached Kabul, ostensibly to protect
the Soviet Embassy.[57] In early July 1979 a Russian airborne battalion
was based in Bagram to provide extra security against rebel raids.
The Afghan army was suffering from mutinies and diminishing loyalty, and American diplomats considered that only 25 per cent of the
country was controlled by regime forces. Another serious mutiny took
place on 5 August, in the outskirts of Kabul; it was soon put down, but
this dramatic episode led US intelligence to issue a warning memorandum arguing that the possibility of a Soviet military intervention

increased as the Afghan army's reliability diminished.[58] (However, this argument was misguided – it merely claimed a possible Soviet role in counterinsurgency, rather than predicting the overthrow of the Afghan regime.)

In any event, the visit to Kabul on 17 August of 13 generals under General I.G. Pavlovskii, the deputy chief of the Soviet General Staff and commander of the Soviet Ground Forces, seemed to support the thesis that the Soviets were seriously considering involvement in counterinsurgency, and examining the performance of the Afghan forces in depth. (There was an ominous detail here – noted by US analysts: Pavlovskii had commanded the Soviet force that invaded Czechoslovakia in August 1968).[59]

However, it seemed to the Americans that the Soviets had opted to put up with Taraki and Amin, and had no wish now to replace them; the Pavlovskii visit was not interpreted as a sign of immediate changes on the Afghan front. In late August the CIA concluded that 'the deteriorating situation does not presage an escalation of Soviet military involvement in the form of a direct combat role'.[60] Meanwhile, the movements of some components of the 5th Guards Motorised Rifle Division at Kushka (in the USSR's Turkestan military district) were seen as exercises only, with no link to policy over Afghanistan, and preparations detected in some echelons of the 105th Guards Airborne Division were assumed to be for a rapid reinforcement of Kabul in case of a rebel attack.[61] On 14 September CIA Director Stansfield Turner informed Carter that 'the Soviet leaders may be on the threshold of a decision to commit their own forces to prevent the collapse of the regime and to protect their sizable stakes in Afghanistan'. The Soviet deployments were assumed to be incremental, focusing on strengthening the contingent of military advisers and providing extra security for their facilities.[62] But the director was as yet unaware that another coup had taken place in Kabul that same day.

While during the reign of Zahir Shah the Chinese invested in the country, signed a border demarcation agreement and donated substantial aid, their presence under Daoud and Taraki was no more than marginal, and was reduced further in the period 1978–79 due to Taraki's strong pro-Soviet/anti-Chinese declarations.[63] Chinese construction teams left Kandahar in early 1978, discontinuing the building of a local hospital. In Bagram the construction of a textile factory was also abandoned; the same happened with an irrigation system in Parvan which China had undertaken to build. In 1979, Chinese civil-engineering and construction specialists left the country, and China's Embassy staff were cut by half.[64] But Beijing was seriously contemplating backing the Mujahedeen. On 4 April 1979 the CIA reported that the Chinese had discussed with Afghan rebel leaders the arming of the mujahedeen.[65]

2

WRONG ESTIMATES AND THE INVASION

On 10 September 1979, Taraki met Brezhnev and Gromyko in Moscow. Officially, the Afghan was asking for more aid. In secret Brezhnev told him (according to KGB archivist Mitrokhin, who reviewed the KGB's memorandum on the meeting) to get rid of Amin because he had accumulated too much influence in the military and security forces. Taraki wilfully accepted this instruction.[1] The KGB had recommended to Brezhnev that Amin should be replaced:

> 1. [A] way should be found to remove Amin from the leadership of the country, as he is guilty of pursuing a flawed internal policy. He personally should be held responsible for the ungrounded mass punitive measures and the failures of internal policies, 2. Taraki should be persuaded that it is essential to establish a democratic coalition government ... an unofficial meeting should be arranged with K. Babrak ...[2]

The KGB had not yet undertaken any attempt against Amin's life. It seems that with the above memorandum they were seeking authorisation, but still hoped Afghan leaders rather than a Soviet agency would undertake such a task. It may be inaccurate to argue that 'the KGB had overseen several Soviet bids since the summer to remove Amin from the Afghan leadership, including two assassination attempts'.[3]

As we will explore in this chapter, while the KGB had developed plans for assassination, it had not received an authorisation by autumn. In the summer the Kremlin had already pressed Taraki to reshuffle his cabinet, but Taraki had failed to dismiss Amin.

For some time the KGB had been piecing together circumstantial evidence of Amin's contacts with people loyal to King Zahir Shah, and now claimed that Amin was a deep-cover CIA agent.[4] British diplomats thought (wrongly) that there had been a measure of disagreement between Brezhnev and Taraki during their meeting, because the Afghan chairman had referred to 'frank' talks in his interview with the Tass news agency. A member of the Czech Embassy in Moscow confirmed to the British that Taraki had been 'stubborn'. Four days later, on 14 September, Taraki was overthrown by Amin, but the UK Embassy in Moscow assumed (this time correctly) that there had been no direct Soviet complicity in the coup.[5]

From US intelligence, it emerged later that Amin, accompanied by 'six bodyguards' (in fact it was four), was about to visit Taraki to argue about the dismissal of four ministers implicated in an attempt against Amin's life while Taraki was abroad. It seemed that Taraki was about to shoot Amin on the spot, but the latter was warned by a bodyguard, while climbing the staircase to Taraki's office, and was protected by his security detail after the first shot was fired. Amin escaped in a cinematic exchange of fire in the People's House, returned to the Ministry of Defence, and launched his coup. Ambassador Puzanov was blamed by Amin for persuading him to attend the 14 September meeting (in effect a lethal trap). According to the Americans, it seemed that Amin had launched his coup in direct response to the attempt against his life; only the previous day Taraki and Amin had spent time together trying to reach an accommodation on the fate of the four ministers.[6]

During the tense hours of 13–14 September confusion reigned in Kabul, as it also did in Washington and London. The first US analyses argued that Amin's coup 'may have been a pre-emptive move to forestall a Soviet plot to have Taraki remove him'. Unconfirmed reports alleged that in Moscow Taraki had discussed the overthrow of Amin, but the US Embassy in Kabul discounted this possibility – indeed, the Americans, in following the political feuds in Kabul, faced serious gaps in intelligence despite their vast resources and expertise. Thomas Thorton of the NSC wrote to Brzezinski on 17 September 1979 to the effect that 'simply we don't know' what was really going on in Kabul. There was 'no evidence' to back the hypothesis either that the Soviets had instigated the coup or that Amin had acted on his own. Thorton's assessment was that the Soviets were trapped in Afghanistan, working through surrogates who fought each other rather than stabilising the security position.[7]

The crisis of 13–14 September showed that neither the KGB and the CIA were able to follow hour-by-hour the intrigue, assassination plots and quarrels among the authoritarian Afghan leaders, nor to predict Amin's intentions. Amin retained the initiative, and may have felt that he should allow Taraki to believe him sufficiently naive as to cancel any military alert on 13 September, and to visit him again the following day 'without bodyguards', as Taraki had asked; but Amin took a security detail with him. The coup was the catalyst that changed Soviet perceptions about the limits of military deployment in Afghanistan. If the KGB wanted Amin dead, it would have had to arrange for the assassination days or even weeks earlier. Moscow wanted to see a cabinet reshuffle and a trial for Amin. Obviously, Taraki and his bodyguards assumed in Amin the mentality of a Chicago gangster, who, once saved from the shooting episode, seized the pretext to launch his coup, ignoring the Kremlin's call for unity and restraint. The KGB had no accurate assessment of the forces loyal to Amin, and were unable to avert the course of events that led to the coup.

As for the US intelligence community, again taken by surprise, an inter-agency memorandum claimed on 28 September that

Moscow probably views the situation as even more unstable [and] may fear that this coup might fragment the Afghan army and lead to a breakdown of control in Kabul ... [t]he threat raised by the Muslim insurgency to the survival of the Marxist government in Afghanistan appears to be more serious now than at any time since the government assumed power in April 1978.[8]

This was the dominant assessment until December; it went on to argue that only if the Afghan army collapsed would the Soviets, in a 'multidivisional operation' (meaning more than four ground and one airborne division – the 105th Guards), move in to help the regime against the rebels. The Soviets would try to replace the Khalq faction, but if they failed they would sponsor a moderate regime (as yet unidentifiable). The tactical and political disadvantages of occupying Afghanistan were listed. The conclusion of this memorandum (which examined hypotheses without much solid intelligence) was that 'Moscow would not believe that saving the current Khalq regime or even another communist regime was worth the price.' But the prospects of 'a foreign military intervention', 'prolonged political chaos' and 'the advent of an anti-Soviet regime' would make the Soviets opt for invasion. For the time being, 'We have not seen indications that the Soviets are at the moment preparing ground forces for large-scale [multi-divisional] military intervention.'9

London and Washington recognised the new regime, congratulating Amin on being 'elected' president by the Communist Party. M.E. Howell, the UK chargé d'affaires, had a meeting with Amin on 30 September. It this first post-coup contact, Amin took a friendly line towards the West, and 'went out of his way' to state three times that he wished to pursue friendly relations with Britain, and appreciated the economic aid received. Naturally, he blamed Taraki for previous policies, and did not seem to take undue umbrage at the BBC's criticism of human rights violations. Howell was invited to visit the new president 'any time ... his door was always open to me'. However, the diplomat added drily, 'The poorly re-plastered bullet holes by the stairs were not exactly an incentive to pursue this invitation.' Howell concluded his telegram with some perceptive remarks:

> I doubt whether these avowals of friendship and understanding mean a great deal but they were stressed more than mere courtesy demanded. The Americans got the same message. It may be that Amin is not yet confident that he has the firm Soviet backing that he needs and is looking to a time when he might need

any friends he can make. Amin looked horribly tired, eyes deep
sunken and with every appearance of badly needing sleep. There
was no indication of worry, just simple fatigue.[10]

Meanwhile, in the FCO's South Asia Department the prevailing view
was that the Soviets feared trouble with Amin's rise to power. It was
also considered that Soviet paratroopers had been transferred to Kabul
for the security of the Soviet Embassy, and did not constitute a deployment of additional forces in the country.[11] In their turn, the Americans
were confused by this transfer of forces; their intelligence analysts produced only vague estimates. In the NATO Political Committee the
American assessment was presented in order to draw the attention of
the European allies to what had being going on in Afghanistan. It was
argued that the coup deposing Taraki had cost Afghans' support for
the socialist regime, and that now Amin would face the opposition of
the military, the Communist Party and Taraki's supporters. Besides,

> The US had noticed some increased military activity north of
> the Soviet–Afghan border, which could indicate preparations
> for the movement of some air force units out of garrisons, how-
> ever, the US had not (repeat not) noticed any build-up of Soviet
> forces north of the border. The US had not (repeat not) concluded
> that the Soviets intended to intervene in Afghanistan, but the
> increased military activity was disturbing.[12]

This was hardly a statement that would make the Europeans worry
much over the developments in far-distant Afghanistan, preoccupied
as they were with other issues – among them the question of how to
re-integrate Greece into NATO after sustained Turkish vetoes and the
deployment of Pershing II missiles in Europe. (The Pershings – a total
of 108 missiles, coupled with 464 ground-launched cruise missiles –
were not scheduled to be deployed until December 1983, and thus
presented no immediate threat to the Soviets.)

On 26 September 1979, the *Pravda* daily gave an ominous hint
about real Soviet intentions over Afghanistan and the new regime.
It was explicitly stated that 'the sovereignty of individual socialist

countries must not run counter to the interests of ... the world revolutionary movement'.[13] Indeed Sir Nicholas Keeble, the British ambassador in Moscow, assessed the cool reaction of the Kremlin to Amin's coup, and concluded that the Soviets did not have a direct hand in toppling Taraki. They had assessed Amin's leadership, and certainly would wish him to become more moderate, but there was no evidence that they had deemed the situation more serious, demanding an increase of their forces in Afghanistan.[14]

The precedents of the invasions of Hungary in 1956 and of Czechoslovakia in 1968 (which demonstrated the 'Brezhnev doctrine', as it was termed in the West) were part of the Soviet legacy of intervention. Washington, however, failed to pay much attention to the evolving situation in Afghanistan until the very last moment, surprised and confused as it was by current developments in Iran. Meanwhile, the Iranian crisis was intensifying. On 4 November 1979 students stormed the US Embassy in Tehran, taking the staff hostage, diverting any attention from Afghanistan, and leading Carter to the desperate, doomed rescue attempt of 24 April 1980.

Back at the FCO, by mid-October a heads-of-mission conference had been concluded, and Lord Carrington, the foreign secretary, had dispatched to Sir Curtis Keeble his own views, together with a statement of the UK's main policy aims. Carrington was of course unaware of Soviet intentions over Afghanistan, yet he was able to paint a rather accurate picture of the American and Soviet leaderships. Carrington's view was that the Soviet Union aimed to maintain 'reasonably good' relations between East and West. Nonetheless, 'détente is a misleading word; the Soviet meaning is very restrictive, different from the usual Western interpretation'. In any case, the Soviets intended to defeat the West 'by all means short of war.' According to Carrington the Soviets understood that détente was not about limiting their arsenal or supporting regional dictators, while they regarded subversion as a means of frightening the Europeans and other countries so that one day the Soviet Union would become the dominant power in Europe.[15] Britain should not speed up contacts with the Soviet Union, as the French and the Germans were doing with the conclusion of a number of agreements. The main aim was to 'seek the respect of the Soviet

Union, rather than its good opinion'. The absence of strong leadership in both Moscow and Washington provided a window of opportunity for Britain to play a more active role in international politics defending Western interests. The foreign secretary then produced a rather contradictory remark: 'Leadership changes are imminent in the Soviet Union. The transition until a new primus inter pares is established could last several years.' The Soviet Union would remain a superpower only in military terms; economically it was weak. His view of the United States was critical enough:

> The US is in an uncertain period which has lasted since the withdrawal from Vietnam. In the final years before the presidential election, Mr Carter may need to show that he is not soft on the Soviets. The pursuit of stability in East–West relations requires firmer and more sophisticated leadership than he has given and the Soviets themselves show signs of having lost confidence in his chances.[16]

Britain supported NATO's bid for Long Term Defence Planning (LTDP) and Theatre Nuclear Forces (TNF), as well as the development of the US Rapid Deployment Force and the possible stationing of a US task force in the Indian Ocean.[17] British diplomacy also backed SALT II, and hoped this would be ratified so as to open the way for SALT III.[18] Nonetheless, Carrington – aware of the Carter administration's policy of engaging China against the Soviet Union – warned against any thought of playing an oversimplified strategy game with the USSR and China: 'The growing Western relationship with China is a constraint on the USSR, but any deliberate attempt to exploit the Sino-Soviet disputes would be risky and its effects unpredictable.'[19]

In mid-October, London and Washington had to assess the impact of yet another Afghan army mutiny, only nine miles from Kabul. The mutiny was soon put down, but it was another indication that the loyalty of the military was disintegrating. Afterwards, US intelligence noticed that the Russians' 105th Guards Airborne Division was undertaking some sort of preparations; there was also some activity (training or otherwise) in the 5th Motorised Rifle Division at Kushka, the 108th at Termez and the 58th at Kizyl Arvat (all in the USSR's Turkestan military district). Diplomatic and secret-intelligence reports disclosed Russia's intention to replace Amin; it was confirmed that Amin was aware of this.[20]

Meanwhile, American diplomats asked Turkey to share its assessments of the Afghanistan situation. In late October, Karaosmanoglu, a high-ranking official in the Turkish Ministry of Foreign Affairs, confided that the Soviets would not send more troops into Afghanistan unless Soviet lives were under threat. Amin had only a narrow support-base and the Soviets were looking for someone to replace him. The Turks believed that Ahmad Nur Etemadi, the former prime minister and ambassador in Moscow (now in jail) was the person the Soviets were seeking to approach for such a task. Karaosmanoglu also disclosed information about a mutiny two months earlier: 20 Afghan pilots had been ordered to attack rebel positions in downtown Herat, but had intentionally dropped their bombs outside the target zone. On their return, they were summarily executed by Amin's regime, and a new bombing mission was undertaken by Soviet pilots.[21] Eventually Etemadi would be tortured and executed at the order of Amin.

The incremental deployment of Soviet troops to Afghanistan did not alarm Whitehall. On 8 November 1979, a memorandum by C.L.G. Mallaby, the head of the FCO's Eastern European and Soviet Department, claimed that the Soviets would not move forces en masse into the country, suggesting that they treated the progress of SALT II separately from the situation in Afghanistan: the reason they had not invaded was because they did not deem it necessary. They would do so only if they assumed that their policy of backing the Afghan regime had not paid sufficient dividends. In any case, if an invasion occurred, 'it was clear that the West could not stop [it]'. Nonetheless, it would provide an excellent opportunity for taking advantage of this aggression in furthering anti-Soviet propaganda, especially in the Third World. Mallaby's argument was cynical:

> Soviet invasion might be to our advantage in the sense that, if the Soviets are going to get a grip of Afghanistan, they should be seen to be doing so and should be forced to pay the maximum political and military price. The risk at the moment may be that they will get away with doing it quietly. On the other hand,

an open Soviet takeover would underline the West's inability to stop it and would strengthen the impression that the Soviet Union has a potentially successful long-term plan for taking over Third World dominoes.[22]

K. White, head of the FCO's South Asia Department, considered that the Soviets were far from happy with Amin, an 'embarrassingly zealous disciple' whom they did not trust. An assassination and a coup against him would not be viewed by Moscow as a defeat but as the continuation of the socialist revolution, at a suitably moderate pace. But if an Islamic regime similar to Khomeini's took over, the Soviets would not tolerate it and would invade. The problem was that, in the event of an invasion, the Third World and the non-aligned nations (especially India) would not back the West, because the non-aligned bloc 'seems to have great capacity for swallowing Soviet camels whilst straining at Western gnats'. Britain should avoid arming the rebels so as to avoid the Soviet response; besides, the Mujahedeen retained enough arms for their operations.

> In short, what is happening in Afghanistan is essentially a problem for the Soviets and not us [sic], and is not wholly unwelcome. But it is a mixed blessing, and we exercise no control on events. Things could get messier [with the reaction of Pakistan] ... Pakistan is building up trouble for herself anyway [with its interference in Afghanistan, its nuclear programme and the burning-down of the US Embassy in Islamabad by protestors on 21 November 1979].[23]

Another official in the South Asia Department agreed that an invasion was unlikely. Moscow was definitely not happy with Amin, and its military had 'what is probably an unassailable hold on airfields and [was] therefore in a position to augment any attack on dissidents from the air'. On the other hand, Western diplomacy did not favour any particular Afghan leader:

> There are no obvious alternative leaders for the West to identify with even if these were desirable ... Western interests would

probably be best served by the establishment of a stable government which could establish good relations with the Soviet Union
but without becoming nothing more than a Soviet satellite.[24]

What was also clear was that unless the security situation within
Afghanistan improved there would be a serious spill-over effect in
Pakistan, with large numbers of refugees and the Afghan insurgent
bases.[25]

By late November, US intelligence had reported that the USSR's
105th Guards Airborne Division was still on increased readiness. In
addition, the three motorised rifle divisions appeared to be on the
move again, though below the imminent deployment threshold.
Nonetheless, the hostage crisis in Tehran blurred the analysts' picture;
they argued (wrongly) that the Soviet military activity could be linked
to a Russian fear that US forces might move against Iran.[26]

In early December, the CIA station in Kabul reported that
Soviet special forces were infiltrating the city; there were flights
from the Soviet Union whose purpose remained unclear; 'numerous
reports from the field also indicated some covert operations seemed
to be afoot'. The 'on the spot senior intelligence officer [the CIA
station chief] concluded that some Soviet military operation was
being readied'.[27]

On 4 December 1979, Brzezinski met Russian Ambassador
Anatoly Dobrynin in the White House. They discussed SALT II, the
national security advisor remarking that ratification by the following March seemed possible. Other issues addressed were the visit of
Brezhnev to Washington, planned for July 1980, and the reduction
in the number of medium-range missiles. There was no reference to
Afghanistan.[28]

On 8 December, a second Soviet airborne battalion landed
at Bagram airbase; it was assumed that their task was to boost
security. The top-secret National Intelligence Daily received by the US
president claimed that the extra troops were for security tasks, to repel
any rebel attacks. The new battalion could also help in the event of an
evacuation of Russian subjects.[29]

On 11 December, US intelligence disclosed the arrival of a motorised rifle battalion at Bagram. The assessment remained unrevised; it

was possibly meant for security. The DIA revealed its lack of intelligence on the Soviets' real intentions:

[I]t is also possible, although much more speculative, that the airborne and motorised rifle elements now at Bagram are merely the first increment of a much larger combat force that may be deployed to Afghanistan during the coming year ... It is not certain that Moscow has embarked on such a plan ... but it is clear that the Soviets have made a qualitative increase in their military presence and capabilities ...

The same day, at a senior analysts' panel under the national intelligence officer for warning, the majority agreed that the extra forces deployed in Kabul were tasked only with security, especially in the event of an evacuation after a rebel attack. A minority of analysts, however, examined a curious detail that could have revealed the actual Soviet intent. The motorised battalion included an anti-aircraft component although there was no possibility of foreign aircraft attacking the regime's forces; thus the Soviets' motive in bringing this anti-aircraft artillery must be linked to an assumption that their operation (whatever it was) might 'risk a reaction by at least parts of the Afghan military [and the Afghan air force]'.[30]

Eventually, on 11 December, Warren Christopher, the acting secretary of state, met the Soviet chargé d'affaires in Washington and raised the issue of Soviet intentions over Afghanistan – Washington 'was aware of quantitative and qualitative changes' in Russian forces there. He received no reply.[31]

The same day, Peter Barker, a high-ranking British diplomat in Kabul, wrote: 'However long [Amin] stays in power his alliance with the Soviets will be an uneasy one – although since based on mutual self-interest there is no immediate reason why it should not last.' The Afghan leader was 'a true Machiavellian' who throughout the autumn had waged a campaign of terror to wipe out any potential rivals in the party.[32] R.D. Lavers, now head of the South Asia Department at the FCO, noted an earlier report by the British air attaché in Tehran. The latter had visited Kabul, and claimed that Amin had told a closed audience (though not including this RAF officer) that at some point in the future he would break with the Soviets.[33] On 18 December, however, Barker replied to Lavers denying any knowledge of the officer's intelligence; he could neither confirm nor deny that Amin had made such a statement. He assumed, however, that if the Afghan leader had made such a remark, it 'was made out of bravado; even Hafizullah Amin must realise that without Russian backing – particularly military – his government would have trouble surviving'. The diplomat insisted on his previous analysis that both the Kremlin and the Afghan regime, each serving its own interests, would continue with their alliance.[34]

The US Embassy in Kabul reported the discreet deployment of Spetsnaz (Russian special forces) around the capital, and on 15 December that the 5th Guards and 108th Motorised divisions were at full strength, the latter leaving its barracks. There was also a build-up of military aircraft – transports, helicopters and fighters – in the Turkestan military district.[35]

Information on a new deployment (the 2nd Paratrooper battalion) was presented by the US press as 'armed for combat', but the State Department downplayed this status.[36] On 17 December, the ABC news network aired a report claiming that 10–20,000 Soviet troops were being transferred to Afghanistan due to the crisis in Iran. The deputy assistant secretary of state, however, found no link between the deployment in Afghanistan and the crisis in Iran; the numbers mentioned by ABC could not be confirmed, but Washington 'was convinced that there were "major elements of an airborne regiment" and an additional land-based battalion, possibly a motorised rifle unit, at Bagram air base'. In addition 'there were signs of Soviet military activity north of the [river] Oxus.' Still, the Americans were 'puzzled by some curious features of this build-up': there was no propaganda campaign to justify a possible intervention, and also no worsening of the internal security situation involving raids by Afghan rebels against government forces. Meanwhile, US intelligence analysts warned that it was the first time Soviet troops had been deployed outside the Warsaw Pact area[37] (though this failed to take into account the Soviet military presence in Cuba, Ethiopia, Angola and South Yemen).

The same day, the Special Coordination Committee (SCC), under the chairmanship of Vice-President Walter Mondale, discussed the hostage crisis and the prospect of bringing the issue to the Security Council in a bid for sanctions to be adopted under Chapter VII. Ironically, it was agreed that Russia should be asked to use its vote against Iran, and if Moscow were unwilling to do so, American diplomats would work to persuade it to abstain from the voting. In addition, a Soviet veto would have very negative effects on SALT II (still undergoing the ratification process in the Senate). Lloyd Cutler (a special counsel and consultant to the president on SALT II) wisely argued that Washington should move immediately in the Security Council to adopt a finding under Article 39. However, the State Department was against moving too fast, preferring first to seek the reactions of other countries to the International Court of Justice (ICJ) ruling strongly condemning the Iranians' actions. The SCC would therefore wait 'for several days' to review such reactions, as well as to assess the outcome of the discussions between Mansour Farhang, the Iranian foreign minister, and the UN secretary-general, before Washington invoked Chapter VII.[38] Ironically, in the week when the Soviet invasion of Afghanistan took place Washington was forced to respond, thus losing the opportunity for a Security Council resolution against Iran. Cutler's advice should have been heeded. The State Department should have started work immediately on a resolution. The Soviets would have abstained, opening the way for sanctions (perhaps with the Soviets assuming – wrongly – that their action in Afghanistan would not be subject to strong American criticism). The Americans would not have been constrained by any potential quid pro quo, and would have won their resolution before the KGB special units had stormed the Kabul palace. Cutler had grasped that successful diplomacy must move with all due speed – too much debate and procrastination (the 'wait and see' approach) lost time, and with it momentum, and a new crisis created new realities.

As the SCC meeting progressed, CIA Director Stansfield Turner presented a reassuring estimate (which in the event turned out to be ill-founded): despite the establishment of two new command posts near their borders with Afghanistan, the deployment of aircraft, and the fact that two divisions may be on the move ... the CIA does not see this as a crash build up but rather a steady, planned build-up, perhaps related to Soviet perceptions of a deterioration of the Afghan military forces and the need to beef them up at some point.

Certainly the Soviets would give military backing to a communist regime in Kabul, and would have liked to replace Amin, but for the time being they had not found an influential leader. The SCC approved a three-stage strategy: to continue with private démarches to the Soviets on their build-up in Afghanistan; to consider – with the British and Pakistanis – the secret arming and further financing of the Mujahedeen; and to urge the allies and their media to concentrate their attention on Afghanistan, publicly deploring Russian policy and persuading the Muslim countries of Russian anti-Muslim policies. Backing the rebels was no easy or straightforward task. At the SCC it was noted, 'we are hamstrung by the divisions within the tribes and an effort to organize them would be a mammoth undertaking'. The number of Russian troops in Afghanistan was now up to 5,300. Moscow, according to Turner, had reached a decision to maintain a pro-Soviet regime: 'They either give this a higher priority than SALT II or they may believe it is irrelevant to SALT.'[39] Nonetheless, 5,300 Soviets were too numerous and too well-armed to be less than a threat to Amin.

On 19 December, a dispatch from the UK Embassy in Kabul claimed that the Russian troops that had arrived in the capital 'strengthen the theory that the Afghan army is using all available manpower in its push against the rebels'. Purportedly, the Soviets were assuming garrison duties, but there was some speculation that they had deployed in Kabul and decreased their presence at Bagram due to strong rebel pressure.[40] This was another wrong assumption.

On 19 December at the White House, Thatcher had discussions with Carter, Brzezinski and Vance on the Middle East, Southern Rhodesia (which would become the independent Republic of Zimbabwe the following year), the evolving situation in Iran, energy issues, defence cooperation and Northern Ireland. They also discussed the situation in Afghanistan, the president emphasising the massive scale of Russian troop movements in the country, and stating that a new battalion had reached Afghanistan only the previous day. Brzezinski revealed that the two Soviet divisions previously located north of the Oxus river (within Russian territory), 'had disappeared. The evidence was derived from ... [not declassified]. It was not now known where the two divisions were but it was obviously possible they had moved into Afghanistan.' Carter told the prime minister that his administration had already expressed in public its concern about the troop movements, and urged her to make a similar statement in public. Vance referred to the four Soviet battalions in the area near Kabul airport (a total of 1,800 men, plus their headquarters). Carter stated that these troops had at their disposal armoured personnel carriers and fighter aircraft, and claimed 'there was evidence that they had participated in air-strikes and in suppressing groups of opposition guerrillas'.[41] He offered to send the British regular intelligence reports; Thatcher accepted.[42] Both he and she seemed unsure of Russian intentions; the 'disappearance' of the two Russian divisions called into question the performance of US intelligence-gathering assets.

The same day (19 December), the US ambassador in Moscow informed his British counterpart, in confidence, that he had asked Soviet Deputy Foreign Minister Maltsev about the intentions behind the Russian deployment in Afghanistan. The Soviet official, though 'normally a courteous man, [refused] in fairly disagreeable terms to discuss the matter, [spoking] of American "invention" and [saying] that in any case the matter was no business of the United States.'[43]

Meanwhile (still on 19 December), US imaging and signals intelligence revealed that large stocks of petrol and other fuels, in mobile containers, had been pre-positioned near key crossing points on the Soviet–Afghan border, and that bridging equipment had been unloaded from a train near one of these points. Also, the 5th Guards Motorised Rifle Division had been transferred to the border. Confirmed intelligence showed that preparations were being made for special forces, based in three places in West Russia, to fly to the Turkestan military district where transport aircraft were continuing to amass. Intelligence also disclosed that a Russian motorised division within Afghanistan, which had recently reached Bagram, was now moving to occupy the

Salang Pass, a key stretch of the road from the USSR to Kabul. All this detailed information, however, did not change the analysts' assessment that the incremental Soviet reinforcement was intended solely to boost security. A 19 December alert memorandum stated:

> The pace of Soviet deployments in recent weeks does not suggest that the Soviets are responding to what they perceive as a time-urgent contingency, but rather that they are reacting to the continuing deterioration of the security situation in Afghanistan. [Once the Soviets had introduced more forces they would be able] to hold other key points, engage insurgents in selected provinces, or free Afghan Army units for operations elsewhere.[44]

On 20 December, the US chargé d'affaires in Kabul notified his British counterpart that earlier that day the Americans had received intelligence to the effect that a third battalion had arrived in Bagram. The US diplomat argued that the Russian deployments were aimed at defending Bagram from rebel attacks, assisting Russian forces in Kabul in case of need, and 'filling the breach' if an Afghan army unit was to suffer defeat by the insurgents. Any Soviet missions and troop requirements, and any possibility of heavy casualties in the fight against the rebels, were matters for debate.

All these assessments constrained the analysis and failed to allow for the examination of the hypothesis that the Kremlin was seeking to topple Amin. The British Embassy stated:

> We do not have (but then we would hardly expect to have) any evidence of a move to topple Amin, who appears to be well in control of the government machine. Again without any firm evidence our reading is that it is in the Soviets' interests to keep Amin in power.[45]

On 21 December, W.K. White, of the FCO's South Asian department, found the deployments in Bagram and elsewhere 'distinctly disturbing ... a disturbing picture but a little puzzling'. He assumed that the reinforcement of the Bagram base was a defensive requirement for the Soviets, occupying key sectors to counter rebel mortar attacks against the base. He did not worry about paratroopers being involved in action against the regime, and questioned an American comment on the 'qualitative' upgrade of the Soviet presence in Bagram. But he wondered (without elaborating further) if deployments outside that sector had been tasked with participating in a coup against Amin.[46]

The White House was still confused, but an anonymous national security aide spoke of evidence in the Afghan situation that paralleled the preparations in 1968 for the Russian invasion of Czechoslovakia.[47]

The NSA was the first to warn explicitly about the invasion. On 22 December its director, Vice-Admiral Bobby Ray Inman, telephoned both Brzezinski and Secretary of Defense Brown telling them 'there was no doubt' that a major military intervention would commence within the next 72 hours. Two days later, on 24 December, he called again, informing the White House and the Pentagon that the infiltration would begin within the next 15 hours.[48] In the evening of 24 December, the flights of Soviet transports to Kabul airport peaked. Inman wrote in his alert memorandum that the preparations were complete, and that the Soviets were probably already on the move in Afghanistan; their supposed intention was to help Amin with the security of his regime.[49]

On 25 December, the NSA issued a warning arguing that a major Russian deployment to Afghanistan was 'possibly imminent'. Confirmed information indicated that both the 105th and 103rd Guards Airborne Divisions, as well as units based in the Moscow military district, were on the move; transport flights to Kabul, Bagram, Shindand and Kandahar were recorded. However, by the end of the day both the DIA and the CIA were still insisting that the Soviet presence was being incrementally boosted to provide security for their advisers in Kabul and other cities. On 26 December, the *National Intelligence Daily* referred to field fuel deposits near the borders that could supply mechanised divisions. But the current daily reporting on 26 and 27 December still led to false conclusions: that the Soviets would commit few forces to the Amin regime's counter-insurgency effort.[50]

On the morning of 26 December (New York time – 27 December in Afghanistan), US Ambassador to the UN McHenry told his British counterpart that according to the latest intelligence the situation in Afghanistan was 'very bad' and that 'something might happen in 24 to 72 hours'. Inbound flights from the USSR to Afghanistan had reached 50 on previous days, and there were some airborne exercises taking place, linked to the deployment in the country. The US could have brought this issue to the Security Council, but preferred that Pakistan did so (the Carter administration's preoccupation with Iran was continuing).[51] Confusion still reigned in the Washington diplomatic and intelligence apparatus about what the Soviets were up to.[52]

Later the same day (26 December in New York), news of the Soviet operations against Amin and his regime took US intelligence and the White House by surprise. Hastily the State Department – equally surprised – publicly deplored the invasion. However, the UK Embassy in Washington informed the FCO that

> The [US] administration are being cautious about making any firm analysis of Soviet intentions in Afghanistan, partly because intelligence of what is happening on the ground is still incomplete and partly because they are concentrating primarily of the Security Council and the economic measures against Iran. Analysts in the intelligence community here are impressed by recent evidence of continuing deterioration in security [in Afghanistan] ...[53]

Washington urged the international community to condemn the intervention; this was interpreted by British diplomats 'as a measure both of [the US administration's] concern and of their determination not to be left alone to carry the baby. They will want to get others involved in dealing with the problem ...'[54]

The Soviets (with a long-established practice of deception and disinformation in military operations) managed to hide their real intentions until the raid on Amin's palace. All the interpretations of tactical information on Soviet deployments gathered by Anglo-American intelligence were still based on the hypothesis that the Russians were boosting the security of their facilities in Afghanistan against rebel attacks. The CIA and the DIA supported this estimate right up to the invasion itself, and must have lost credibility in the eyes of Carter and his staff. Neither did the NSA escape blame: Inman's warnings on 22, 24 and 25 December were about an imminent and massive Soviet intervention, but the NSA failed to predict that Amin was about to be overthrown and assassinated.

At noon on 26 December during the State Department's press briefing, it was made known that five divisions had gathered on the Soviet–Afghan border: 'It appears that the Soviets are crossing a new threshold in their military deployments in Afghanistan.'[55] The same day (26 December in New York, 27 December in Kabul) the UK Embassy informed the FCO that, starting on 24 December, Russian transports had been landing at Kabul airport at three-minute intervals for almost 48 hours or more, carrying troops and armoured personnel carriers. The estimate was that 5,000 new troops must have arrived; rumours were spreading to the effect that the Soviets were planning to replace Amin with Panjshiri, the minister of public works, who had just returned from Moscow.[56]

A few hours later, the UK Embassy in Kabul reported the beginning of the coup:

There has been heavy cannon and machine-gun fire from the direction of the Darulaman palace since about 19.00 local time (1500 GMT). Afghan tanks have passed behind the [UK] Embassy moving in the direction of Darulaman. There is also more distant gunfire in the direction of Rishkur.[57]

Since 1600 GMT there has only been isolated small arms fire in the distance. There has been considerable movement of heavy tanks near the embassy into the town, perhaps heading for the old People's House and also a number of light tanks or armoured cars, presumably Russian, estimated at about 150, coming from the airport road and going in the direction of Darulaman.[58]

Next day (28 December), US intelligence confirmed that the 108th Motorised Division was driving through the Salang Pass to Bagram and Kabul, and that the 5th Guards Motorised Division had crossed the border into Afghanistan, moving through Herat to Kandahar.[59] Carter and Thatcher discussed the situation by telephone, the president condemning the intervention as similar to the invasion of Czechoslovakia in 1968. The turning of Afghanistan into a puppet state entailed serious strategic consequences for the region, and it was up to the free world to make the Soviets understand how costly their decision would prove to be. However, 'the administration did not intend to allow their concern about the signings of SALT II to interfere with their taking a strong stand against the Soviets for what they have done in Afghanistan'. He would send Brezhnev a personal letter, expressing his 'deepest concern' at the situation. The prime minister agreed with Carter that 'swift action was needed'.[60] Next day, Thatcher wrote to Brezhnev:

> I have been profoundly disturbed at recent developments in Afghanistan ... I have seen the statement by the Soviet government handed to the Foreign and Commonwealth Office late on 26 December by the Soviet Embassy in London and am frankly puzzled by the assertion that recent Soviet action was at the invitation of the Afghan government. After all, the new government was only announced on 28 December. Nor can I see that Soviet action is justified in terms of Article 51 of the UN Charter.[61]

From Kabul, UK Embassy officials admitted that US intelligence was their main source, since 'the Americans have the best sources of intelligence regarding general disposition of Soviet troops'. The Soviet troop transfers were concentrated on the capital in order to defend the city from outside attack. The reinforcement of the defence of Kabul hinted that other Russian units might be dispatched to deal with the rebels. The Afghan army had suffered from Amin's coup, and earlier from mutinies. Very few Afghan troops carried arms; they would not be able to fight the rebel forces. The Soviets ran the risk of being called upon to do so themselves, when 'they would find themselves in the same sort of stalemate as the Amin government'. It was an accurate forecast.[62]

An FCO report titled 'Afghanistan: Soviet Occupation', compiled in February 1980, was an attempt to give the first full description of the invasion. It mirrored the understanding of events by top decision makers in Downing Street and Whitehall. Of course, this report suffered from mistakes and inaccuracies. According to FCO estimates (possibly coupled with MI6 analyses), after the signature of the 1978 Treaty of Friendship, Good Neighbourliness and Cooperation between Russia and Afghanistan almost 5,000 Soviets (of whom half were military personnel) penetrated the Afghan government and military. Russian generals (like Pavlovskii and Epishev) visited regions to assess the potential of government operations against insurgents. When Taraki was overthrown by his party rival Hafizullah Amin on 14 September 1979, Moscow did not react to the coup but gave sanctuary to three high-ranking officers and party members; one of those was Babrak Karmal, a party member and an opponent of Amin. Amin unleashed an unexpected wave of violence against any party member who might stand against him, and soon demanded the recall of Russian Ambassador Puzanov for supporting opponents of the regime. On 6 October 1979, at a conference of communist countries, Shah Wali, Amin's chief deputy, accused the ambassador of being implicated in a failed assassination attempt against Amin. Puzanov was declared persona non grata, and recalled; Moscow seemed unmoved by this, and replaced him with Fikryat Tabeev, who presented his credentials on 1 December. This 'suggested that the Soviet leaders were reconciling themselves to Amin', said the FCO report. Three days later, on the anniversary of the signing of the 1978 Afghan–Soviet Treaty, Amin received a friendly message from Moscow.[63]

In early December, the landing of 2,500 Russian troops at the Bagram air base and their transport to Kabul was noted by the foreign press. 'This seems to have been the first contingent of Soviet combat troops to arrive in Afghanistan', remarked the FCO. Still, the description of events remained vague: 'Tension apparently revived after the arrival of the troops. On 17 December Asadullah Amin, the President's nephew and head of the intelligence service, was shot, wounded and taken to Moscow – it appeared as an attempt against Amin.'[64]

Amin, fearful of his personal security, moved from the People's palace to the Tajbeg Palace, on the outskirts of Kabul ... on

26 December the Afghan media announced [Minister of Public Works] Panjshiri's return (presumably earlier) from Moscow, reinforcing the rumours that the Soviets intended to replace Amin with some of the Afghan leaders they had been protecting.[65]

Foreign (including Indian) press sources reported that new Russian troops had been deploying north of the Oxus River since mid-December. The Indian Embassy in Kabul made it known that Russian troops (infantry and armour) had been moving there as early as 24 December. On Christmas night some 5,000 troops flew into Kabul airport, moving close to the People's Palace, and stationed in the vicinity of the airport and the suburbs near the Darulaman Palace.[66]

At 19.15 hours (local) on 27 December the lethal violence began. Soviet troops stormed the Ministry of the Interior, destroyed the main post office, and directed fire against the Darulaman Palace and the radio station:

> According to eye-witnesses, the military side of the coup was a purely Soviet operation. There is evidence that Soviet advisers, who were present certainly down to company level in the Afghan army units in Kabul, had taken action to neutralise these units. Meanwhile the flow of troops continued by air and more Soviet forces entered Afghanistan by road.[67]

Babrak Karmal made a radio broadcast from Russia announcing the coup at about 16.15 hours. At 19.45 the Tass news agency transmitted Karmal's declaration in Russian, and at 21.00 Moscow Radio broadcast it in English. A couple of hours later, Kabul Radio gave it full coverage, announcing the names of the members of the new Revolutionary Council under Karmal (who had assumed the post of PDPA secretary-general and president of the Revolutionary Council) and the execution of Amin after a decision of the 'Revolutionary Tribunal'. At 02.55 hours the new government of the Democratic Republic of Afghanistan declared that, on the basis of the 1978 treaty, 'It had requested the USSR to render urgent political, moral and economic assistance, including military aid, and ... the Soviet government had agreed to do so.'[68]

By the morning of 28 December (after the broadcast of new government appointments), the British Embassy in Kabul was describing the situation:

> There is still intermittent firing at Darulaman palace and Rishkor barracks south of Kabul. This morning MIGs have been making air passes but not engaging targets. Town [Kabul] is quiet with large numbers of Soviet troops and tanks as well as civilian militia.[69]

The FCO report of February 1980 pointed out that the Russian troops had been deployed in Kabul at least four days before the coup, and had been attacking government buildings at least nine hours before Karmal's 'invitation'. 'The Soviet combat units could not have entered and acted so swiftly had not detailed arrangements been made and planned by advanced units', concluded the report.[70] Karmal did not hold any official post at the time he called in the Soviets, and there was no evidence that he was actually in Afghanistan, claimed British diplomats. He made another broadcast on Afghan television on 1 January 1980, while Soviet sources insisted that the day of the 'invitation' was 28 December. A story spread that Amin had called the Soviets on 26 December, but this was equally unconvincing (concluded the FCO report) since the coup cost him his own life:

> There had been ample evidence of Soviet antipathy to Amin in the months before, and his experience on 14 September [the day of the attempt against his life] had warned him against Soviet assurances. The suggestion that he requested troops on 26 December is therefore unlikely and becomes even more absurd in the light of claims now being made by Babrak Karmal that Amin was planning an anti-Communist coup [to take place] on 29 December – a plan that would have been sabotaged by the arrival of Soviet troops.[71]

In spite of 'ample evidence', the UK Embassy did not examine the possibility of a coup against Amin. Beyond foreign policy and the attitudes of Amin and Brezhnev, the moving around of Russian troops, armour and military trucks in Afghan city avenues would certainly have captured the attention of British diplomats and intelligence officers, and made them question Moscow's intentions. In any event, the Embassy continued to argue that, out of self-interest, Russia and Amin would maintain their alliance; it failed to take seriously the hypothesis of a Russian intervention against Amin – the lack of intelligence as well as the fixation on a single analysis hampered a clear appreciation of the evolving situation. Kremlin must have felt assured that London and Washington were in the dark; the direct queries as to its intentions put to Russian diplomats by Acting Secretary of State Warren Christopher and other American officials showed a depressing lack of intelligence, to the extent of needing to ask their opponents directly what the latter were up to.

Once it was known that there had been an attempt on the life of Amin's intelligence chief (on 17 December), analysts in London had to choose between two estimates: Moscow was planning either to help Amin or to overthrow him. The key to this riddle might have been provided by signals intelligence (UK signals-intelligence files have not been declassified, and we may therefore form only a plausible hypothesis). US satellite and signals intelligence targeting low-level communications within and between the two divisions in the Turkestan military district might have disclosed the magnitude of Russian preparations for troop transports to Afghanistan. But Brzezinski's remark (on 19 December) that two Soviet divisions had 'disappeared' showed serious intelligence gaps at a critical moment.[72] The key to the riddle should have been provided by the interception of the communications of the KGB 'Zenith' unit preparing a raid against Amin.

It seems that the Soviets, since the GRU mission and the dispatch of the paratroopers, had been sending too many special forces troops to confine themselves to a friendly attitude towards Amin. The debate about the defence requirements of the Bagram base diverted the FCO's analysis 'from the woods to the trees'. We could argue that by 20 December an invasion warning might well have been issued if the FCO had been convinced that the shooting incident on 17 December was indicative of Russian intent against Amin.

But could London or Washington actually have decided to deter Russia from invading Afghanistan, even if they had known of Soviet intentions by that date? After all, Amin was no ally of the West. There was no time to mount a military deterrent on the ground – Carter and Thatcher did not have sufficient time first to agree on a common approach and then to bring the issue to their allies in NATO and the Security Council. The only possible option for military-backed deterrence (rather than deterrence backed by words alone) would be a naval task force deploying in Pakistani waters. There could be no ground deployment to the north (for example, to the Pakistani–Afghan border), since a move into non-aligned Afghanistan would look like a Western invasion. But the Americans could not open a new front; they could scarcely take the Afghanistan issue to the Security Council alone, because they had been focusing on sanctions against Iran to compel the Khomeini regime to free the American hostages. On 30 December, Vance told Sir Anthony Parsons (now the UK ambassador to the UN) that Carter was interested first in securing sanctions against Iran, and only then in proceeding with the condemnation of the Soviet invasion in the Security Council; to this the British diplomat replied that there was little time left for such a strategy.[73]

Could the Politburo of Brezhnev, Andropov, Ustinov, Suslov and Gromyko be deterred by Carter (who until then had shown great interest in détente and SALT II, but who now looked weakened by the Iran crisis) and Thatcher (who, in their eyes, was still learning the ropes in international politics while fighting for reforms in the economy)? Soviet leaders might have also underestimated Thatcher, since no woman had ever reached the top echelons of power in the USSR. The Soviets believed that neither the ideologue peanut farmer from Georgia who spoke of human rights nor the shopkeeper's daughter who was obsessed with liberalism would confront them on Afghanistan. The group in the Politburo were too confident of their power to reject the notion of an invasion. Besides, they were frustrated with the Afghans' feuding; they assumed that an obedient communist like Karmal would be the solution, and would save Afghanistan from either Western influence or the Islamist rebels.

The second part of this chapter will examine the accuracy of Anglo-American intelligence reporting, as well as of the FCO's February 1980 report, by taking into consideration the declassified files that describe KGB operational planning and the Politburo's deliberations, confirming that the KGB considered Amin a CIA agent. According to one Soviet account, Amin spread this rumour himself, having admitted to the Soviets earlier that, while in the United States, 'he was just playing with the CIA because he needed money to continue with his studies'. Nonetheless, US intelligence later dismissed this allegation.[74]

The Soviet part of the story

According to the Kremlin's perceptions, the Afghan army mutiny of March 1979 in Herat (when an artillery and an infantry regiment joined the rebels) revealed the impotence of the Taraki regime in dealing effectively with the Islamist guerrillas. Protests against reform, especially education for women, were the pretext for the mutiny, with mobs turning against Russian advisers and their families, murdering them indiscriminately.[75]

On 17 March 1979, at the Politburo meeting in Moscow under the chairmanship of Andrei Kirilenko, the secretary of the Central Committee – Brezhnev did not attend – there was a clear reference to the need for contingency planning to be completed by the introduction of a large Russian contingent into Afghanistan. Kirilenko was absolutely against any intervention, though he was no admirer of Taraki or Amin, remarking:

We gave them everything and what had come off? Nothing of any value. After all, it was they who executed innocent people for no reason and told us that we also executed people in Lenin's time. You see what kind of Marxists we have found?[76]

Defence Minister Ustinov presented a plan for the 105th Guards Airborne Division and a motorised rifle-regiment to move by air to Kabul at a day's notice. In addition, two motorised divisions near the borders could (if the green light was given) enter Afghanistan within three days; these were the 5th Motor Artillery Division and the 68th Motorised Division (which US intelligence had mistakenly listed as the 5th Guards Motorised Division and the 108th Motorised Division, respectively). Two days later, at another Politburo meeting, Ustinov referred to a third division under preparation in the Central Asian military district. Kosygin, Andropov and Gromyko were in favour of an intervention, if this became expedient. Gromyko boasted:

We must proceed from a fundamental proposition in considering the question of aid to Afghanistan, namely: under no conditions can we lose Afghanistan. For 60 years now we have lived with Afghanistan in peace and friendship. And if we lose Afghanistan now and it turns against the Soviet Union, this will result in a sharp setback to our foreign policy.[77]

This Politburo meeting deferred any decision on intervention, but Ustinov was authorised to draft a further contingency – for two motorised divisions to move close to the borders. But next day in the Politburo, the policy recommendations were altered. Now Andropov and Gromyko sounded less than eager to press for intervention. The KGB chairman was emphatic:

It's completely clear to us that Afghanistan is not ready at this time to resolve all of the issues it faces through socialism. The economy is backward, the Islamic religion predominates, and nearly all of the rural population is illiterate. We know Lenin's teaching about a revolutionary situation. Therefore, I believe that we can suppress a revolution in Afghanistan only with the aid of our bayonets, and that is for us entirely inadmissible. We cannot take that risk.[78]

Gromyko concurred: '[I]ndeed the situation in Afghanistan is not ripe for a revolution. And all we have done in recent years with détente, arms reduction, and much more – all that would be thrown back.'[79]

The foreign minister realised the impact an intervention might have on US–Soviet relations, but his stance is perplexing since the previous day, together with Andropov, he had been an ardent supporter of intervention if there was a need. At the 19 March Politburo meeting, Brezhnev himself admitted:

The question was raised as to the immediate participation of our troops in the conflict that has arisen in Afghanistan. In my view, the Politburo has correctly determined that the time is not right for us to become entangled in that war.[80]

This did not mean that contingency planning no longer took place. Ustinov stated that he had taken prudent measures forming two divisions in the Turkestan and one in the Central Asian military districts. He did not support intervention, but sought to demonstrate the military's readiness, which was why he was requesting authorisation to conduct exercises; forming new regiments meant he needed to call up reservists. The Politburo concurred.[81] (We have seen above that US intelligence followed the exercises in the Turkestan military district throughout 1979, but could not discern Russian intentions.)

Meanwhile, Taraki and Amin pleaded repeatedly not only for more arms but for Soviet military personnel to man tanks and fighters. After the mutiny in Herat, they both feared the increasing disloyalty of the Afghan armed forces; essentially, they wanted Moscow to fight their war. On 17 (or 18) March 1979, in a telephone conversation between Taraki and Alexei Kosygin (the Russian premier), the Afghan leader requested Russian crews to man helicopters. Kosygin refused, leaving no room for doubt by warning that Soviet personnel playing a combat role would bring international protests about Russian 'interference'. He asked about all the Afghan officers trained in the Soviet Union, and was dismayed by Taraki's answer – that most of them were Muslim reactionaries, disloyal to his regime. Taraki spoke of Russian tank crews of Uzbek and Tajik origin, operational in civilian clothes or in Afghan army uniform. But Kosygin would not allow himself to be persuaded.[82] On 20 March he met with Taraki in Moscow, just before the latter was to see Brezhnev. Kosygin repeated:

> [I]f our troops were introduced, the situation in your country would not only not improve, but would worsen. One cannot deny that our troops would have to fight not only with foreign aggressors, but also with a certain number of your people. And people do not forgive such things. Besides, as soon as our troops cross the border, China and all other aggressors will be vindicated.[83]

Taraki took refuge in exaggeration, claiming not only that Muslim Brotherhood members had infiltrated the country, but also that 'entire sub-divisions (from Pakistan), dressed in Afghan military uniforms' were fighting his regime. Kosygin replied that he had just received a reassurance from Pakistani dictator Zia ul-Haq that his country was seeking good relations with Afghanistan, would not interfere in domestic affairs, and was merely providing humanitarian aid to Afghan refugees. Taraki insisted that the Pakistanis were setting up 'commando training camps'. Kosygin answered: 'We are not so naive as to believe every word of Zia ul-Haq, but whatever the case may be, the [Pakistani] statement has been made and it is binding.' As the conversation developed, Taraki once again raised the issue of Soviet tank crews. Kosygin again replied: 'I believe that it is unlikely that socialist countries will agree to this. The question of sending people who would sit in your tanks and shoot at your people – this is a very pointed political question.'[84] In his later meeting with Brezhnev, Taraki was bluntly reprimanded by the chairman: 'I said directly to Comrade Taraki that repression is a sharp weapon and it must be applied extremely cautiously, and only in cases when there are serious legal grounds for it.'[85]

By the end of May the new Soviet military aid, 'free of charge', included 140 field guns and mortars, 90 armoured personnel carriers, 48,000 machine guns, 1,000 grenade launchers, and 680 aircraft munitions (but 'the delivery of gas bombs with a non-toxic poison gas is not considered possible', wrote Gromyko to Ambassador Puzanov).[86]

Later, on 29 June 1979, the Politburo authorised the dispatch of an airborne battalion to provide security for the Bagram base. Also, more KGB Spetsnaz operatives of the elite, 150-strong 'Zenith' unit were assigned to guard the Soviet Embassy in Kabul; and it was decided that a GRU unit – possibly Spetsnaz – would be sent to Bagram in August.[87]

Taraki continued relentlessly to press Moscow for Soviet tank crews, and he continued to meet with rebuffs. The Afghan leader tried to play up the Pakistani threat, but Puzanov and the KGB were not unduly alarmed. Puzanov made it clear to Taraki, in a meeting on 10 July 1979, that

> The Pakistanis must not be given grounds for breaking the dialogue [with Kabul on Pashtunistan] ... [I]n any case the Afghan side must demonstrate reasonable restraint; if the Pakistanis set out to break off the negotiations, let the blame for that fall entirely on them.[88]

Taraki and Amin asked the Russian representatives to have two divisions ready on the border, to enter the country and fight the rebels in case of need. On a visit to Kabul, Boris Ponomarev (the head of the International Department of the Politburo's CPSU Central Committee) gave a short answer: 'The Soviet Union cannot do that.' In another conversation, Taraki asked for a parachute division, but again his request was turned down.[89] Meanwhile, Ustinov was preparing the two mechanised divisions near the border.

KGB resident Sergei Bogdanov was sending reports of growing discontent among the Afghan cabinet members. He was told by Sarwari, the AGSA chief, that the head of the general staff, General Shakhur, was plotting a coup under the direction of a superior, and with American support. He was hinting at Minister of Defence Abdul Qadir, who belonged to the rival Parham faction. Ambassador Puzanov did not believe this intelligence, so was duly taken by surprise when Qadir was arrested and later executed.[90] (Qadir was a trusted KGB source who had participated in the coup against Daoud; the Soviets tried in vain to save him).[91]

Puzanov heard of Amin's complaints that Taraki had so concentrated power in his own hands that Amin could not launch effective
counterinsurgency operations. Puzanov replied that a special group of
five or six officials, including Amin himself, could take operational
command, while Taraki's authority would be preserved. The ambassador just tried to present a workable resolution while the KGB was
collecting incriminating information on Amin.[92] The latter once again
raised the issue of Russian participation in combating the Islamists, in
a 25 August discussion with Soviet Deputy Defence Minister General
Ivan Pavlovskii. The general followed the Politburo line: '[T]he introduction of our troops might lead to the complication of the military–
political situation and the strengthening of American assistance to the
rebels.'[93]

Throughout the autumn of 1979 the Soviet policy of not intervening in the civil war in Afghanistan was gradually altering. Amin
unleashed a wave of terror unprecedented even by Afghan standards,
shocking the Kremlin and crippling the PDPA apparatus. In response,
as early as 10 September 1979, Andropov was authorised to bring
Karmal from Czechoslovakia and to discuss a coup, with the latter as
its leader. Andropov now seemed to favour an invasion, but wanted
first to commit Brezhnev; he spoke of a coup by 'healthy forces' to be
supported by the Soviet military.[94] The KGB's 'Zenith' had already
drafted a plan to kidnap Amin and bring him to the Soviet Union.[95]
Karmal was deemed an obedient person; according to his GRU file,
updated in December 1979, he was 'a skilful orator ... emotional, with
a tendency towards generalisation rather than concrete analysis. He
has a poor command of economic problems, and is interested only in
their general outline.'[96]

It seemed that the KGB and the Soviet Embassy in Kabul, despite
their resources, were unable to keep track of the complex web of evolving intrigue between Amin and Taraki. Indeed, on 10 September,
while Taraki was on a visit to Moscow, Sayed Tarun, his chief of staff,
confided to Bogdanov that he sided with Amin and would help him
defend himself, since Taraki wanted to kill him.[97] In any case, Taraki
was warned of Amin's intentions by Brezhnev, and, after his return to
Kabul, by a KGB officer. Taraki reassured the Soviets that no coup

could take place, since 'nothing could happen without my knowledge'.
Taraki did not know that Amin, fearful of what the Soviets might
have told Taraki in Moscow, planned for an anti-aircraft battery to
shoot down Taraki's plane as it approached Kabul. But Taraki loyalists
got wind of this plot and arrested the battery's crew. Amin waited in
vain for the noise of gun-fire and of the aircraft crashing.[98]

Russian files offer a more detailed picture than that available to
Anglo-American intelligence at the time, enriching our understanding of the September coup and the invasion.

On 11 September, Taraki returned to Kabul, confident of being
able to implement Brezhnev's recommendation to oust Amin. Next
day, Amin accused four cabinet ministers of planning to assassinate
him while Taraki was abroad; the latter sought a compromise would
mean not replacing them. On 13 September, Taraki and Amin met,
but without reaching an accommodation. After the meeting, Amin
allegedly told Jandad, the head of the National Guard, that he was
relinquishing his premiership and assuming the position of minister
of defence, in charge of all the armed forces. Ambassador Puzanov
reported back to Moscow that 'at 9.30 pm, 13 September, the situation was critical. The possibility that H. Amin might order the military units loyal to him to take up arms against Taraki could not be
excluded.'[99] Both Taraki and Amin sought Russian support. At the
former's residence, Soviet officials delivered a message from Brezhnev
and the Politburo urging unity.[100] At the same venue Taraki and
Amin held discussions until 1.00 am; the order alerting the National
Guard, issued earlier by Amin, was cancelled, and Amin returned to
his home. The four ministers accused of plotting his murder hid in the
Soviet Embassy (whence they would later be transferred, in disguise,
to the USSR).

At 1230 hours on 14 September, Ivanov and Bogdanov paid a
visit to Amin at the Ministry of Defence. In the presence of the two
Russians, Amin spoke by telephone to Taraki, who deplored his stance
as insubordinate, given his own wish to appoint a new minister of
defence, and asked Amin to come to his residence again without bodyguards. Amin asked the Soviets for advice; they urged calm and compromise.[101] That evening, after his coup had succeeded, Amin told

the Russian delegation that he considered them 'the most responsible
people in Afghanistan. He was prepared to follow any advice from his
Soviet friends, fully, even if he did not agree with it.'[102] Eventually,
however, he was to show no mercy towards Taraki.

On 13 September (the day before Amin's coup), the Politburo
made it clear to General Pavlovskii, Lieutenant-General Gorelov
and KGB resident Boris Ivanov: 'We cannot take it upon ourselves
to arrest Amin with our own battalion, since this would be a direct
interference in the internal affairs of Afghanistan and would have far-
reaching consequences.'[103] Soon, however, the Politburo would change
its approach.

Amin went to see Taraki in his office, despite a secret warning
from Tarun that the president and his loyalists would attempt to
murder him there. Accompanied by four bodyguards, he reached the
palace, and while climbing the stairs he met Tarun. The guards at the
entrance to the meeting room insisted that no armed man could enter.
An argument erupted and Tarun, who was himself carrying an assault
rifle, ordered them to step aside. One of the guards then opened fire,
killing him. Amin rushed for cover, while his bodyguards returned
fire (one of them was injured). Amin and his party escaped to the yard
and fled in one of their cars. Reaching the army general staff building, he telephoned Taraki to demand an explanation. The president
replied that 'there was a misunderstanding between the guards', and
again invited Amin to his office. The exasperated Amin accused the
guards of having intended to kill Tarun in the first place. Puzanov,
Bogdanov, Gorelov and Ivanov (responsible for KGB liaison with the
Afghan Ministry of Defence), finding themselves in the midst of the
Afghan feud, left Taraki and walked to the office where Amin had
remained, to persuade him to meet the president. This was a futile
exercise, since Amin, his suit stained with his bodyguard's blood, was
convinced Taraki wanted him dead.[104]

The situation got further out of hand when Taraki ordered a jet
fighter to bomb the general staff building while the Soviets were holding talks with Amin. Taraki knew that the Soviets were inside, and
allegedly said, 'It doesn't matter.' But the air force refused Taraki's
order, and Amin, who was in de facto control of the armed forces,

launched his coup. Soldiers surrounded the president's residence, and he was arrested.[105] Amin's coup proved one thing clearly: that the Soviets, despite the resources and intelligence apparatus they had deployed in Afghanistan since the early days of the Cold War, remained no more than confused observers of Afghan feuding, still unable to react promptly.

Amin claimed that, 'for reasons of health', Taraki (now under arrest) was about to resign as chairman of the Revolutionary Council, and the Central Committee plenum would elect himself in two days' time. All the Soviet pleas were to no avail.[106]

On 15 September, the Politburo decided the Soviet representatives should talk again with Amin to dissuade him from persecuting Taraki's supporters. The Russian military advisers would not take part in any activities that involved persecuting Taraki's cadres. Arms supplies would be curtailed, save only for spare parts and ammunition.[107] Two days later Russian officials were to congratulate Amin on his appointment as secretary-general of the PDPA and chairman of the Revolutionary Council.[108] For the time being Moscow had no other choice.

An angry Brezhnev, at the Politburo conference of 20 September, admitted that the KGB had failed to give advance warning of Amin's coup:

> Events developed so swiftly that essentially there was little opportunity for us, here in Moscow, to somehow interfere in them ... Right now our mission is to determine our further positions in Afghanistan and to secure our influence there ... Evidently, Amin will continue to follow, at least outwardly, the recommendations we made earlier (under Taraki) ... But [our] job will be difficult and delicate.[109]

Two weeks later, on 4 October, Brezhnev confided to Erich Honecker:

> Frankly, we are not pleased by all Amin's methods and actions. He is very power-driven. In the past he repeatedly revealed disproportionate harshness. But with regard to his basic political

platform, he has decidedly conformed to the course of further development of the Revolution ...[110]

The Politburo considered that Amin would soon be toppled by dissidents, supported by the four ex–cabinet ministers who had escaped with the help of the KGB's 'Zenith' flying out on 14 October to Sofia, Bulgaria. Purges in the Afghan military soared, and a special three-month officer-training course was instituted to replace the purged personnel. The new regime boasted a list of 12,000 executions, but some believed that a greater number had been killed. Meanwhile, the Islamist rebels resisting reforms now controlled 90 per cent of Afghan territory.[111]

There were widespread Russian fears that the unpredictable Amin would turn Afghanistan towards the West: memories of losing Egypt, Chile and Somalia were still alive,[112] and Amin was not polite to the Soviets, despite his pleas for military aid. On 6 October 1979, he leaked to the ambassadors of communist countries via Akbar Shah Wali, his foreign minister, that Puzanov was behind the assassination attempt of 14 September. On 9 October, Puzanov and the KGB station chief met Amin to protest against Wali's statement. But Amin was unfriendly and arrogant. It was reported to Moscow that

During the talks H. Amin was brash and provocative. He sometimes contained his fury with difficulty. He interrupted the Soviet representatives and did not give them a chance to state their point of view calmly. At the same time there were moments when he appeared to collect his thoughts, and gave the impression that he did not want to spoil his relations [with the Soviet Union] completely.[113]

On 8 October, Amin ordered Taraki's execution – but kept it a close secret. The KGB, however, suspected the murder and informed Brezhnev, who, though ill, was personally affronted at the killing of his protégé. The chairman had earlier promised Taraki more help, but now he was apprehensive: 'Can [other communist leaders] really believe Brezhnev's word if his assurances of support and protection remain [just] words?' Foreign Secretary Gromyko and the influential Andropov, the KGB chairman, were equally shocked at Taraki's murder.[114]

At the end of October, Ustinov, Gromyko, Andropov and Ponomarev submitted a joint memorandum to the Politburo, warning of new 'signs' of 'a more balanced policy' towards the West on the part of Afghanistan. Soviet intelligence had revealed that 'representatives of the USA, on the basis of their contacts with the Afghans, are coming to a conclusion about the possibility of a change in the political line of Afghanistan in a direction which is pleasing to Washington'.[115] The Russian leaders admitted that the situation in Afghanistan was 'extremely complicated', and recommend continued consultations with Amin, 'not giving grounds to believe that we don't trust him and don't wish to deal with him. Use the contacts with Amin to assert appropriate influence and simultaneously to further expose his true intentions.'[116]

The KGB continued feeding the Politburo with intelligence on Amin and his regime. The Afghan leadership almost openly asserted that the April 1978 revolution would have been achieved 'perfectly without Russian machine guns, rockets and tanks. Afghans do not need the beggarly Russian socialism and Russian politics' (but it was true that Moscow had not facilitated the 1978 coup). There was also

> political targeting of Soviet citizens on the personal orders of Amin, and gradual pressure on Soviet specialists with a view to using them to transmit slanted information to Moscow through unofficial channels, bypassing the embassy and leadership of other departments ... covert searches and surveillance of Soviet citizens, threats and blackmail.[117]

Intelligence from the Soviet Embassy in Belgrade revealed that the temporary Afghan chargé d'affaires had told a group of diplomats in Belgrade:

> These models [of socialism] are unacceptable to Afghanistan. Afghanistan's attachment to the USSR is only a short-term tactical step caused by the internal situation [the war with

the Islamists]. When the situation has been consolidated, Afghanistan will rely on effective aid from Muslim countries. It will follow the example of Egypt and come out openly against the presence of Soviet advisers in the country.[118]

Indeed, throughout the autumn 1979, Amin's elder brother and cabinet members spoke of the Sadat option, while KGB disclosed Amin's secret conferences with the US chargé d'affaires in Kabul. The Kremlin grew anxious at the possibility of Afghanistan under Amin allying itself with Islamist clerics and fundamentalist Iran, expanding their influence. Intelligence also suggested that Amin was seeking to approach rightist opponents belonging to the faction of the exiled king, Zahir Shah. Finally, there was intelligence that Amin had fabricated anti-Moscow rumours, and that loyal government and party members seemed free to talk against the Soviets in closed party meetings. In November 1979, the Cuban ambassador in Kabul spoke of Amin's starting to follow a policy independent of Russia.[119]

The KGB also reported an alleged meeting between Amin's representatives and Islamists in Logar province in early September. But the Soviet spies were wrong in assuming that the secular Amin was thinking of siding with Khomeini's Iran and of establishing an Islamic regime.[120]

The fear of a nuclear war interrupted the focus on Afghanistan. On 9 November 1979, at 3 am, Brzezinski was woken to be informed that 250 Soviet nuclear missiles were heading to the United States. He did not have the time to inform Carter. Two calls later it was confirmed that it was a false alarm. Upon getting the news of the false US alarm, Moscow grew anxious. On 14 November, Brezhnev sent a message to Carter expressing his 'extreme anxiety' at the 'tremendous danger' of a nuclear war that might result from retaliation after a false alarm. He took note of press reports that top US decision-makers had not been informed on time that the warning was erroneous. Washington simply rebuked Brezhnev's claims. Three other false alerts of US missile-warning systems occurred on 28 May, 3 June and 6 June 1980.[121] Evidently, the paranoid fear of the Kremlin that the United States would launch a surprise attack (see Chapter 4) grew after the false-alarm episodes of 1979–80.

In early December (the specific date has not been revealed) Andropov submitted a memorandum to Brezhnev repeating the allegations that Amin was dealing with the Americans:

Alarming information [has] started to arrive about Amin's secret activities, forewarning of a political shift to the West: contacts with an American agent about issues which are kept secret from us. Promises to tribal leaders to shift away from the USSR and to adopt a 'policy of neutrality.' Closed meetings in which attacks were made against Soviet policy and the activities of our specialists. The practical removal of our headquarters in Kabul, etc. Diplomatic circles in Kabul are talking widely of Amin's differences with Moscow and his possible anti-Soviet steps.

It was enough finally to persuade Brezhnev to give the green light for the operation to topple Amin and replace him with Karmal. Andropov claimed that the two battalions that had arrived in Kabul were sufficient for a coup, 'but as a precautionary measure in the event of unforeseen complications, it would be wise to have a military group close to the border'.[122] (In fact, two divisions had already been deployed and conducting drills since mid-1979; Andropov merely reminded Brezhnev of this.)

Meanwhile on 2, 3, 12 and 17 December, Amin issued more requests for Moscow to help him fight the rebels. He touched on the issue of being invited to Moscow during his 6 December audience with Ambassador Tabeev. The diplomat was non-committal, while appearing willing to satisfy Amin's requests for war materiel – to assuage any suspicions that the Kremlin might be seeking to have him removed.[123]

On 6 December, the Politburo authorised the dispatch of 500 GRU troops to Afghanistan. In a private discussion between Andropov and Ustinov reviewing the KGB chairman's plans for an intervention, the minister of defence joked, 'You are quite the adventurist, Yura.'[124]

At about the same time Andropov agreed with Ustinov's full-scale plan for deploying 75,000 troops in Afghanistan to secure an easy victory over Amin. Soviet forces would also be positioned near the borders with Iran and Pakistan, to deter any support for the Islamist rebels and to help the new government under Babrak Karmal to deal with internal security.[125]

On 8 December, Andropov, Gromyko, Ustinov and Michail Suslov (the influential chief ideologist of the Politburo) met in Brezhnev's office to consult on the advantages and disadvantages of an invasion. In their assessment they took into consideration the previous US decision to deploy Pershing II missiles in Europe (fearing that a future deployment in Afghanistan could threaten the air defences in south-east Russia and the Baykonur cosmodrome). They also believed some intercepted CIA reports from Ankara arguing in favour of a (far-fetched) plan for creating a 'New Great Ottoman Empire', to include the Muslim populations in the south of the USSR. In addition, they worried about the possibility of an Irano-Pakistani intervention in Afghanistan to seize alleged uranium deposits for the construction of nuclear weapons. Andropov and Ustinov were unequivocally in favour of the invasion; soon the others joined them.[126]

On 10 December, Ustinov alerted the two mechanised divisions to be ready to move. He requested Marshal Nikolay Ogarkov, chief of the general staff, to have 75–80,000 troops in readiness for the intervention. On 12 December, key Politburo members (Brezhnev, Andropov, Gromyko, Ustinov, Suslov) decided to depose Amin and to introduce 'limited' forces into the country. On 23 December, Western radio broadcasts disclosed the arrival of the Russian forces; some commentators assumed this meant Amin was getting support against the insurgents. Between 25 and 27 December, 7,700 troops reached Afghanistan by air; the 108th Motorised Rifle Division moved to Kabul. On 25 December, the evening edition of the English-language *Kabul Times* contained an article entitled 'The will of the people will be the deciding factor', hinting at anti-Moscow attitudes with the slogan, 'Down with the interventionists!' According to one KGB source, this article had been sanctioned by Amin himself, who sought to make the West interested in his case and to help him by directing its propaganda against the Kremlin (while other accounts discounted the possibility that Amin feared an intervention, as will be seen below). Bogdanov, KGB resident in Kabul, had meetings with Amin on 12 and 17 December. The Afghan leader insisted that Russian troops participate in combat against the Islamists; he wanted them deployed in the northern regions, where they could set up garrison whenever they deemed necessary, guard the lines of communication, and command joint Soviet–Afghan units.[127]

On 14 December, KGB 'Zenith' snipers were ordered to shoot at Amin while he was in his limousine, but they aborted the attempt because his car accelerated.[128] Next day a plot was initiated to poison him and his entourage, his nephew Asadullah, and Mohammad Yaqub, the chief of the general staff. The Russian cooks who provided lunch to the president laced his food with poison. The lethal substance would start taking effect after six hours. The KGB started the countdown, observing any movements (for example, ambulances, guards placed on alert) in the presidential palace that could disclose the success of the plot. If such nervousness was discovered, then the paratrooper battalions and KGB 'Zenith' would take over key military and communications buildings in Kabul. But it turned out to be a quiet night; Amin avoided poisoning because of a refreshment he had drunk that had a direct mitigating effect on the poison. His nephew, however, was not so lucky, and Russian medical staff were called upon to provide treatment. The KGB asked for directions from Moscow, which replied that a routine cable should be delivered to Amin by hand, to allow the Russians to enter the palace and check on his condition. At about midnight a GRU officer and an interpreter reached the palace, and asked to meet Amin to deliver the message. Amin, who looked rather pale, was handed the message and listened to the translation. He replied by sending greetings to Brezhnev. His nephew felt unwell the next day, and was transported to a Moscow clinic. Once the news of the failed attempt became known in the Kremlin, the dispatch of a second paratrooper battalion to Bagram was cleared; the mechanised divisions, the KGB, the GRU and the paratroopers all geared up for the invasion. A request from Kabul also urged sending more troops; this, according to Liakhovskii, was the start of a full-scale invasion, after the failed assassination attempts and the piecemeal Russian deployments in Afghanistan that had commenced the previous May.[129]

On 25 December, Amin chaired a PDPA Politburo meeting to discuss the political and military issues arising from the planned spring campaign against the Islamists. Later he confided to Sultan Ahmad, 'All my efforts to improve relations with the USA and other Western countries have been fruitless. Our possibilities have been exhausted; I consider myself free from any obligations to the West.'[130]

Under 'Operation Storm-333', three KGB units – 'Zenith', 'Alpha' and 'Grom' ('Thunder') – would assault the presidential palace. The raiders would have at their disposal BTRs with heavy machine guns, and would be supported by the Muslim Battalion.[131] Since November, at Amin's request, the Soviets had provided part of his personal guard; a Spetsnaz unit termed 'the Muslim Battalion,' composed of men from Soviet Central Asia, was based next to the palace; a total of 520 troops with BTR-60 vehicles and heavy anti-aircraft ZSU 23-4 machine guns were stationed at the palace's eastern defence perimeter. Amin's personal bodyguard detail also contained KGB officers acting as advisers.[132] (The 'Zenith' had prepared to storm the building on 13 December – the day of the failed attempt to poison Amin – but the operation was postponed.)[133]

Amin suspected nothing. A rather alarmed Yaqub told him on 26 December that 'the Soviet troops were arriving in quantities that exceeded the [Afghan–Soviet aid] agreement'. The KGB intercepted their call and confirmed Amin's relaxed attitude; he told Yaqub not to worry: 'So what, the more they come, the better for us.'[134] He assumed that the Soviets had poured in more troops to help him with the insurgency – which he believed to be the purpose of the airborne units arriving in Kabul and Bagram. On the morning of 27 December, Amin called for a PDPA Politburo meeting at the Tajbeg palace, and was about to make a speech to the general staff at 1400 hours. The cabinet and Afghan Politburo members had been invited to lunch an hour earlier; but the KGB cooks had again slipped poison into the food, and soon the Afghans were ill or comatose. The unconscious Amin remained at the Tajbeg palace. Ambassador Tabeev was called to provide medical assistance, and he dispatched two Russian army doctors, who quickly realised that the Afghan leaders had been poisoned.[135] Amin was now in a coma, and breathing with difficulty. After an hour or so, Tabeev called to ask how Amin was feeling, ostensibly to inform him of the deployment of the Soviet forces. Associates of Amin, like Ekbar Waziri, the Afghan political directorate chief, understood that Tabeev wished to check if Amin was still unconscious. Meanwhile intelligence had revealed that the KGB would have to deal with 2,500 guards from Amin's Afghan Security Brigade, backed by 12 100-mm anti-aircraft guns, 16 dual-barrelled DShK heavy machine guns and three tanks; the guards were all either in the palace or at posts around it.[136]

On 25 December, the officers of the Muslim Battalion invited their counterparts in the Security Brigade to a reception in nearby barracks, that overlooked the palace; this was a Russian ploy to get more information on Amin's security arrangements. During the reception an Afghan deputy political commissar, drunk, became talkative and revealed that Taraki had been suffocated on Amin's orders, thus confirming KGB intelligence on how the former president had met his end. The KGB draft assault plan required that the Muslim Battalion, together with a company of Russian paratroopers, would cut off the Afghan troops from reaching their armour and anti-aircraft batteries near the palace. Then a Soviet armoured company would transport the 'Zenith', 'Alpha' and 'Thunder' teams to the palace for a direct assault. On 26 December, Amin's KGB security advisers led KGB Spetsnaz officers around the palace to reconnoitre the rooms and corridors they would raid the next day; a detailed floor plan was produced.[137]

Early in the morning of 27 December, a request was passed to the head of the Afghan Security Brigade to release the KGB advisers and the Russian cooks – who had already slipped poison into the food to be served at a scheduled grand reception for Amin. The request was granted by the unsuspecting Afghans (though some cooks stayed on even after the poisoning of the Politburo members' food). Kremlin then twice changed the timing of the raid, first from 1500 to 2200, then to 1930 hours.[138]

The 'Zenith' troops wore Afghan army uniforms, with a white armband to distinguish themselves from their unsuspecting opponents. According to the plan, KGB operatives would blow up a main underground communications shaft in Kabul, cutting off communication with the outside world and signalling the start of the operation. The explosion took place at 1930 hours, as the KGB troops approached the Tajbeg palace.[139] The guards opened fire on the Russian column, knocking out the leading vehicle. The Muslim Battalion, in a hail of fire, intercepted and destroyed the Afghan Security Brigade's reinforcements. Meanwhile, the rest of the KGB, GRU, paratroop and army units attacked 12 key military targets and ministry buildings in Kabul.[140]

By the time Storm-333 had started, Amin felt better, leaving his bed, while the two Soviet medical officers treated his five-year-old son; they had already helped his young daughter, who had also been poisoned. Once the first shots were fired, the doctors assumed that Afghan rebels were storming the building, and chose to withdraw, having done all they could for Amin and his family.[141] Amin was in a dismal condition, in his underwear and still holding his IV packs. A Russian doctor removed them. Amin's son, crying, hugged his father's legs as the latter tried to calm him down.[142] The Soviet officers left, but soon found themselves trapped in a room when the Spetsnaz stormed the building; they heard soldiers speaking in Russian and replied in kind, but one doctor was mortally wounded in the chest by a Spetsnaz, who was firing indiscriminately. The Alpha team burst into Amin's room where an officer shot him and then tossed a grenade at him, killing both him and his son. The other family members were also shot. Later, Amin's body was wrapped in a carpet.[143]

At the Darulaman palace, where the Afghan army general staff were to be found, a high-ranking Russian delegation asked for a meeting; they reached the office of General Yaqub, accompanied by 14 Zenith Spetsnaz, at 1900 hours. The meeting with General Yaqub was polite, but when the explosion of the communication shaft was heard, Yaqub realised the danger of the situation. He made for his submachine gun but a Soviet officer, a Major Rozin, wrestled him to the floor. Soviets and Afghans joined the fight, and the ensuing exchange of fire resulted in the wounding of Yaqub and the killing of one of his assistants. Yaqub escaped into a nearby room, where armed

Afghan soldiers and the deputy minister of internal affairs remained, but eventually, realising they were trapped, they all surrendered. Soon Soviet paratroopers from outside joined the fighting, which continued in the corridors and rooms of the General Staff for about an hour.[144]

The whole operation of taking Kabul had cost the KGB more than 100 casualties; in the palace raid five KGB Spetsnaz, including their commanding officer, were killed, and all 36 remaining 'Zenith' members were wounded. About 150 Afghans were killed and 1,700 taken prisoner. On 27–28 December, the 5th Motorised Rifle Division entered Afghanistan.[145]

On 27 December, the Politburo authorised the start of a diplomatic campaign for the justification of the invasion; the main line was that the USSR had 'granted military help to Afghanistan under the 1978 Friendship Treaty in accordance with Article 51 of the UN Charter on self-defence'. Next day, Ambassador Vinogradov met with Ayatollah Khomeini in the Iranian holy city of Qom, and attempted to explain the reasons for intervention, while reassuring him of the Kremlin's friendly intentions towards Iran. He allegedly revealed Carter's appeal to Moscow to show understanding with regard to speculation about US interference in Iran; this could not be, claimed the ambassador. He invited Khomeini to examine why the Soviet Union was compelled to act in Afghanistan. But Khomeini was blunt: 'There could be no mutual understanding between a Muslim nation and a non-Muslim government.'[146]

In October 1980, the CIA concluded a review of the intelligence community's performance in forecasting the invasion; it was claimed that US intelligence and decision-makers ('the warnees') were, in general terms, not taken by surprise. However, the authors of the report admitted that the Russian intention to kill Amin and install another leader had not been anticipated. The 25 December NSA report warning of an imminent Soviet move in Afghanistan had not rung alarm bells among either the intelligence community or the decision-makers: 'the movement of airborne forces was not assessed as the beginning of an invasion'. CIA alert memoranda of 16 and 27 December claimed that the Soviets were introducing more forces into the country to protect their own missions there, and possibly to contribute to counter-insurgency.[147] No 'strategic warning' was issued, since no attack against the United States, or a country where US forces were based, was forecast. In any event, 'The Defense Department has unique and specific responsibilities for warning of attack. In the Afghanistan situation, no such warning was issued.'[148] A 'tactical warning' was issued by the NSA on 25 December, and an alert memorandum by the CIA two days later. No 'warning of attack' was issued; the explanation for this was:

> We had no specific information on Soviet intentions to move forces across the border, nor did we know when, where, or with what forces a move would come. This probably was due to the remoteness of the area and to the unopposed nature of the Soviet move.[149]

It was also made clear that the decision-makers were preoccupied with the hostage crisis in Iran, and assumed that a move by Russian troops in Afghanistan would be a contingency to counter any US intervention in Iran:

> Many of the preliminary Soviet actions in the Turkestan [Military District] were interpreted as contingency move in case of a US retaliatory venture against Iran. In addition to Iran, operations in support of refugees in Southeast Asia were also absorbing a great deal of attention, particularly with the Joint Chiefs of Staff.

Decision-makers did not receive specific warning (as to either place or time) of the invasion, but

> were not surprised when the initial warning of an imminent major Soviet move was given by NSA on 25 December 1979. It did appear that the key staff officers of most decision-makers relied on their own review of individual SIGINT and IMINT reports to determine that the Soviets were getting ready to intervene.[150]

In its turn, GCHQ, in close collaboration with the NSA, tried to offer decision-makers a full coverage of the Russian deployments. Aldrich writes that 'GCHQ's intelligence about the Soviet invasion of Afghanistan in the last days of 1979 was excellent'.[151] This was accurate only after the killing of Amin and the confirmation that the Russians had ousted his regime. Russian intentions had indeed surprised the intelligence community, since, given Moscow's stance on improving relations with the US after the signing of SALT II,

> even the idea that the Soviets would actually pay the price of invading seemed so outrageous, that it was estimated that only a small force would be committed [in Afghanistan]. This idea persisted through the beginning of the invasion, when the initial assessments viewed the airborne troops at Kabul and Bagram as merely additional security forces.[152]

Finally, any Russian move against China, Pakistan or Iran could have been predicted from indications of immense Russian preparations and logistics support. Nonetheless, the Soviets did not fully follow their own logistics doctrine in the case of Afghanistan.[153] Nor were they interested in Pakistan, Iran or China.

3

INTERNATIONAL
REACTIONS

On 26 December 1979 Vance, Jones, Brzezinski and Turner attended a meeting of the Special Coordination Committee (SCC), where it was highlighted that 215 military transport aircraft had reached Kabul the previous day:

> This size airlift, it is speculated, could raise the Soviet combat force level in Afghanistan to somewhere between two-thirds and one and one-half divisions ... thus we have an unusually large air movement but no ground reinforcement. There is [not declassified] direct Politburo supervision of parts of this operation.[1]

It was considered that the 'greatest risk we face is a quick, effective Soviet operation to pacify Afghanistan', damaging the image of the US world-wide. Thus covert action should be aimed at making the Soviet occupation of Afghanistan 'as unsustainable as possible'. The covert action that President Carter had authorised (the preceding summer) had been 'very slow in getting off the ground'.[2]

After a 26 December State Department press briefing that called for the international community 'to condemn such blatant military interference into the internal affairs of an independent sovereign state', American diplomats informed their British counterparts that they sought to portray the invasion as a dispute between the Soviet Union and the rest of the world, rather than as within the framework of US-Soviet antagonism. This option was similar to the American diplomatic strategy towards Iran encouraging other countries to denounce the hostage-taking. The news reports from Kabul revealed that the Soviets had now turned against Amin, and had not intervened in his favour. Sir Nicholas Henderson, the British ambassador in Washington, wondered whether the Soviets might be interested in a trade-off with the Americans at the Security Council – with Washington not protesting too strongly about the invasion in return for Soviet backing of sanctions against Iran. Nonetheless, the Americans wanted Iran and Afghanistan to be treated as totally separate issues, feeling that it would be preferable to obtain a Security Council resolution against Iran before taking the Afghanistan issue to the UN. In any event, Washington had the opportunity to portray the Soviet Union to the Muslim world as the enemy of Islam. After the invasion, the defence of Pakistan would come to the forefront.[3]

Secretary of State Cyrus Vance acknowledged that before the invasion he had discussed the Soviet build-up in Afghanistan with the Chinese; they were cautious and did not disclose what position they would take, but simply asked what the American response would be in the event of a Russian intervention. Vance also sounded a pro-Pakistan note in his recommendations to Carter: 'The US should accept the facts of nuclear life and be content with what they had been able to extract so far from the Pakistanis'.[4] Islamabad did not yet have the capability to construct a nuclear weapon, and it would neither share nuclear technology with other states nor test a nuclear weapon (if one were in due course developed) while Zia remained in power. In a move to maintain the fragile Indo-Pakistani status quo, Vance would clear the sale of nuclear fuel to India, and would offer 'certain technologically advanced [military] equipment to smooth any reactions of New Delhi'.[5]

On 27 December Keline, the minister-counselor in the Soviet Embassy in London, paid a visit to FCO minister Julian Bullard's home, handing him the Soviet government's statement justifying the invasion as a response to 'outside interference in Afghanistan', but

declining to answer any questions, his manner being 'even more nervous and uncertain than usual'.[6]

In his first analyses of the evolving situation, Brzezinski considered that there was a regional crisis: Iran, Afghanistan and an
unstable Pakistan had put US strategic interests in jeopardy. He feared
that if the Soviets established themselves in Afghanistan, and if the
Pakistanis followed a policy of appeasement, the 'age-old dream of
Moscow to have direct access to the Indian Ocean will have been ful-
filled'. For the time being, the invasion showed the world Moscow's
determination, and unless Washington reacted it would demonstrate
timidity rather than prudent restraint: 'With Iran destabilised there
will be no firm bulwark in Southwest Asia against the Soviet drive
to the Indian Ocean'. His words were somewhat alarmist, though
he could hardly be blamed for this. Since the US intelligence community had still not understood what was going on, the erstwhile
professor of strategic studies re-adopted the appealing theory he had
aired almost two years earlier: a crescent of crisis in the region. In
his policy recommendations he disclosed that SALT II was now in
jeopardy, and Washington should now approach China and Pakistan.
Though the US non-proliferation policy was incompatible with helping the latter country with its nuclear development, the National
Security Advisor hesitated to call Afghanistan 'Moscow's Vietnam'.
The Mujahedeen were badly organised and led; they lacked the sanctu-
aries, the army and the central government of the North Vietnamese,
as well as enjoying (at least for the time being) only limited external
support.[7]

In the White House situation room the vice-president consulted
with Vance, Christopher, Brown (the secretary of defense), Turner and
Brzezinski. It was evident from Turner's vague statements that the
CIA could not cope with the confusion:

One unknown at this point [in the crisis] is the extent of Soviet
activity and their full intentions. They have brought in perhaps an additional 4–5,000 troops. We know that Babrak is a
Parchamist who has been in Prague as Ambassador ... resistance in Kabul has died out for the night ... [the Soviets]

probably felt that they had to replace Amin; we don't know whether they have made a broader commitment. The forces in the Turkestan military district may just be to support this move ... In Kabul [the Soviets] are engaging in combat. We do not know what is going on in the countryside. There are reports of Soviet flights in Herat and Kandahar ... we do not know exactly [the total number of Russian troops in Kabul] – perhaps it is 10,000 men.[8]

Next day (28 December), Carter and Thatcher held a telephone discussion, the President condemning the intervention as similar to the invasion of Czechoslovakia in 1968. The turning of Afghanistan into a puppet state entailed serious strategic consequences for the region, and it was up to the free world to make Moscow understand how costly its decision had been. However: 'The administration did not intend to allow their concern about the signings of SALT II to interfere with their taking a strong stand against the Soviets for what they have done in Afghanistan.' Carter would send Brezhnev a personal letter, expressing his 'deepest concern' at the situation. The prime minister agreed with Carter's analysis and with the judgement that 'swift action was needed'.[9] (Ironically, the KGB had marked Carter down as an indecisive leader; a dossier – also passed to the GDR's Stasi – referred to him as having 'mismanaged the economy, reduced the morale of American business, and weakened the United States' position worldwide'.)[10] The president told Thatcher that he was in favour of taking the matter to the UN but wanted others, not his own diplomats, to take the initiative.[11]

Thatcher wrote to Brezhnev in strong terms:

I have been profoundly disturbed at recent developments in Afghanistan ... I have seen the statement by the Soviet government handed to the Foreign and Commonwealth Office late on 26 December by the Soviet embassy in London and am frankly puzzled by the assertion that recent Soviet action was at the invitation of the Afghan government. After all, the new government was only announced on 28 December. Nor can I see that Soviet action is justified in terms of article 51 of the UN Charter.[12]

In addition, the prime minister, in her consultations with her closest advisers, had 'expressed particular interest in using the crisis to get the Ayatollah [Khomeini] to come closer to the Western point of view'. This seemed a sensible stratagem, but Tehran was in no mood to negotiate over the hostages, and Carter (reasonably enough) wanted a Security Council vote for sanctions against Iran. The FCO favoured 'developing a channel' to Iran via Agha Shahi, the foreign affairs advisor to President Zia of Pakistan.[13] (The FCO was, nonetheless, aware that the Americans were 'unhappy' at the prospect of Shahi's contact with Khomeini putting at risk their effort in the Security Council for sanctions against Iran; they considered that the Shahi option should be examined only after sanctions had been adopted.)[14] A day earlier, the EEC ambassadors in Tehran had held a meeting with Foreign Minister Qotbzadeh which led to his eventually 'losing his temper' and declaring that there was no distinction between the United States and the Soviet Union.[15] On 31 December, the Security Council eventually passed a resolution (no. 461) deploring the hostage-taking in Tehran, deciding to meet again on 7 January 1980 to review the situation and, in case of non-compliance, 'to adopt effective measures under articles 39 and 41 of the Charter'.[16] However, the Anglo-American efforts failed to achieve a second resolution against Iran.

The Carter–Thatcher phone discussion was followed the same day by Vance's with Carrington; they mainly focused on the Iran sanctions, with the foreign secretary reminding his counterpart of the difference between the American and British positions on sanctions. Eventually, Vance instituted a two-phase strategy: on 31 December Washington would table a resolution at the Security Council deploring Tehran's failure to abide by the ICJ's ruling that the hostages should be freed, and clearing the way for the UN secretary-general to visit Iran. No specific sanctions would be included in this resolution; however, a week later, a second resolution would include them.[17]

London sought to avoid the dilemma over recognising the Babrak Karmal government. The Embassy in Kabul was instructed that no British diplomats should attend a briefing by the new Afghan government unless other EEC members were also present.[18] Three days later this directive was changed: Carrington wished no British diplomat to attend any government briefing, or proceed to any action that could imply recognition of the new regime by the British government.[19] Briefly, beyond the issue of foreign intervention, the criteria for British recognition of a foreign government were: a reasonable prospect of a permanent government; control by that government of a greater part of the country's territory; and the submission of the majority of its population. According to current intelligence the situation in Kabul seemed stable, but the Afghan people's reactions were uncertain, and some tribal leaders were hostile to the new regime. In the case of foreign intervention, recognition would be granted only if it could be shown that such intervention was in accord with the will of the people.[20]

On 28 December, the Soviet ambassador in Paris handed Stirn, the minister of state, the text justifying the invasion. London was aware that the French had neither protested officially to the Soviets nor made immediate plans to do so; the government was still consulting.[21] The Quai d'Orsay (the French Ministry of Foreign Affairs) issued a response which, by comparison to other NATO states' announcements, was a milder statement, liable to confuse the reader as to French intentions:

> The French government have noted with great concern the events which have just taken place in Kabul. Whilst the French government have taken careful note of the explanation given to them by the government of the Soviet Union, they consider that the situation thus created arouses legitimate anxiety for peace and stability in the region ...[22]

The Russian ambassador also handed the West German government the official statement on the intervention. A spokesman for the German Ministry of Foreign Affairs remarked that the intervention of foreign troops in Afghanistan was 'a very grave matter, raising fundamental questions in international relations.' Bonn was interested in seeing the EEC member states respond in a coordinated fashion, and abstained from further comment.[23] Denmark received the same text, but the feeling in Copenhagen was against reacting too strongly to this 'gross violation of national sovereignty', ... because of Iran' – until action had been agreed upon by the UN Security Council.[24]

Ireland, which then held the EEC presidency, deplored the invasion and sought 'an exchange of information' between its European partners on the statement they had all by now received.[25] Canada rejected Russian justifications: it 'deeply regrets the Soviet action, which will have an adverse effect upon stability in the immediate region ... and affect the détente, which depends upon mutual confidence and the practice of restraint'.[26]

On 29 December, President Carter announced that within two days Warren Christopher would visit London to consult with representatives of Britain, France, Italy, Germany and Canada on the Afghanistan issue, at deputy foreign minister level; this hastily programmed meeting would be neither a NATO nor an EEC gathering.[27] Carter put the Russian invasion in a historical context: it was the third time since the Second World War that Russia had invaded another country (in 1956, Hungary; in 1968, Czechoslovakia; and now in 1979, Afghanistan). It was also the first time a Muslim country had been invaded 'since the occupation of Iranian Azerbaijan in the 1940s'.[28] Already, Hans-Dietrich Genscher, the FRG foreign minister (unduly alarmed), had disclosed his concern about the Soviets' future policy towards Romania and Yugoslavia; their action in Afghanistan might have set a dangerous precedent for Europe.[29]

The State Department organised a briefing of all NATO ambassadors, plus those of New Zealand and Australia, and in other meetings the ambassadors of Japan, China, Saudi Arabia and Asian states received information from American diplomats. After some ambassadors' queries, an American spokesman stated that his government had not reached a decision on its relations with Karmal's regime; no decision to bring the issue to the UN Security Council had yet been taken, though such a move had not been ruled out. Finally, a North Atlantic Council meeting was called for 29 December.[30]

Sir Antony Parsons, the UK ambassador at the UN, warned that, though the Soviets would be certain to veto any proposed resolution against them, it would not be impossible to bring the issue to a vote. Portugal and Norway were non-permanent members, and had still to reveal their intentions; the French ambassador to the UN was enthusiastically in favour of a resolution, and saw no reason why these two countries should be opposed. Parsons wanted to close the issue of the Iran sanctions first, and then move on to that of the Afghanistan invasion. His argument was that by 1 January the Chinese presidency of the Security Council would have ended, and thus China might feel free to join the West's diplomatic coalition against Russia.[31]

At the North Atlantic Council of December 29, the 'concern' of the allies was noted, with the Turkish ambassador proposing personally (and unofficially) that NATO should urgently consider ways of deterring a further 'deterioration' of the situation in the Afghanistan region. The French delegate blocked an attempt by Joseph Luns, the NATO secretary-general, to include in the final communiqué the 'concern' of the alliance; 'the expression of concern should be left to the capitals', the cautious French said. Luns accepted that any comments he made at the press conference would be attributable only to himself.[32] Thus, 'the Secretary General expressed his strong concern over the Soviet action, which he said represents a gross interference in the internal affairs of Afghanistan and is a matter of major concern to the entire international community'.[33] Carter's letter to Brezhnev remained secret. In his memoirs, however, Carter mentions having described the invasion as

a clear threat to peace ... these actions could mark a fundamental and long-lasting turning point in our relations ... unless you draw back from your present course of action, this will inevitably jeopardize the course of United States–Soviet relations throughout the world. I urge you to take prompt constructive action to withdraw your forces and cease interference in Afghanistan's internal affairs.[34]

Two days later, the Soviet chairman replied; Carter deemed his answer 'devious', and Brzezinski thought it 'mendacious and arrogant'. Brezhnev denied claims of interference in Afghan affairs, pledging: 'As soon as the reasons which prompted the Afghan request to the Soviet Union disappear, we fully intend to withdraw the Soviet military contingents from Afghan territory.'[35]

On 29 December, Brzezinski showed Sir Nicholas Henderson, the British ambassador to Washington, Carter's letter to Brezhnev, but did not allow him to take notes. The current American thinking envisioned a Security Council resolution to be tabled by Britain and other Western allies between the first and second resolutions against Iran. In addition, in the coming two to three days the Muslim countries and the non-aligned would shape their coordinated response.[36]

At the UN Security Council, the Norwegian and Portuguese ambassadors' personal reaction was positive about the idea of backing a resolution against the Soviet Union, but they would have to wait for instructions from their capitals. Parsons 'spoke very privately to the Chinese (who are extremely discreet)'. They suggested that Asians might take the lead on such a motion and doubted if the Pakistanis would do so, since they 'were too close and trembling'. The Chinese thought the resolution would divide the non-aligned nations, but were prepared to speak to Bangladesh. Parsons understood the Chinese argument; seeking to include Asian states in the bid for a Security Council resolution, he had previously met a few non-aligned ambassadors, and 'all of them had 'exhibited varying degrees of embarrassment'. The Bangladeshi ambassador to the UN admitted that the non-aligned had two standards: 'If a single British or American soldier had crossed the Afghan frontier there would have been immediate recourse to the [Security] Council; when the Russians did so, everyone [in the non-aligned bloc] kept quiet.'[37]

In Kabul, British Embassy officials admitted that US intelligence was their main source, since 'the Americans have the best sources of intelligence regarding general disposition of Soviet troops'. The troop deployments were concentrated in the capital, to defend the city from outside attack; very few Afghan troops carried arms; the reinforcement of the defence of Kabul hinted that other Soviet units might be dispatched to deal with the rebels. The Afghan army had suffered from the coup (and earlier from mutinies); they would not be able to fight, and the Soviets ran the risk of themselves being called upon to fight the rebel forces, whereupon 'They would find themselves in the same sort of stalemate as the Amin government.' It was a most accurate forecast.[38]

Carter took the invasion as a personal affront; he went public in admitting that it had changed, overnight, his view of Soviet foreign policy. But one of his senior advisers, Hedley Donovan, the former editor-in-chief of *Time* and an old media hand, was outspoken in a letter to the president:

> I was distressed by your comment on the ABC interview ... that your opinion of the Soviets had changed more drastically in the last week than in all your previous time in office. I see how this can be true, and it could be a perfectly sensible observation for you to make privately. But as a public statement by the President I fear it opens you up to charges of naiveté ... It also troubles me to have you assert the Soviets will suffer 'severe political consequences' but you can't yet say what. This creates an unnecessary and quite uncomfortable resemblance between our stance toward the Soviets and toward the Ayatollah.[39]

On 30 December, Brzezinski was interviewed on a US television programme, *Issues and Answers*. He strongly condemned the invasion, disclosing that, as of the previous day, between 20,000 and 25,000 Soviet troops were deployed in Afghanistan, stating that the administration aimed first to consult with US allies so as to respond in a coordinated fashion, and giving reassurances of American backing for Pakistan. Showing clear determination, he read the relevant passage of the 1959 US–Pakistan treaty allowing for the possible use of force following a Pakistani request for help. He claimed that deliveries of arms would be resumed, and – in light of the invasion – that Congress sanctions on the Pakistanis over their nuclear programme would not overshadow US–Pakistan relations. He went on to say that cash sales to Islamabad could be a way of bypassing any reaction on the part of Congress.[40] Essentially, Brzezinski's resolve was hollow, drawing a hypothetical line in the sand to show the administration's determination to a domestic audience; he was well aware that the Soviet Union had no interest in advancing on Pakistan. Indeed, a close reading of a study compiled by Douglas MacEachin, a former key CIA officer, *Predicting the Soviet Invasion of Afghanistan: The Intelligence Community's Record*, suggests that the community was quite unworried about a post-invasion attack by the Russians on either Pakistan or Iran.

In a vain attempt to show the Carter administration's resolve, Brzezinski denied that Soviet interference in Ethiopia, Cuba, Angola and South Yemen had been met only with rhetoric, claiming that the current administration had done more in three years to improve America's geostrategic position than its predecessors had done in their eight years. He listed the increased defence budget, the stationing of cruise missiles in Europe, the development of a Rapid Deployment Force, the Middle East talks, the normalisation of Sino-US relations; all these initiatives had strengthened US security interests in Asia, Europe and the Middle East. Knowing that this broadcast would be watched by Russian diplomats and the KGB, and understanding that each word and phrase would be thoroughly analysed as to its exact meaning and what it might disclose of US intentions and strategy, Brzezinski stated, reassuringly, that

> The American–Soviet relationship will remain a mixed and complex one for many years to come. We have to cooperate where we can. For example, in strategic arms limitations. But we have to compete over the longer haul and not get mesmerized by specific events and one day conclude that détente is in full bloom because we have agreement and the next day have scare headlines as we saw them today in some newspapers that détente is completely dead. A competitive, cooperative relationship will be with us for many years to come. We have to be willing to compete toughly, assertively, forcefully but also realistically, and we have to be prepared to enhance the operative aspects of the relationship when there are opportunities; and this is what the President has been doing ... SALT is not a favour to the Soviet Union. SALT is not a Soviet favour to the United States. SALT is a strategic accommodation in the most dynamic aspect of the relationship ... SALT introduces strategic stability, which both sides need.[41]

All of this sounded like a professor's lecture on a balanced approach to international politics, leaning towards the realist school, rather than a hawkish speech that would deter a Russian ideologist; Kremlin insiders could read whatever they liked into the phrasing. Besides,

Brzezinski did not anticipate a further Russian move (the next chapter will explore the military intelligence estimates that confirmed this), so he could indulge in the luxury of lecturing. Finally, he made a futile bid to scare off Tehran by remarking: 'There have been Soviet troops in Tehran before. Tehran could be next.'[42] Again he knew that Russia was planning no move against Tehran – in fact Moscow had been trying to accommodate the new regime there.

Brzezinski's remarks set confused and contradictory tasks for US policy: he could not sound too hawkish, because Carter wished to continue with détente and SALT, but Congress was hostile to the expedient arming of Pakistan; and while pleading for the release of the US hostages in Iran, he was calling for Muslims to turn against Russia.[43]

Meanwhile, in a non-attributable lunch meeting with journalists, Carter claimed he had sent a 'strong warning' to Brezhnev over the hot line: the Soviet forces had to be withdrawn, otherwise there would be 'serious consequences' for US–Russian relations. Carter admitted having received a reply from the Kremlin, but said nothing further. Nonetheless, the *Washington Post*, in an 'authoritative-looking' article, claimed that the Russian chairman had 'turned a cold shoulder to Carter's appeal'. At the same journalists' lunch, Carter sounded optimistic about the war-fighting potential of the Afghan guerrillas, but unwilling to discuss the possibility of US aid to them; he gave the impression that such aid would be withheld. Secretary of Defense Harold Brown would probably visit China in the coming week, demonstrating a common Sino-US approach on Afghanistan. After all, the two countries had 'common strategic goals', and the 'China card' could thus be played against Russia. But Carter sounded like he was against allowing arms sales to Beijing.[44] Brown held discussions with the Chinese leadership, who deplored the invasion and sought improvement of relations with Washington; but, as Vance put it, 'The Chinese proved more wisely hesitant than we were. Brown found a near convergence between the United States and China on broad strategic interests, but he also discovered that the Chinese leaders were wary of being used as a counterweight in the US–Soviet geopolitical rivalry. I was not surprised.'[45] The secretary of defense admitted an evolving intelligence link with Beijing, on 29 January 1980 submitting a report to Congress which stated that a Landsat D ground station would be made available to the Chinese military, though 'under safeguards which will assure that it is not immediately usable for military purposes'.[46]

British Ambassador Henderson's assessment was that the Americans were 'emerging from the post-Vietnam chrysalis', and seeking to shoulder the issues jointly with their allies, fearing the effects of the invasion on other countries if there were 'an insufficiently resilient response'. The argument he formulated was a Machiavellian one: the invasion would not be a problem for US domestic politics, because for some time the press and politicians had been blaming Carter for being soft with the Iranians holding American hostages. Indeed:

> The dramatic shift of the public attention to Afghanistan could be helpful in that it enables the administration to argue that the Iranians should be given more time to absorb the significance for them of having alienated US friendship at a time when the Soviets are moving in next door; it gives the Americans a useful counter-argument, of which they can be expected to make much, to the notion that the Islamic revival necessarily represents an anti-American menace, and it may offer an outlet for the calls for action (perhaps with Pakistani help) which they still feel inhibited from taking in Iran.[47]

Parsons, Britain's ambassador to the UN, discussed with Vance a plan for calling on as many Security Council members and non-aligned nations as possible to back a resolution exposing Russia to world opinion. However, he also warned that if this took place on the eve of a Security Council vote on a second Iran resolution, the Soviets might in response exercise their veto; Vance expressed his own concern about such an outcome. Carter had initially sought to deal first with Iran at the UN, and then to move on to Afghanistan. Parsons proposed to move swiftly with a draft resolution in 72 hours, so as not to give time for the non-aligned bloc 'to water it down'.[48] The non-aligned nations would understand the futility of a bid for an anti-Soviet resolution (Moscow would cast a veto) and the cost they would themselves incur later by attracting Soviet criticism and hostility. But still, an important political point would have been made.

The 31 December meeting at the FCO was attended by Warren Christopher, Douglas Hurd (minister of state at the FCO), Alan Gotlieb (Canadian foreign under-secretary), De Leusse (French permanent under-secretary), Dr Van Well (FRG state secretary) and Francesco Malfatti (Italian permanent under-secretary), together with their staffs. Christopher, who opened the conference, wondered why the Soviets had chosen this period to invade, and went on to claim that the Afghan guerrillas were a more effective force than initially assumed. According to his latest intelligence, the number of Soviet troops in Afghanistani had reached between 25,000 and 30,000, while the refugees on the Afghan–Pakistani border already totalled 350,000, a figure which might rise to half a million. Pakistan was worried about Soviet intentions, and might consider approaching Moscow to appease them; but a very positive factor was that Zia was thinking of convoking the Islamic Conference. As for the West's response, Christopher claimed a three-tier approach: modernising weaponry, notably NATO's Theatre Nuclear Force – this 'seemed wise and necessary'; seeking the continuation of détente, and most specifically of SALT II, though this would receive heavy criticism in the Senate; and adopting a stance of 'solidarity and vigilance' on the part of the West in general. The West should increase contacts with Romania and Yugoslavia (both countries having deplored Moscow's action in Afghanistan). He considered that a firm response could deter the Soviets from similar interventions in the future. As the meeting progressed, Christopher admitted that US economic aid to Afghanistan so far was very limited – cutting it would not bring real pressure to bear (in fact it had been suspended since the murder of Ambassador Dubs). The Americans had been reviewing options with regard to their Embassy in Kabul – they could break off diplomatic relations, recall their ambassador or decrease the staff. Meanwhile, no decision had yet been taken as to recognising Karmal's regime, while the policy of US grain and technology exports to Russia was under review.[49]

Hurd spoke of Soviet opportunism, ruthlessness and secrecy, fearing a spill-over of the crisis to Pakistan.[50] He was strongly in favour of taking the Russian aggression to the Security Council immediately, seizing the moment to secure the backing of the non-aligned. He insisted that

> early action was important. It was essential to act when the tide of protest in non-aligned countries and particularly the Muslim world was flowing strongly. Indignation subsided quickly. Fears remained but the inclination to do or say anything faded.[51]

Also it was 'extremely desirable' for Pakistan to address the invasion at the Islamic Conference.[52]

In his turn, Van Well believed that Afghanistan was intended as a kind of 'platform' for the Soviets to spread their influence in the subcontinent, but that it would be difficult for them to win over the Afghan tribes. The Germans saw a crisis not only for the subcontinent but even for the Horn of Africa. They feared that Pakistan was weak and lacked direction, that India would be affected by Russian adventurism, and that China would deplore the invasion, but do no more. As for German domestic opinion and the press, détente was 'losing ground', and they criticised Moscow as a result.[53]

De Leusse sought to block an agreement at this early stage, doubting that the Russian invasion had crossed a new threshold, as the Americans argued. He reminded his counterparts of the Soviets' arming of the North during the war in Vietnam, and of their backing for the Cubans in Angola, as well as of the fact that there had been no protests over Russian involvement in Eritrea. He insisted that the West should not overreact, possibly endangering its own interests. Preferably, the Third World should lead the protest, but currently he saw little response (questioning Hurd's earlier remark). However, it would be 'extremely desirable' for the Pakistanis to take the issue to the Islamic Conference.[54]

Gotlieb thought that public opinion had gained the impression that the credibility of détente was now at stake. He warned of the Pakistanis' perception that they were encircled by India and Soviet-occupied Afghanistan. He also was in favour of the non-aligned and

Third World countries taking the lead in the Security Council, and, if there were wide support, their bringing the crisis before the General Assembly.[55]

What to do with the diplomatic missions was a riddle. The Germans would have liked to recall their ambassador, but it was more useful for them if he were to remain. Besides, it would be difficult to withdraw their mission because it supported many teachers and technical experts scattered around the country. The French did not have an issue with recognising the new regime, given their policy of recognition for states rather than governments. Also, Paris gave almost no aid to Afghanistan. Malfatti wanted the West to persuade the Asian members of the Security Council to call its attention to the crisis. He would also have liked to recall the Italian ambassador, but was willing to wait for a consensus to be reached among the Europeans and Americans.[56]

All agreed for the time being to curtail political contacts with the new regime. The British were 'ready to fall in with any consensus (on this issue)'. A similar line was followed by Christopher (the Americans being eager for coordination). The Germans also sought a consensus to determine their response over recognition. Van Well pointed out the possible reprisals his government would consider, one of them being a boycott of the Moscow Olympics; he was the first official to raise this. He also supported the setting-up of a conference on economic aid to Pakistan, to help the government there cope with the refugee crisis.[57]

Privately Hurd found the meeting 'disappointing ... US ideas were not clear and the French were determined to block any action today.'[58] There was no consensus on bringing Russia before the Security Council, though the delegates agreed that the non-aligned should take the initiative at the UN and then receive the backing of Western diplomacy. An agreement was reached among all Western ambassadors in Kabul to avoid political contacts with the new government for the time being. The allies wanted to continue with détente and SALT II; contacts with the Soviets would be restricted to bilateral relations only, while Christopher listed options for US sanctions, including cutting off grain exports to the USSR. He insisted that it was now time for the regime in Iran to reconsider their relations with the West.

European ambassadors in Tehran agreed to urge the Islamic regime to oppose Russian influence. As for the Pakistanis, the US appeared determined to boost their military, while Canada suggested the country should rejoin the Commonwealth. China was 'to be kept in touch, but handled with care'. Hurd closed his short briefing to Carrington with the words:

> There were thus several loose ends, and our proposal for working groups to tackle specific areas of action was not taken up. A lot of hard work and clear thinking is required if this US initiative is to bear any fruit.[59]

Later the same day (and in the same building), Minister of State Peter Blaker had a meeting with Marshall Brement, the advisor on Soviet affairs at the National Security Council. Brement was asked if the US administration regarded the invasion as part of a pattern of Russian aggression. He admitted that administration members were divided on this, but he personally assumed that this was a consistent pattern, 'a very ominous development'. If the Soviets succeeded in Afghanistan they would boost their status, and would more readily consider the military option in future crises. In any event, the Soviets 'probably regarded a strong US reaction as inevitable', while hoping for a 'muted' European response. Brement was not optimistic about the potential of the Afghan guerrillas; unlike the jungles of Vietnam, Afghanistan's mountains and desert valleys were not suitable for guerrilla operations. The Soviets had already sent up to three divisions to secure the capital and key road networks. They 'were likely to have a considerable military success', remarked Brement, emphasising the administration's willingness to listen to their allies and to adopt a coordinated diplomatic strategy against the Soviet Union. There would also be Anglo-American consultations on how to help the insurgents.[60]

On the last day of the year in Kabul, the ambassadors of the United Kingdom, the FRG, France and Italy met to discuss developments, agreeing that they should urge their governments to condemn the invasion publicly (the British government had already done so).

The German and the Italian insisted that the EEC should implement trade sanctions and boycott the Moscow Olympics; all actions should be directed against Russia, not the new Afghan regime.[61]

At the FCO an assessment was circulated entitled 'Impact of the Soviet intervention in Afghanistan on détente, China, disarmament and arms control'; its authors avoided concluding that the Americans had better intelligence. They listed three possible explanations: the Soviets regarded the invasion simply as 'unfortunate but unavoidable', and remained unwilling to damage détente; the Russian military might have exercised considerable pressure on the ailing Brezhnev; and/or the Soviets might no longer be interested in détente, having been frustrated by the delay in the ratification of SALT II. Up until the invasion, London and Washington had assumed that Moscow was strongly interested in détente, and that the Soviets 'would wish to preserve it in almost any circumstances'. For her part, Margaret Thatcher wanted the West to demonstrate 'strength and vigilance', but she also favoured the ratification of SALT II, rather than the upsetting of prospects for East/West agreements 'on a basis of strict mutual advantage', as well as continued negotiations over an Mutual and Balanced Force Reduction (MBFR) agreement, in parallel with the modernisation of NATO.[62] (It is evident that in this list one task tended to contradict another.) Thatcher wanted SALT II, but the FCO was singularly unimpressed; its assessment, as of January 1980, claimed:

> We do not believe that the advantages of SALT II (e.g., co-operation in measures of intrusive verification, a start on controlling qualitative improvements in missile development) outbalance the disadvantages (the failure to reduce the deployment of warheads, the neglect in dealing with the Soviet heavy missiles, the SS20 and the Backfire [strategic bomber].[63]

Reports from Washington reflected the administration's confusion with regard to strategy and tactics; it was argued that now Carter ought to test overall US–Soviet relations. The administration now believed that strong pressure on the Kremlin could compel the withdrawal of

Soviet forces to pre-November 1979 levels. But the UK Embassy in Washington

> had understood earlier that [the US administration] saw Afghanistan as a bog into which the Soviet Union was likely to be sucked ever deeper, not necessarily to [its] ultimate advantage, and that they were concerned to avoid over-reaction.

As for China, which had taken a strong anti-Russian stance, the FCO report warned perceptively:

> We need to handle the Chinese aspect with prudence and not oversimplify, as Peking itself is prone to do; it would not be practical to think of China as the cornerstone of a new Asian alliance to resist Soviet encroachment.[64]

Another study circulated at the FCO followed Hurd's line, that the three characteristics of Soviet policy were opportunism, ruthlessness and secrecy; that leaders and world opinion had not paid sufficient attention to developments in Afghanistan; and that the intervention was similar to the earlier invasions of Hungary and Czechoslovakia. The Soviets were aware of the risks the invasion entailed to their standing in the Third World and to their relations with the US. Most significantly, however, the FCO – possibly having received relevant intelligence from MI6 – attempted to calm fears: 'There is no reason to revise fundamentally the analysis of Soviet foreign policy contained in the Alliances Study of East–West relations, approved by NATO heads of government in Washington on 30–31 May 1978'.[65]

On 2 January 1980, Carter summoned the National Security Council. Subjects for discussion were the upcoming vote at the UN Security Council on sanctions against Iran, taking the Afghan crisis to the UN, and military aid to Pakistan. The president wanted Afghanistan to be brought to both the Security Council and the General Assembly,[66] but he was realist enough to admit that, while Washington and its allies could not compel the Soviets to leave Afghanistan,

Soviet actions over the next ten to twenty years will be colored by our behavior in this crisis … if the Gulf states and others are too timid, we should go with our NATO allies and China to try to do the maximum, short of a world war, to make the Soviets see that this was a major mistake.[67]

Evidently, Carter too easily assumed NATO support for US policy on Central Asia, as well as a diplomatic alliance with communist China.[68] Earlier in the discussion, Vance (as if he had foreknowledge of Carter's remarks) had mentioned that Ambassador Hummel in Islamabad was against aid to Pakistan coming under NATO; Carter then admitted that the French would also block such action.[69] Interestingly, one question put by the president remains classified: 'The President asked whether we could [not declassified]. The Secretary [of State] indicated that he would rather not.'[70]

The ratification of SALT II stalled in the Senate, but Carter and his cabinet had no wish to abandon the ongoing negotiations on arms control:

[They] should be left alone to proceed as they can … the MBFR ball was in the Soviet court. It was also noted that CTB [the Comprehensive Test Ban treaty] was moving ahead slowly and that the chemical warfare negotiations were in our favour.[71]

Pakistan's nuclear programme was addressed, with the president remarking that Zia had agreed not to test a weapon, but 'he could not bind his successor'. The secretary of state in effect corrected Carter, stating: 'The Pakistanis have pulled back from that commitment by saying only that they would not test a nuclear weapon in the next six months.'[72]

The meeting went on to discuss strategy options, but without estimating threats; Carter merely asked Brzezinski if the Soviets 'might do something' in Berlin to signal resolve. The national security advisor discounted this, appearing keen to back China and finding it a very interesting idea to sell the Chinese over-the-horizon radars and possibly other defensive weapons.[73] As he put it: 'With Soviet tanks moving towards the Indian Ocean, our unwillingness to provide anti-tank weapons was not a contribution to regional stability.' The president was willing to explore the notion of such sales to China, but he did not seem committed.[74]

A close examination of the minutes of this meeting, only five days after the invasion, shows that while the Carter administration weighed up options for a diplomatic strategy against the Soviet Union, it was not afraid of Moscow's driving south to the Persian Gulf or the Indian Ocean. Obviously, intelligence of Soviet deployments – signals intelligence (unfortunately unavailable to researchers) – had reassured the White House that the Kremlin did not pose an immediate or short-to-medium-term threat to Iran or Pakistan.

On 8 January 1980, Carrington wrote to Thatcher that Carter had proceeded with cutting off grain exports to the Soviet Union, a move in the direction of sanctions that the foreign secretary had envisioned. The British urged their NATO allies to coordinate their politico-diplomatic (not military) response, but the French still hesitated.[75] Carrington listed his recommendations for the British reaction. Already London had recalled its ambassador from Kabul, decreased the number of embassy staff and curtailed programmed meetings with Soviet officials. Aid to Afghanistan was also suspended, and the British Council's presence there closed down. He was about to visit Turkey, Oman, Saudi Arabia, Pakistan and India to consult with leaders and to build diplomatic momentum for an international response. Meanwhile, he appeared satisfied with the outcome of consultations in the UN–despite the Russian veto on a Security Council resolution, the non-aligned having been courageously quite critical of Moscow. The foreign secretary sought ways of reacting 'which will demonstrate that aggression brings penalties'.[76] Already, the UK Embassy in Moscow had warned Carrington that unless there was a strong response the Soviets might continue believing that

> they can have their adventures and détente too. The harsher the reaction from NATO – and especially its smaller members – the more clearly the Soviets may understand the damage they

have done both to SALT II and to their hopes of delaying or frustrating Western defence measures ...[77]

Nonetheless, Brzezinski later admitted in his memoirs that the suspension of grain exports to the USSR had lost momentum, and was based on flawed estimates provided by the Department of Agriculture. It had been assumed that no country could replace the US exports; but within days of Carter's announcement, Argentina jumped in, selling large quantities to the Soviet Union and at least partially making up the shortfall.[78] Brzezinski had been unaware of an active and large-scale KGB operation to deceive US intelligence on grain production in the Soviet Union and on the effect of grain imports from third countries. In this complex operation, the KGB cooperated with the Soviet Ministries of Trade, Foreign Affairs and Agriculture. In the first phase, the KGB lured US imagery-satellites and secret agents into locating areas of plentiful harvests and reporting back to Washington that Soviet grain supplies were sufficient for the next few years; the initial US estimates were moved upwards. The second phase entailed giving the false impression that imports from Argentina, Canada, New Zealand and Australia could replace the American harvest, which remained unsold in the United States; the effect was a sharp drop in the price of grain. The third phase was based on disinformation – that the Americans employed a substance in their grain-production process which was harmful to both humans and animals. All these factors contributed to the US losing more money than the Soviets, since quantities of grain remained unsold. Eventually, Reagan decided to have the embargo lifted, and Washington proposed to Moscow that the exports should be resumed. If nothing else, according to the Soviet Ministry of Trade, the KGB, with an operation that had lasted for two years, had saved the country up to 500 million roubles. (The KGB was also hoping, meanwhile, to profit from speculating in the gold market.)[79]

By the autumn of 1980, American academics were criticising the results of the embargo. Robert L. Paarlberg, a Harvard research associate, commented:

The urge to teach someone a lesson seldom inspires sound policy. The lessons learned are too often one's own. So it is with President

Carter's 1980 grain embargo. Soviet food supplies have been little affected. US illusions about its own 'food power' have been properly dispelled.[80]

By 10 January 1980, the FCO's 'best guess' on the basis of relevant intelligence estimates was that the number of Soviet troops involved in counterinsurgency operations in Afghanistan had reached 70,000.[81] The foreign secretary recommended that contacts with the Soviets at ministerial or deputy-ministerial level should be suspended for three months or more. The existing Anglo-Russian credit agreement would expire the following month; he recommended non-renewal. Restrictions on exports of sensitive technology to Russia should be increased, and naval visits and military exchanges postponed. Carrington also wanted to introduce more sanctions, by persuading EEC member-states to cut off grain and butter exports to the Soviet Union, as well as to examine restrictions on sales of sugar. The foreign secretary followed the German argument in favour of an Olympic boycott, claiming that 'few things would hurt Soviet prestige more that the absence of a number of Western countries from the Olympic games this year'.[82] Nonetheless, he was aware that the government could not order British athletes to join a boycott; it was up to them to decide.[83]

Pakistan was an ally to be backed immediately. In his visit to Islamabad, Carrington gained a better understanding of the operational requirements of Pakistani defence. Before the visit, an MoD/FCO/Treasury committee had already discussed the matter, and agreed that Pakistan should be offered soft credit terms to facilitate the procurement of modern weaponry. In addition, a Royal Navy task force in the Indian Ocean would call at Karachi to show Britain's interest in Pakistani security. The FCO was also interested in expanding staff-college training for Pakistani officers.[84] It is noteworthy that in his memorandum, only a week or so after the invasion, Carrington evinced no alarm at the prospect of further Soviet aggression in the region, focusing rather on trade/commercial sanctions. Indeed, on 13 January, in an interview with Omani TV, Carrington explicitly stated: 'I think for the time being a military operation by the Soviet Union outside Afghanistan is not particularly likely.'[85]

Nonetheless, the foreign secretary was aware of facts he could not disclose in his talks with Pakistani officials. An FCO report was clear:

> We have neither the available forces nor the equipment nor the resources to offer large-scale military aid ... a decision now to supply arms (e.g., defensive equipment for use in their North-West frontier area) would therefore have to be on credit, notwithstanding their rating, and the Treasury have so far resisted any extension [of credit].[86]

It would also be difficult to increase other bilateral aid due to budgetary constraints.[87]

Overnight, the invasion altered British policy, which had previously focused on convincing their European allies they should reach a common agreement to put strong pressure on the Pakistani government to stop their nuclear arms programme. As late as 12–13 December 1979 at the European Political Cooperation (Asia Working Group) conference in Dublin, the British delegate revealed 'clear indications that [Pakistan] was carrying out nuclear weapons research work and constructing nuclear explosive test facilities'. The Indian response to current Pakistani policy could cause instability in the subcontinent. There was also the danger of a nuclear arms race, and the possibility that other states might also fail to continue abiding by the non-proliferation treaty, given Pakistan's stance on the matter. He called on his counterparts to coordinate their response and to frame it in the context of Pakistan's relations with the whole free world.[88]

A letter was sent by UN General Assembly members to the president of the Security Council calling for the invasion to be examined as a threat to international peace and security (the letter being signed jointly by the representatives of Australia, the Bahamas, Belgium, Canada, Chile, Colombia, Costa Rica, Denmark, the Dominican Republic, Egypt, El Salvador, Ecuador, Fiji, the FRG, Greece, Haiti, Honduras, Iceland, Italy, Japan, Liberia, Luxembourg, New Zealand, Norway, Oman, Pakistan, Panama, Papua New Guinea, the Philippines, Portugal, Santa Lucia, Saudi Arabia, Singapore, Suriname, Sweden, the Netherlands, Turkey, the UK, Uruguay, the US and Venezuela). From 5 to 9 January 1980, the Security Council (the permanent five members, plus Norway, Portugal, Colombia, the GDR, Bangladesh, the Philippines, Tunisia, Zambia, Niger and Jamaica) duly held consultations on the issue.

Russia and the Afghan regime promptly denounced the meeting as interference in the domestic affairs of a sovereign state, but on 7 January the non-aligned group sponsored a Security Council resolution condemning the invasion, and calling for the immediate withdrawal of troops and the respecting of Afghanistan's sovereignty. Naturally, the Soviets vetoed this motion, with the support of the GDR. (Only the Eastern bloc countries and Vietnam sided with Russia, while at a conference of communist states in Sofia on 6–7 February, Romania and North Korea implicitly criticised the Russian move by not subscribing to the final communiqué's declaration of solidarity with the new Afghan regime.)[89]

The diplomatic momentum was now sufficient for another bid at the UN (despite initial British pessimism that a motion would not get nine votes in favour), thus prompting the 'Uniting for Peace Procedure' – instituted back in 1950 – and thereby taking the issue to the General Assembly.[90] The UK, the US and their allies worked for the adoption of a new resolution (SCR 462), which, while 'taking into account the lack of unanimity' among the Security Council members, secured a majority of 12 (with Russia and the GDR opposed and Zambia abstaining) calling for the General Assembly to examine the Afghanistan crisis in an emergency special session.

In response, Russia questioned whether it was legitimate for the General Assembly to examine the Afghanistan crisis, declaring that it was the 'invitation' of a sovereign member state that had cleared the way for the Soviet deployment. Eventually, with the non-aligned group influencing other General Assembly members, Resolution ES-6/2 was adopted (with 104 states in favour and 18 abstaining):

[The General Assembly] strongly deplores the recent armed intervention in Afghanistan [and] appeals to all States to respect the sovereignty, territorial integrity, political independence and non-aligned character of Afghanistan and to refrain from any interference in the internal affairs of that country [and] calls for the immediate, unconditional and total withdrawal of the foreign troops from Afghanistan in order to enable its people to determine their own form of government and choose their economic, political and social systems free from outside intervention, subversion, coercion or constraint of any kind whatsoever.

Meanwhile, Western European communist parties remained in a state of confusion and embarrassment; those of Britain, Italy, Spain, Sweden and Belgium were to varying degrees critical of Moscow; the invasion was backed by the communist parties of France, Finland, Portugal and Luxembourg.[91]

China deplored the Russian intervention in the strongest and 'most sustained terms', as described by the FCO. On 30 December 1979, a Chinese government statement was circulated at the UN declaring:

The Soviet Union brazenly made a massive military invasion into Afghanistan, grossly interfering in its internal affairs. This armed intervention wantonly violates all norms of international relations ... The Soviet Union has long planned for this military invasion of Afghanistan. This is its grave step for a southward thrust to the Indian Ocean and the control of sea lanes; it is also an important part of the Soviet strategy for seizing oil-producing areas, outflanking Europe and so gaining world hegemony ... it is utterly preposterous for the Soviet Union to invoke the United Nations Charter in defence of aggression. Peoples remember how the Soviet Union pretentiously proposed the inadmissibility of hegemonism at this very session of the United Nations General Assembly ...[92]

Vice-Premier Deng Xiao-ping stated that the invasion was 'by no means an isolated case but a component of the global strategy of Soviet hegemonism'. The *People's Daily* claimed (inaccurately, but convincingly enough in these post-invasion weeks) that the Soviet Union was now closer to the Indian Ocean, and a further move of Russian troops could facilitate interference with oil supply-lines to Europe and Japan. The conclusion of the article was a clear message to Washington: 'All countries concerned with international peace and security must unite and co-ordinate their actions ... in order to resist and oppose every aggressive move by the Soviet Union.'[93]

On 31 December Sir Percy Cradock, Britain's ambassador in Beijing, had a very informative conversation with Vice-Foreign Minister Zhang Wen-jin. The Chinese official argued (erroneously) that the invasion was a long-planned operation, a step in the Russian drive into the Middle East and Asia with the aim of controlling the Gulf and the sea lanes. Beijing did not compare this invasion with the one in Czechoslovakia, which was a member of the Warsaw Pact and thus 'fair game' for the Soviets. With the clear intention of raising fear levels, Zhang asked the rhetorical question: 'Who will be the next Amin and which country the next Afghanistan?' The invasion reminded the West that Russia's real intentions would affect US–Russian relations and SALT II. The Chinese (who made no reference to help for the guerrillas) backed the diplomatic campaign at the UN, with the West and the non-aligned bloc taking the initiative; China would simply follow.[94]

The Chinese were soon actively involved in the secret arming of the Mujahedeen; furthermore, they realised that their anti-Soviet policy paid dividends. Brzezinski persuaded Carter to expand defence sales to China: 30 types of defence support-equipment were to be licensed for export, including air-defence radar, transmitters, tropospheric-communications and electronic-warfare equipment, transport helicopters and tractor-trucks. On 1 April 1980, the US transferred China to a category of countries allowed to receive exports of transport aircraft, long-distance communications equipment and military helicopters. More liberalisation followed in July, and in September a high-level Pentagon delegation paid a visit to Beijing, clearing the way for some 400 items of advanced-technology 'military support-equipment' to be exported.[95] Essentially, in his bid to build a coalition against the Soviet Union, Carter had taken the first big step in the upgrading of Chinese conventional capabilities. The sharing of crucial knowhow and advanced technology (especially in communications, electronic warfare and counter-measures) enabled the Chinese to examine US systems, imitate them, and boost their own research. Another hidden aspect of developing Sino-US relations was an agreement on the sharing of electronic intelligence on Soviet missile sites, following the loss of US stations in northern Iran; joint US–Chinese signal intelligence stations were also established in western China.[96]

Nonetheless, at this point we should note the evolving Chinese policy: while political talks with the Soviets were abandoned, communication continued (signalling a medium-term intention of improving relations). The talks on navigation on the border rivers were held as scheduled from 5 February to 19 March 1980. Some friendly signals had been sent to the Kremlin as early as September 1979, when at a conference on Soviet literature in Harbin the majority of the delegates characterised the Soviet system as 'essentially socialist', rather than la-belling it 'revisionist', as Mao and his supporters had done.[97]

Strong condemnation of the Soviet invasion came from all Europeans. All NATO and EEC members deplored the invasion. On 16 February the Parliament of the European Community voted for an official advisory to the national teams of the member-states boycotting the 1980 Moscow Olympics. Nations of the Middle East and Africa also joined in the criticism of the Soviets.

Throughout the debates in the Security Council and the General Assembly, Cuba (the then chairman of the non-aligned movement) remained silent – something that caused the Cubans, according to British diplomats, to lose potential support for their candidacy as a non-permanent member of the Security Council (the eventual winner being Mexico).[98] Cuba appeared the odd man out among the non-aligned nations, with Havana Radio attempting to justify the invasion as a joint Russian–Afghan 'measure for the sole purpose of stopping the counter-revolution promoted by the imperialists, [which] in no way affects the interests of third countries'.[99]

Pakistan was the 'third country' most worried and most affected by the Russian invasion. Islamabad, under General Zia, feared a Soviet move against his country, whose foreign and defence policy had been focused on India for decades. On 29 December, the Pakistani gov-ernment issued a statement deploring the 'external military interven-tion' against a member of the Islamic Conference, and a neighbour of Pakistan. The hope was expressed that 'the far-reaching negative consequences of such foreign intervention will be clearly realised and that foreign [Soviet] troops will be removed from Afghanistan'.[100] Sir Oliver Forster, the UK ambassador in Pakistan, met with Shah Nawaz, the foreign secretary, whom he found in a 'rather jumpy and emotional state', blaming the West because it had not listened to Pakistan's warning regarding previous Russian involvement in Afghanistan. He wanted the Americans to open channels for military and economic aid. Within the Pakistani government, there was a degree of fear – when the Russian ambassador had been presented with statements deploring the invasion he had 'reacted very belligerently', identifying Pakistan as 'the external aggressor' for protecting Afghan guerrillas on its soil. Levels of tension during the conversation between the minister and the ambassador escalated, with the latter employing 'threatening language', warning of Russia 'responding to the Pakistani statement'.[101]

The Pakistanis also held talks with China, which took a supportive line, being well aware that Beijing was preoccupied with the Vietnam/ Cambodia crisis. Beyond diplomatic support, Islamabad did not expect much from the Chinese; it had received 'a lot of [Chinese] material assistance over the years and there was not much more they could do'. At that time (30 December) Islamabad had not yet decided to bring the issue to the UN, being inclined first towards the option of calling for the support of the Islamic Conference and the non-aligned bloc; but the foreign minister admitted that the Islamic Conference 'was much weakened because of the Iranian business' (the hostage crisis). However, he claimed that the Iranian government's strong statement against the invasion was heavily influenced by Agha Shahi's visit to Tehran.[102] (Nonetheless, the FCO was aware that the Americans were 'unhappy' with Shahi's contact with Khomeini, thinking it could put at risk their effort at the Security Council for sanctions against Iran, and that Shahi's démarche should have been deferred until after sanctions had been adopted.)[103]

On 12 January, Zia himself spoke of the plight of almost 430,000 Afghan refugees reaching Pakistan, turning it into a buffer zone 'against further Soviet expansion.' He claimed that his country would help the refugees but would not support the Afghan guerrillas; meanwhile, his regime played up the Russian menace in a bid to get more aid. On 19 January, the *Karachi* daily argued (erroneously) that

> Moscow's military intervention is seen as an early warning of a southward thrust of Soviet power. This leads towards the central region of the Islamic world – the area in which the Arabian Peninsula is situated. Even if the southward thrust does not materialise in the near future the region faces the risk of political destabilisation.[104]

India, Pakistan's strategic rival, viewed the Soviets' bid to expand their influence in Central Asia with hostility. Until then, Afghanistan had belonged (at least nominally) to the non-aligned bloc. On 31 December 1979, Prime Minister Charan Singh met the Russian ambassador in New Delhi, warning him of the 'far-reaching adverse consequences for the region' and joining with other regional leaders in requesting the withdrawal of the Russian troops. Indira Gandhi, a contender for the premiership, condemned the invasion but also played up the notion of Western interference in the region. By mid-January, Gandhi had been elected prime minister and maintained her stance on the invasion, though adding that the Russian troops had been 'invited' by the 'Afghan Revolutionary Council'. India focused on pressure for troop withdrawal, and this issue was addressed during Gromyko's visit to New Delhi on 12 February, with Narasimha Rao, the Indian foreign minister, calling for all countries to respect national sovereignties as the only way to uphold peace and stability. The joint communiqué following the visit made no mention of Afghanistan, but the Indian government made it known that the Soviets 'had not disagreed' with its position on a troop withdrawal, but that 'there may be differences in interim perceptions as to how it is to be achieved.'[105]

Interestingly, on 31 December 1979 the first secretary of the Indian embassy in Islamabad told his British counterpart, in confidence, that his country would not object to the arming of Pakistan by the United States (Carter having lifted the embargo on arms sales to Islamabad) in the light of the present situation, but the Pakistanis had to understand the Indians' 'very real concerns' about the use of Western arms against them in the past. The British diplomat commented that Islamabad would not take kindly to this remark, 'given the traditional Pakistani paranoia about the threat to their security from India'.[106]

Back in New Delhi, Under Secretary Krishnan appeared apprehensive of the arming of Pakistan, and complained at the absence of an official statement by the Americans on their planned military aid to Pakistan. He and other members of the Indian government considered that the region could be destabilised not only by the Russian invasion but also by the arming of Pakistan. The Indians aimed for the further normalisation of their relations with Pakistan, but now this 'could suffer a setback or even a reversal if the US went ahead with a massive arms supply'. Indeed, they feared that there were some in Islamabad who were assuming that Pakistan could go ahead with its nuclear programme.[107] In his turn, the American ambassador in New Delhi (who had urged that nuclear fuel should be sold to India) complained that the initial 'weakness of the Indian reaction' to the invasion 'made it very difficult' to persuade the US administration that beyond Pakistan there was genuine concern in the region about further Soviet adventurism and India's apparent unwillingness to take a stand against it.[108] Krishnan's anxieties had already found their way into the Indian press, which claimed that the Indo-Pakistani arms race was being revived.[109]

The Islamic government in Iran, meanwhile, sent a letter to the Kremlin denouncing the 'military intervention', declaring that it was an attack against all Muslims and calling in parallel for the withdrawal of troops 'to prove [Soviet] support for Iran's anti-imperialist movement'.[110] According to the official announcement,

> This act of the Soviet Union has deeply worried all the Moslem countries and in turn will provide the pretext, opportunity and permission to imperialism and international Zionism to continue their aggressions against the Mostazafs [oppressed and unprivilleged persons who had done nothing wrong] of the world in a more intensified manner ... [T]he invasion would be interpreted as] a gross and unjustified aggression against a weak

country and people who have risen against their government ...
the Islamic republic is astonished that the Soviet Union has not
learned from the swamp in which US imperialism was caught in
Vietnam and has committed the same act as the US in Vietnam
... [T]he occupation of our neighbouring country by the army of
the Soviet Union is in effect weakening our struggle against US
imperialism and is considered a hostile act against the Iranian
nation.[111]

Abdulhassan Bani-Sadr, the Iranian president, worried that the Kremlin
planned 'to exploit ethnic differences in Iran', with the final aim of getting access to the Indian Ocean. At a 27 January press conference, he
declared that it was the duty of Muslims 'to help our Afghan brothers
fighting for independence from foreign domination'. On 12 February,
Khomeini wrote to Brezhnev emphasising that 'any aggression against
countries of the Third World and in particular Islamic lands in this
region was contrary to the correct standard for relations between
nations'.[112] (Nonetheless, the Shiite regime in Iran would not be willing
to help the predominantly Sunni mujahedeen backed by Pakistan.)

In Baghdad, the early post-invasion period passed with some media
coverage, but no official commentary and no reference to Russian
involvement. It was reported that the US and Pakistan intended to
supply the Afghan guerrillas with arms.[113] On 6 January Saddam
Hussein, the new absolute ruler of Iraq (soon to launch his war against
Iran), spoke of the invasion in his Army Day speech as a 'dangerous
phenomenon which cannot be justified or excused'. An editorial in the
Al Thawra daily had already claimed (on 4 January) that the Soviet
occupation was 'now causing widespread concern to friends of the
Soviet Union as well as every other country in the world'.[114] On 13
January another daily, Al-Iraq, assaulted the Soviets, stressing that
Moscow's strategy against the non-aligned Afghanistan had given rise
to universal concern; the international reaction to the invasion had also
surprised the Soviets, and there was 'a formidable moral force' backed
by world opinion to end the occupation.[115]

In a statement on 30 December, the government of Saudi Arabia
called the invasion a 'disgraceful interference', identifying (rather

improbably) 'direct Soviet involvement in Afghanistan as a further step in the Soviet plan to encircle the moderate Arab states'.[116] Soon the Saudis were urging action, their foreign minister calling on other Muslin countries to take 'a clear position' against the Russian aggression, because 'all Islamic and Third World countries were threatened by the danger'. The *Al Riyadh* daily had already (on 5 January) asked Muslim countries to support the Afghan guerrillas both morally and materially.[117] By the end of January the government had set up a committee, under the governor of Riyadh, to handle private donations for the 'Afghan freedom fighters', while national donations would be collected by the World Islamic League.[118]

The Kuwaitis followed, making it clear to the Russian ambassador that they were dispatching humanitarian aid to Pakistan to help the refugees: 'As a Muslim country, Kuwait is committed to the Muslim people of Afghanistan.' The ambassador was summoned by Foreign Minister Sabah Al Ahmed to be told the Kuwaiti position, which claimed that the invasion provided "other big powers" with the justification to undertake similar military operations elsewhere. Kuwait would object to the Americans using force in the region over the hostage issue.'[119] A spokesman for the Kuwaiti government denied the existence of any plan for the defence of the Gulf in the event of further Russian aggression, but he claimed states in the region were in constant communication 'on measures which could help strengthen the security and stability of the areas, blocking all means for any foreign intervention'. Since the fall of Daoud in 1978, the Kuwaitis had feared that Afghanistan might become – like Cuba – a 'cat's-paw' for intervention in the region, fomenting unrest among the Afghan populations of Iran and Pakistan. For the worried Al Rashid, the under secretary for foreign affairs, 'It would be child's play' for the Soviets to send Afghan communist fighters to Africa, and 'they would be good fighters too'.[120]

Bahrain also condemned the invasion, as did Oman and Qatar, with the latter's statement claiming that 'a Soviet military expansion into this and neighbouring regions was already manifested in events in the Horn of Africa, Southern Yemen ...'.[121] Leaders of the 'big powers [had to] halt the military action in Afghanistan, though by legitimate, peaceful channels'. The Qataris showed themselves unusually outspoken against the Soviet Union, which could only be interpreted as concern at Soviet plans for the region, while the United Arab Emirates condemned the invasion as 'conspicuous meddling in the internal affairs of the Afghan Muslim people'.[122] They appeared willing to back a UN resolution, but would abstain from any meaningful aid to the Afghan guerrillas unless Saudi Arabia or another country took the lead. Foreign Secretary Mohammed Heikal had spent ten days in Iran visiting Khomeini, and considered that the invasion 'was a God-send for the United States' in diverting attention from Iran. Heikal was of the opinion that skilful American diplomacy could secure an unequivocal Arab condemnation of the invasion,

> a breathing space over Iran and a chance to let the question of Security Council action [against Iran] drop without losing face. When the Afghanistan news fades and Iran comes again to the forefront, Washington would have more supporters than today.[123]

On 28 December 1979, the Egyptian daily *Al-Ahram* quoted an official source deploring the invasion and calling for support for the Muslim people of Afghanistan 'who were struggling against the externally supported forces of atheism'.[124] Sadat sided with Russia's critics, making it known that he would facilitate American military aid to the Gulf states in case of a general war, though he would not grant any bases. Cairo limited its contacts with Moscow, while the Grand Mufti advocated assistance for the Afghans 'in defending their religion, themselves and their country'. Muslim hatred focused for years on Israel and the US was now directed at the Soviets.

Turkey, a NATO member-state, condemned the aggression as dangerous interference and 'a threat to peace and stability in the region and the world'. Nonetheless, Ankara did not take the lead in further criticising Soviet policy,[125] fearing that events in Afghanistan would make an American move against Iran more probable.[126]

In their turn, the Greek government deplored the invasion: 'The armed intervention against the territory of independent and sovereign states constitutes a danger to international peace and security.' The Russian ambassador visited the Greek minister of foreign affairs in order to provide a justification for the Kremlin's action; the latter promptly reminded him of Turkey's invasion of Cyprus in 1974. The problem for Greek diplomats was that the ever-increasing anti-Americanism in their country constrained them from condemning Russian actions more openly, for fear of sounding pro-US. Indeed, Andreas Papandreou, the major opposition leader, spoke of 'the danger for the area constituted by the threats of military intervention by the US and NATO imperialists' without any direct reference to Afghanistan. The Greek Communist Party, meanwhile, accused the government of 'siding with the imperialists who are attempting to create the preconditions for intervention in Iran'. Essentially, the party's position was that the invasion had been justified.[127]

On 3 January, the Soviet embassy in Khartoum was besieged by demonstrators. The Sudanese foreign minister denounced Russian explanations, warning of the 'dangerous precedent [of the invasion]'.[128] However, while almost all Muslim countries took a strong anti-Russian stance, this could not be said of Algeria, where the government faced a serious dilemma. The people were Muslims, and felt a religious bond with the Afghans. But the Algerians could not publicly deplore the Kremlin's action because for years they had been enjoying its vital military and economic aid; the Soviet Union was officially regarded as 'an ally of the Third World'. Somewhat hesitantly, the Algerian press spoke of Russian 'aid' to the new Afghan regime, while a French-language newspaper, in a brief article, produced a more balanced comment: 'The Socialist countries have approved the changes brought about in Kabul while other countries, including Iran, have expressed their anxiety in the face of the situation prevailing in Afghanistan.'[129]

On 29 December, the government of Japan issued a strong statement demanding the 'immediate cessation' of the intervention;[130] even the Japanese Communist Party deplored the invasion.[131] The members of the ASEAN, namely Thailand, Malaysia, Singapore, Indonesia and the Philippines, all came out against the Soviet Union, each choosing different words; it took time for them to adopt a common position. Initial angst led to improbable conclusions: Singapore's foreign minister rushed out a statement that Russian strategy in

Afghanistan 'was a signal to Asia that in the 1980s it will be the target of Soviet ambitions ... neither non-alignment nor pro-Soviet policies have saved Afghanistan's independence and dignity'.[132] Similar fears were expressed by the Thai prime minister and the Malaysian Foreign Ministry, while President Suharto of Indonesia declared that the invasion 'shakes the foundations of world peace and infringes on the principle of peaceful co-existence and mutual respect'.[133] At a 3 January press conference, the vice-president of the World Islamic Congress, Mohammed Nassir, declared that the case of Afghanistan was similar to the invasion of Czechoslovakia, urging Muslims all over the world to take 'concrete steps and other kinds of firm action'.[134]

Among the non-aligned nations, Yugoslavia played a role second only to India's; the government under Tito, with the support of the press, backed the strong criticisms of the intervention:

> In connection with the military action of the Soviet Union in Afghanistan ... Yugoslavia expresses its deep concern over the serious consequences that such a development can have, not only by causing greater instability in that region, but also by affecting international relations as a whole.[135]

The UK ambassador in Belgrade commented: 'Though it is usual for Yugoslavs to wait on the feelings of other members of the non-aligned movement, their official statement is by local standards unusually prompt and forthright.'[136] The daily newspaper *Borba* (of 6 January 1980) wrote of Yugoslavia's respect for 'the sovereign right of nations to independence, autonomy, territorial integrity and their own way of life'. The Slovene daily *Delo* (of 4 January 1980) described 'the destruction of balance of forces in the so-called crisis crescent'.[137] On 8 January, the Yugoslav foreign minister assailed the Russian explanations, denouncing 'the unacceptability of nations resorting to policies of force, military interventions, pressure and interference in the internal affairs of other countries in order to preserve their privileged interest and various forms of outside domination and hegemony'.[138]

Finally, Malcolm Fraser, the prime minister of Australia, in the 19 February session of the House of Representatives, warned against appeasement: 'If the lesson which the Soviet Union is allowed to draw is that all it has to do is to sit tight and allow the storm of protest to blow itself out, the consequences will be disastrous'.

Carrington returned to London having visited the governments of Turkey, Oman, Saudi Arabia, Pakistan and India, gaining some impressions of their rulers' attitudes. In his 19 January 1980 memorandum to the prime minister, he reported a general feeling that the Western response was disappointing, observing that Oman, Saudi Arabia and Pakistan 'probably underestimate the threat of internal subversion'.[139] Turkey was encountering a severe economic and internal-security crisis, and feared the disintegration of Iran given the Soviet subversion in Azerbaijan and elsewhere.[140] The Saudis were willing to provide financial aid to Turkey, and to assume a leading role among Muslims in deploring the invasion of Afghanistan; but they wished for no Western military presence in the region. The Pakistanis feared 'Soviet retaliatory raids' in their country, while criticising the US stance in charging too high a price for defence-aid credits.[141]

Carrington urged Thatcher to adopt a consistent stance towards the invasion, warning (rather vaguely) that 'any repetition of it, e.g. in Yugoslavia, could be disastrous'. He set out a number of political and economic measures which might be taken by an international coalition, with the participation of the non-aligned bloc, to punish Russia as well as the Afghan regime.[142] By 1 February the FCO, in an analysis titled 'Soviet Foreign Policy after Afghanistan', had discounted the possibility of a Russian move against Yugoslavia:

> The Soviet leaders are not likely to invade Yugoslavia when Tito goes. They will seek to play on economic problems and the differences between nationalities, in the hope of creating opportunities for reintegrating Yugoslavia into their sphere of influence, even in time by invasion, although the Soviets will be watching carefully for a military response by the West.[143]

Carrington took the view that the Americans should be encouraged only to arm Pakistan to an extent which would not raise India's fears. Meanwhile, he urged, 'we should conclude as rapidly as possible' UK defence sales to Pakistan, Oman, Saudi Arabia, and other Gulf states.

He insisted that a European initiative at the United Nations should focus on acknowledging Palestinians' rights in return for their recognition of Israel. Carrington also advised the prime minister on intelligence-related schemes: 'We should provide friendly states in the Gulf and Pakistan with more information about our assessments of Soviet activities and intentions in the area. We should also provide these states with assistance in counter-subversion'. With reference to arms for China, the existing policy should be reviewed. Most significantly, Carrington was in favour of covert action in the region: 'We should consider the practicability of promoting insurgency in Soviet-dominated areas such as [the People's Democratic Republic of Yemen], Ethiopia and Afghanistan itself'.[144] Indeed, an FCO study submitted to him earlier had noted that the 'exposed nerves in the Soviet Empire' were Angola, Cabinda, Cuba, Guinea and Congo; action should be taken to disrupt Russian influence there. Nonetheless, it should be borne in mind that the Soviets could strike back in Pakistan, the Gulf, Iran, Rhodesia, Turkey, Morocco-Sahara, Thailand, Yugoslavia, the Basque country, Puerto Rico, Jamaica, Belize, El Salvador, Namibia, Zaire and Oman. This study hinted at Russian subversion and secret service operations rather than full-scale invasions. All these hypotheses (most of which it was improbable would ever be realised) were reflections of the British authorities' limited understanding, and of their resultant apprehension in the face of the Soviet occupation of Afghanistan.[145]

On 15 January, Cabinet Secretary Sir Robert Armstrong held talks in Paris with Brzezinski, Whal (director-general at the Quai d'Orsai) and von Staden, the latter's FRG counterpart, on the possibility of covert aid to the Mujahedeen guerrillas. The German official took a negative view of involving the West German secret services in Afghanistan. It turned out that

[h]e was anxious to make it clear that the German government was constitutionally debarred from exporting arms, and could not therefore give direct military support to Afghan guerrillas. The German intelligence service was also under charter restraints which were likely to prevent it from taking any part in activities of that kind.[146]

Nonetheless, he 'accepted' that his government could do nothing to stop funding for humanitarian aid 'in substitution for other [foreign/allied] funds which might then be in practice diverted' to the guerrillas.[147] Staden was helpfully disclosing the limits of German involvement in covert action, but also that Bonn would tolerate others financing the guerrillas. However, Chancellor Schmidt, who met Thatcher in 10 Downing Street on 25 February, favoured drastic action, in parallel to diplomacy. He told Thatcher:

> The dialogue between the American and Soviet government had to continue. The need for the Soviets to save face had to be borne in mind. There should be no pinpricking and no sabre-rattling. At the same time the West should find a way of doing something that really(s) hurt the Soviet Union. This meant pushing them out of some country in which they were already established – Angola, Ethiopia, the PDRY or some similar country (Schmidt noted that this was the kind of point that he could not put to anyone in writing: he asked that it should not be recorded or disseminated).[148]

He also criticised the American response as 'inadequate': Washington had not realised the need for continuous consultation and coordination among the allies. The Americans should not talk about punishing the Soviet Union, but work with the other allies to compel the Kremlin to withdraw its troops from Afghanistan and to deter them from any adventurism in Yemen.[149]

In the Paris meeting on 15 January, officials also hinted at fears of a Russian intervention in Yugoslavia; Tito's ill health might lead the Kremlin into following an adventurist policy. Contingency planning among the ministers of state for foreign affairs of Britain, France, West Germany and the US, in the light of a possible crisis after Tito's death, was scheduled for 31 January. Brzezinski told the Europeans that Washington was examining plans for rapid military aid to Yugoslavia in the first fortnight after the death of the Yugoslav president.[150] (Tito eventually died on 4 May 1980, but no contingency plan was ever implemented. In any case, an FCO minute dated 1 February had considerably downgraded the threat of a Soviet bid against Yugoslavia: 'The Soviet leaders are not likely to invade Yugoslavia when Tito goes. They will seek to play on economic problems and the differences between nationalities, in the hope of creating opportunities for reintegrating Yugoslavia into their sphere of influence').[151]

The single most important factor that led to the build-up of consensus among the non-aligned and key countries in Asia and the Middle East was the fear that followed their surprise at the Soviet invasion of the Afghanistan. Uninformed and alarmist strategic assessments of Kremlin's further intentions ignited consultations, and in January 1980 provided Anglo-American diplomacy with much-needed backing. In any event, the non-aligned were seriously angered by the invasion of the seemingly non-aligned Afghanistan. Washington and London did nothing to calm their allies, at least in January. Evidence shows that British and US diplomats did not deceive the non-aligned by claiming that the Soviet Union intended to reach the Persian Gulf or to upset the balance of power in Asia. In May the NATO ambassadors understood from a briefing by Edmund Muskie, now US secretary of state, that the Soviets were not as belligerent as initially assumed by the non-aligned and other countries in Asia and the Middle East (as we will see in the next chapter). Lord Carrington was confident that there would be no Soviet thrust in Asia or the Middle East. Fearful allies, and most importantly the non-aligned among them, were the protagonists at the UN, ready to channel their fury against the invasion into a General Assembly resolution. Did this international reaction deter Russia from further adventurism? The answer is no. In the first place, the Soviets were not interested in a military thrust in the region – and they could hardly be deterred from action they had no intention of carrying out. Neither the minutes of the Politburo's 17 January conference nor the recommendations submitted to its new meeting ten days later made any mention of a Russian intent to challenge the regional balance of power by invading Iran or Pakistan. The Kremlin regarded Afghanistan simply as a 'backyard problem', and would not be compelled to reduce its presence there.[152]

The KGB historian-archivist Mitrokhin claims that Moscow had discounted any danger of a Western over-reaction 'as early as January

1980'. The KGB maintained a secret source in FRG government circles who disclosed details of the visit by Egon Bahr (the Social Democrats' executive secretary) to Washington, where he met Carter, Vance, Brzezinski and Kissinger. The source passed on Bahr's impressions to the Soviets: 'Three factors govern the situation: uncertainty, the desire for strong leadership and a growing fear of war with the Soviet Union'. The reason was 'the general loss of faith in the power of America politically, economically and militarily'. Widespread disappointment was reported at the way Washington had reacted to the crises in Afghanistan and Iran, with Carter seemingly absorbed in his bid to win a second term. The US president was 'incurable, with his inconsistency and flawed decisions, which he takes on the spur of the moment for reasons of prestige'.[153] Brzezinski had boasted of having surprised the Soviets with the American response, but when in a conversation with Bahr he was told that Moscow had anticipated such a reaction to the invasion, he asked in a surprised tone: 'Didn't we catch the Soviets unawares?'[154]

The national security advisor assumed that the war would be over in six months, at which time Washington and Moscow could agree on a neutral Afghanistan without Russian bases; then they would continue with SALT II. He wanted Bonn and London to cultivate further relations with Turkey and Pakistan, respectively, helping them with defence aid. Bahr's comments (which found their way to the Soviets) concluded: 'Brzezinski was full of anti-Sovietism as before and would try to use any opportunity to damage relations between the US and USSR and to flex American muscles'. Vance view was pragmatic but pessimistic, complaining to Bahr that the State Department's reputation had been damaged by the opportunism implicit in Brzezinski's ideas. Vance withdrew the SALT II treaty from the Senate to save it – he still believed in its importance. Carter had stated that he would honour the terms of the treaty even without ratification, a stance which was maintained up to 1986, when the Reagan administration withdrew from it citing Russian violations. Kissinger sounded openly criticical of Brzezinski, 'the Polish saviour of America who was biologically repugnant to him'.[155]

A hard-nosed Russian ideologist could have interpreted the report of the German spy as indicating a lack of decisiveness in the

Carter administration (coupled with the usual hawkish statements from Brzezinski); therefore, this lack of resolve could mean no escalation to confrontation.

A close examination of Gromyko's speech at the 17 January 1980 Politburo conference shows that, with KGB, the foreign ministry tried to play down the international diplomatic reaction deploring the invasion. Gromyko claimed

> The international situation around Afghanistan has taken a turn for the worse. The ruckus, which has unfolded particularly broadly in the USA, has also assumed a somewhat weakened form. In NATO there is no unity regarding measures towards the Soviet Union. In any case, the Western interests – in particular, the FRG, Italy, Turkey and other countries – did not follow the Americans, are not in agreement with the sanctions [the cutting-off of grain and technology exports] which the USA is applying. The General Assembly session ended. Many delegates spoke over the three days. But it is necessary to say that of the 104 delegations which voted for the resolution, many voted without soul, 48 countries abstained and voted against. That is a full one-third [that] think there will be some kind of momentum in the American press of other countries. But at the same time, countries like Argentina and Brazil do not agree with the Americans, for example, on the sale of grain to the Soviet Union. Canada, too.[156]

It was clear that Gromyko, with his usual shrewdness, had decided to present the Politburo with a distorted assessment, to avoid causing panic among the Russian leadership (though the remark about voting 'without soul' was a somewhat childish touch). At the same session, Ustinov stated rather prematurely that the military situation in Afghanistan was 'basically satisfactory, there are now significantly fewer hotbeds of resistance by the rebels'.[157]

Carter found himself following two simultaneous tactics at the UN: on the one hand he wanted to give Moscow a hard time, and on the other he aimed to secure a second Security Council resolution (which he failed to do) for economic sanctions against the Khomeini regime in Iran. The president was also seeking to continue with détente and SALT II. Thus, as we have seen, in the first post-invasion weeks Washington spoke with more than one voice: while Carter referred to the 'most serious threat since the Second World War',[158] the hawkish Brzezinski issued reassurances about continuing with détente. Margaret Thatcher, meanwhile, never wavered in her determination to pursue sanctions against Russia, nor at the same time to aim for SALT II and détente.

The Pakistanis looked forward to the invasion opening the gates for the resumption of US military aid (and also, importantly, to an easing of the pressure on their nuclear programme). Islamabad took the initiative at the Security Council, and in talks with Muslim and non-aligned countries in the General Assembly helped with the work of Anglo-American diplomacy. Finally. the boycott of the Olympics divided the West: while the UK team would take part, together with those of France, Greece, Luxembourg, Sweden and Switzerland, the US, Norway, Turkey, the FRG, Canada and China abstained.

By mid-January 1980, the intelligence community had been tasked with confirming a report by William Holstein, the UPI correspondent in Kabul, to the effect that a 10,000-strong Russian division was deployed near the Afghan–Iranian border, close to Iranian oilfields. Other UPI sources named this unit as the 66th Motorised Division, one of the seven divisions occupying Afghanistan. In the National Security Council there was some anxiety about Soviet intentions towards Iran, but the intelligence agencies reassured the White House that the Russians would not intervene in Iran. Brzezinski referred to the 66th Division and its intentions in his subsequent January meetings with the CIA, the State Department and the president. Meanwhile, the CIA reported that apparently the Mujahedeen were opening the floodgates to stop Russian forces and supplies moving to Jalalabad.[159]

On 14 January, at a Special Coordination Committee meeting, Brzezinski remarked: 'Whatever the Soviet motives for their actions in Afghanistan, they have created an objective threat and a dynamic development in the area as serious for our security and vital interests as Soviet actions in Greece in 1947.[160] (This analogy was utterly wrong: Stalin had effectively abstained from backing the Greek communists, who received war supplies mainly from Yugoslavia. While 1947 had been a dramatic year in the Greek civil war, there was only a piecemeal and cautious Soviet involvement, since Stalin respected the October 1944 'percentages' agreement with Churchill. By 1947 Britain could no longer afford to provide aid to Greece, and had called on the United States for assistance.) Carter had a meeting with the Pakistani foreign minister, and Brzezinski admitted that there was a problem in defining American commitment to the defence of Pakistan under the 1959 agreement (in fact all US administrations encountered this issue once Pakistan's security affairs hit the headlines.) The National Security Advisor admitted:

> If there is a major Soviet aggression, the US will respond within the limits of our Constitutional authority. The US will not however, become involved in border skirmishes. We want our support to help Pakistan to take a firm stand against Soviet forces in the region even if they are faced by a Moscow/Kabul/ New Delhi axis. In that case, the US will develop a US/Saudi Arabia/PRC/Pakistan and eventually Iran axis as a counter.[161]

General David Jones, the JCS Chairman (who favoured providing the Pakistanis with A7 aircraft) presented an estimate of the distances to be covered by Afghanistan-based Russian forces in the event of operations in the Gulf. If unopposed, Russian forces would need between ten and twelve days to reach the Straits of Hormuz via Baluchistan.[162] They could also reach Kuwait within the same time-frame. Airborne troops could seize the Suez and then reach the Gulf within an estimated deployment period of 21 days. One airborne division (8,000 troops) could land anywhere in the vicinity of the Gulf in two to three days, if all available means were employed.[163]

The chairman of the JCS spoke of Russian capabilities and of prudent US planning, but he gave no hint that the Soviets intended to proceed with these operations. He recommended reducing the US naval presence in the Arabian Sea to one carrier – Egypt, Saudi Arabia and Jordan could facilitate the stationing of US fighters. His recommendation entailed dispatching (during the coming three months or so) two ro-ro (roll-on, roll-off) ships – vessels specially designed for transporting vehicles that could be driven on and off the ship under their own power – which would pre-position materiel to equip one mechanised brigade and to provide ground-support installations for three fighter squadrons. Three leased cargo ships would carry other war materiel for pre-positioning, and additional shipments would be facilitated by eight SL-7 vessels. Thus heavy weapons would be in the region in case of need, and the time taken up by the logistics would be effectively reduced.[164] In addition, two US Marine units would exercise in Oman and Somalia in March 1980 to demonstrate to local regimes Washington's active interest in their security. Jones warned that the deployment of US airborne troops would be very expensive; he had already requested $450 million for the ships carrying war materiel.[165]

A few days later, on 17 January, Vance and Brzezinski discussed the issue of the 2,000 marines exercising near the region to signal American resolve. Vance argued that the regional leaders might be publicly embarrassed by an alliance with the United States, but in private they would be content. He considered the exercises should be held in Diego Garcia. Brown, the secretary of defense, disagreed with this, arguing that the exercises should be held in Oman, Egypt or Saudi Arabia. Brzezinski intervened, proposing Oman and Saudi Arabia, and that if either refused the American invitation, the Americans could turn to Egypt – a positive answer from Cairo was thought certain. Brzezinski then raised the issue of another exercise, involving an airborne brigade and taking place in the coming spring or summer. The US paratroops could train together with the Saudis and Jordanians. Again Vance was negative: 'The political problems are simply too great for us to attempt this'. Brzezinski deferred any decision, asking the Pentagon to prepare a study on costs, planning and other details.[166]

Nonetheless, as the discussion progressed, he surprised his colleagues by revealing that (despite the secret aid to the Mujahedeen initiated by the CIA, a programme he had called for) he did not yet have a full understanding of the Afghan insurgency's potential, nor of the possible strategic effects on the region. The latter was true particularly of Pakistan, whose foreign minister, Agha Shahi, referred to the insurgency as 'a dangerous lighting rod', but also of US interests and US–Russian relations in general. Brzezinski claimed: 'A massive insurgency at present is probably not in our best interest. Rather a low-level and enduring insurgency is essential to keep the Islamic states mobilized against the Soviets in Afghanistan'.[167]

By early February, he had been animated by his visit to Islamabad and his talks with Zia ul-Haq; the dictator brought a number of Mujahedeen, hand-picked by Pakistan's Inter-Service Intelligence. Brzezinski wrote to Sir Robert Wade-Gery of Thatcher's Cabinet Office:

I am impressed by the determination of the Pakistanis, and also with the Afghan resistance fighters – the Mujahedeen – whom I encountered during my visit to a refugee camp on the frontier. I am convinced that we have something solid to work with in frustrating Soviet ambitions towards the South.[168]

But Brzezinski tried to explore a parallel policy. In secret, via Ambassador Dobrynin, he reassured Moscow that the United States was interested in a neutral Afghanistan 'friendly to the Soviet Union like Finland, but not another vassal like Mongolia'.[169] Britain agreed with this. Later Dobrynin claimed in his memoirs that some Politburo members in early April 1980 found this concept useful for a settlement, but soon the chief ideologist Ponomarev rebuffed the whole idea, asking: 'How can one compare Afghanistan and Finland? Finland is a capitalist country'.[170] In any case, this episode showed that Brzezinski was not as hawkish and confrontational with Moscow as he may have wanted to appear in interdepartmental and international conferences.

4

ASSESSING THE KREMLIN'S INTENTIONS, AND ITS FEARS

Anglo-American intelligence agents were not to enjoy a family New Year's Eve. After the surprise of the invasion, they had to move up a gear – it was crucial to discover Soviet intentions beyond Afghanistan, and to provide their political masters with accurate intelligence. It soon became evident that the Soviets were not planning to advance into Iran or Pakistan, nor to threaten the Persian Gulf, nor to reach the Indian Ocean.

In his memoirs, Brzezinski wrote that on 26 December 1979 he had reported to the president, 'in my judgment the Soviet action had initiated a regional crisis of strategic significance'.[1] Over a two-year period, he had been advancing the theory of a 'crescent of crisis' in Southwest Asia, carefully ascribing this view to his own personal 'judgment', and without mentioning any support for it from secret intelligence. Besides, as noted in the previous chapter, the intelligence community was itself confused as to what had actually been going on in Afghanistan during the immediate post-invasion period.

In his State of the Union Address on 23 January 1980, Carter made a seemingly clear statement:

Let our position be absolutely clear: Any attempt by any out-side force to gain control of the Persian Gulf region will be regarded as an assault on the vital interests of the United States of America, and such an assault will be repelled by any means necessary, including military force.[2]

This was to become known as the Carter Doctrine. But the intelligence community, with all its spies, back-channels to the Kremlin, latest technology signal equipment and imagery-intelligence assets had supplied no information, thus raising concerns over the security of the Gulf. In the previous chapter, we examined the January minutes of the discussions between Vance, Turner, Brzezinski and Brown. They had focused on policy options for responding to the invasion – there was no new intelligence warning of a Russian thrust to the south. In essence, the resolve expressed in the Carter Doctrine appeared hollow in light of the reassurances the president had received that the Soviets were not interested in the Gulf. His hawkish stance played to a domestic political audience.

Brzezinski had already briefed key newspaper editors in Washington; indeed, a year earlier (on 15 February 1979) *Time* magazine had published a front cover of the Russian bear staring at the states of Southwest Asia and the Gulf (arranged in the shape of a crescent) under the title 'Crescent of Crisis: Troubles beyond Iran.' It was a public presentation of Brzezinski's crisis theory. In his memoirs, Brzezinski wrote:

> I had stressed [to the editors in their late December 1979 meeting] that the issue was not what might have been Brezhnev's subjective motives in going into Afghanistan but the objective consequences of a Soviet military presence so much closer to the Persian Gulf.[3]

The national security advisor now admitted that, in effect, the Soviets did not pose any immediate threat to the Gulf. He confused the editors by talking about subjective motives (thus recognising the actual scope of the Soviet intervention) and 'objective consequences'. He considered that the need for a US response to the invasion could be met simply by limiting grain exports to the Soviet Union (though eventually they would all be cut off) by transferring military technology to China and by providing military aid to Pakistan. All these 'I felt would be both sufficiently punitive and strategically significant'.[4] Had there in fact been a real threat to the Gulf, Brzezinski would have mentioned the immediate dispatch of a naval task force, together with considerable fighter squadrons to be based in allied Arab states. As noted in the previous chapter, Washington's military planning for joint exercises to signal its resolve to Moscow were delayed until spring/summer 1980. This is more evidence that there was no rush to set up short-term defence arrangements for the defence of the Gulf; there was no rush because there was no threat.

The lack of intelligence pointing to an immediate or short-to-medium-term threat to US interests in the Gulf opened the way for a debate between Vance and Brzezinski on the strategic implications of the Soviet presence in Afghanistan. These very experienced and key players in the Carter administration came in the end to the wrong conclusions. Vance wrote in his memoirs (published in 1983) of two theories aired during the administration's consultations. The first argued that Moscow could not tolerate a regime (Amin's) which leaned increasingly towards Islamism, which was boosted by Khomeini's rise to power in Iran and which constituted a long-term threat to the Soviet republics in Central Asia. Thus the Soviets were interested in Afghanistan only to preserve their own national security and to forestall any troubles their Muslim citizens might foment.[5] This theory, however, did not stand up: Amin was secularist, and leaned towards a Sadat-type of leadership for the long term. The majority of Afghan tribes were Sunnis, who hated the Shiites of Iran and were always suspicious of their bigger neighbour. The Soviets (as is disclosed by the December 1979 meetings of Gromyko, Ustinov, Brezhnev and Andropov) feared that Afghanistan would become a new Egypt eventually deploying US missiles.

The second theory held that Russia had become frustrated by the slow pace of détente, and had decided to launch a thrust in Southwest Asia to gain strategic advantage following the improvement in US–Chinese relations and the deployment of Pershing II missiles in Europe. By occupying Afghanistan, Moscow could influence events in Iran and Pakistan. Thus, there were local and global considerations in understanding the Russian decision to intervene.[6] This theory also was flawed: it treated Afghanistan as a cornerstone of détente, and assumed that the Soviet Union was no longer interested in it. In fact, though the Soviets were frustrated with the decision to deploy the Pershings, they viewed Afghanistan as a separate, local issue on their southern borders.

Nonetheless, Carter felt impelled to abandon SALT II – he could not urge its ratification after the invasion, and this was the best face-saving device he could find. In his memoirs, however, he admitted: 'Our failure to ratify the SALT II treaty and to secure even more far-reaching agreements on nuclear arms control was the most profound disappointment of my Presidency.'[7] The president was persuaded by Brzezinski of the strategic effects of the invasion. Nonetheless, he also admitted in his memoirs that the threat was non-existent, and thus the means of response would not be military: 'Direct military action on our part was not advisable ... [the Soviets] might be tempted toward further aggression. We were resolved to do everything feasible to prevent such a turn of events.'[8]

In London, meanwhile, the chief of defence staff submitted his estimate of Soviet intentions (on 20 January), incorporating in his draft the assessments of the chiefs of the Army, Royal Navy and RAF. He assumed that the Soviets had accurately calculated their strategic interests and the possible Western reactions to their intervention in Afghanistan:

> While we do not think that the Soviet invasion of Afghanistan should be characterised as the first of a series of pre-planned steps in a military advance into Iran and Pakistan, we believe that they will retain their general aim of expanding their sphere of influence.[9]

He also assumed that the Soviets saw Pakistan, 'unlike Afghanistan', as an area of strategic interest to the West, and that they would thus anticipate a harsh response in the event of a further military advance.

Characteristically, he worried that the situation in Iran might become more 'chaotic', given the secessionist movements, and he did not discount the possibility of a coup by the communist Tudeh party. This shows that a year after the fall of the Shah and despite the coming to power of the fundamentalist Khomeini, the chiefs of staff had still not realised the strength of the Islamic regime's grip on Iran.[10]

The 'immediate dangers' for the UK's and the West's interests focused on Pakistan, in the form of possible Soviet intervention against the Afghan guerrillas who had found refuge there; a conflict on the Afghan–Pakistani border could lead to a superpower confrontation.[11] It was important for the West to understand that its response to the invasion could not compel the Soviets to change their strategy over Afghanistan; rather, the need was to demonstrate the credibility of deterrence in the future. Indeed, there was

> [a] danger that the Soviets could conclude that their success in Afghanistan, giving them the strategic wedge into the region, was cheaply bought and that this could lead them to underestimate the dangers of any future military adventure they might contemplate.[12]

Washington had been leading the international response to the aggression, but suffered from a 'strategic disadvantage' – Pakistan was too far for the US to deploy adequate forces in time should the need arise. Besides, American strategists knew only too well that, 'With few exceptions governments [in the Gulf] are reluctant to welcome [US forces] overtly, even though they are privately reassured by their presence.'[13] This was why Washington was hurriedly seeking to establish a network of bases in Oman, Kenya, Somalia and Djibouti, and to expand its facilities on Diego Garcia.[14]

The chief of defence staff presented the hypothesis (unsupported, however, by any intelligence or military analysis) that Moscow might put the blame on the Americans for seeking to interfere in the region with a rapid reaction force, reminding world opinion of the legacy of their pro-Shah policy. Moreover, 'a more promising initiative' might entail stirring up trouble in the Caribbean, Central America, Saudi Arabia or Africa. But Russia would not move against Yugoslavia, nor attempt to take advantage of the precarious condition of Turkey's economy. In any case,

> We believe that the Soviets will first concentrate on consolidating their position in Afghanistan; they will want to take more time to weigh up the risks involved before considering any options listed above [i.e. in the Caribbean, Central America, Saudi Arabia or Africa].[15]

The Kremlin could be deterred from future adventurism, it was thought, if the reaction to the invasion of Afghanistan could be 'coordinated and sustained'.[16]

Planners would always have to be reminded of the 'unpredictability of events' affecting Britain's security; the crises of the revolution in Iran and of the Russian invasion of Afghanistan demonstrated this clearly. Until this latter event, NATO had not addressed the question of out-of-area operations, and the invasion acted as a catalyst for military studies of such operations. However, 'it is too early to anticipate either the results of these studies or the reaction of allies', the chief of staff remarked.[17]

The British military were willing to act in a supporting role with respect to US military deployments and future operations, and could propose to deploy forces 'in a number of areas [where], in view of our previous presence, a UK initiative may prove to be more acceptable than that of the US'.[18] For the British military to be deployed in out-of-area NATO operations, however, the secretaries of state at the MoD and the FCO had to be informed of the three levels of activities: the first entailed training, small-scale military exercises and the loan of personnel ('we regard this form of support [conducted now] as low in profile and adaptable to meet local requirements. If it is to be effective, some costs are inevitable, but they need not be high').[19] The second level addressed 'over-the-horizon presence' and large-scale deployments signalling Britain's determination to support the Americans. Finally, the third level encompassed the earmarking of UK forces for actual operations.[20] The major difficulty for this was that the 1974 Defence Review

> has led to the loss of our strategic reserve air transportable division, a large proportion of the air transport force and the assault capability of our amphibious and parachute forces. We thus have no national capability for opposed [sic] intervention.[21]

The MoD was currently assessing the required UK capabilities for out-of-area NATO operations, 'in particular whether [the forces] need any form of assault capability'.[22]

At NATO headquarters Allied Supreme Commander General Bernard Rogers treated the invasion of Afghanistan as a similar case to the invasion of Czechoslovakia, warning against appeasement and adding an alarmist element to Washington's 'considerable political pressure' on the alliance to show some teeth. In his 'lessons learned' from the invasion, he urged the allies to understand that NATO's strategic interests were linked to the regions and resources of the Third World. He confidently (but pessimistically) claimed:

> I believe that there is a possibility of conflict occurring as a result of political instability or competition for needed resources in the Third World ... one of the things we have learned, if anything, in the whole of history is that aggression condoned is aggression encouraged. I do not need to remind those of you who represent countries of Western Europe of that fact.[23]

He was particularly worried about the security of Iran and Pakistan, concluding that there was a need for intelligence-sharing among alliance members. General Rogers also called for the establishment of intelligence organisations at headquarters and in subordinate units – fully-manned military intelligence agencies that would work in peacetime as they would in wartime.[24] In addition, the alliance had to improve the balance of forces vis-à-vis the Warsaw Pact. He addressed many areas the allies should attend to (repeating previous US policy positions): the obligations of all allies under the Long Term Defence Programme (LTDP); the long-range-theatre nuclear force programme; AWACS; the acceptance of force level goals by each nation, and of the commitment of national resources; the enhanced training of nations' reserve forces; the upgrading of day-to-day training and levels of readiness; an increase in national ammunition stocks to NATO standard levels; the requirements of pre-positioned war-reserve stocks to replace materiel lost on the battlefield (in case of a war with the Warsaw Pact); and the upgrading of logistics (there was a need for an integrated and coordinated NATO system). Finally, he insisted on arming Turkey, re-equipping a Portuguese brigade (earmarked for operations in northern Italy) and reintegrating Greece within the alliance.[25]

Washington called for a NATO consensus on a show of determination, and on gearing up the alliance for out-of-area operations. The Carter administration's apprehension was noted when the US military representatives in Brussels submitted a study entitled 'Strategic Implications of Afghanistan'. (This study is not included in the declassified DEFE 25/350. However, UK memoranda criticise the paper in some detail, giving us an insight into the American positions.) The FCO and the MoD warned their representatives in Brussels not to accept the paper without the necessary alterations. The US wished to avoid protracted debating among the allies, but the British feared that agreeing with the Americans' 'apocalyptic analysis' of events 'could later [be] use[d] to justify more radical changes of policy and demands on their allies.'[26] Indeed, the American draft was

unsatisfactory for four main reasons: 1. There is no clear assessment of Soviet motives in intervening in Afghanistan; 2. The analysis is ambiguous. It fails to distinguish between the threat to Western interests in the area from Soviet invasion and local factors (eg. the instability and anti-Western feeling) which existed long before; 3. It concentrates unduly on the military dimension of the threat, whilst paying scant attention to the political implications of the Soviet intervention, in particular the effect and attitude of regional countries to the Soviet Union and the West; 4. For this reason, it exaggerates the appropriate Western military response (both in NATO and in the region) and undersells the political response.[27]

One scenario included in the study examined for example the possibility of oil producers curtailing oil exports to Europe (by 5 million barrels per day). The Americans were obliged to elaborate on this scenario, because it did not explain whether what was entailed was the Soviet occupation of Saudi Arabia or simply Russian political pressure on Riyadh. There was no overall assessment of Soviet policy towards Middle East oil-producing states, nor of why they should bow to (hypothetical) Russian pressure and reduce their supply to the West.[28]

The NATO allies needed to agree on an assessment of the Kremlin's motives. The available US estimate was 'surprisingly diffident and confused', and there was no explanation for the timing of the invasion. In any event: 'It is a mistake to imply, as the paper does, that the Soviets would be better placed to mount a military operation against the oil states from Afghanistan than from southern Soviet Union.'[29] Moreover, the analysis of the threat to the West needed some 'balancing'. The political threat (the rise of communist governments) was discounted, as was the cost of the invasion to Moscow's prestige among the communist parties of Western Europe. Indeed, the Soviets in their turn needed to resolve their policy contradictions as communists all over the world watched closely: the Kremlin's Marxist propaganda on world peace and progress ran blatantly counter to their aggression in Afghanistan.[30]

British planners believed that the communist threat to the West came in the form of 'subversion, sabotage and internal collapse', and that the Americans should have included in their analysis the political dimensions of the threat. The warning to the British representatives in Brussels was explicit:

It seems from this paper that the Americans are in danger of building up exaggerated expectations in arguing that we should all do more than envisaged in the [Long Term Defence

Programme]. The US paper also goes too far in arguing that there is an additional military risk in Western Europe as a result of Afghanistan. The analogy between Afghanistan and Turkey/ Norway is completely misplaced.[31]

Treating Southwest Asia as a 'third theatre' in the implementation of deterrence strategy, and thereby diverting resources from Europe, was 'not marketable' among the NATO allies.[32] As far as tactics were concerned, P.J. Goulden (head of the FCO's defence department) recommended that:

> We should not do a hatchet job on it [the US paper]. Nor on the other hand can we afford to be too forward in urging everyone to do more. I recognise that this boils down to a rather unexciting neutral steer.[33]

Reflecting on US-European differences, Vance remarked in his memoirs that some allies did not see the invasion as having set a precedent for Soviet behaviour. Some European countries (and NATO partners) had not taken strong action on trade and export sanctions.[34] To some European states, the Americans appeared too eager to lead by confrontation, and to scrap détente for the sake of Afghanistan. The Europeans had no wish to increase their own defence spending to cover for US forces earmarked for future operations in Southwest Asia. In his consultations with British, French and German officials, Vance remarked:

> We (the Americans) encountered serious concern that the administration's reaction to Afghanistan was exaggerated and threatened to wreck the framework of East-West relations ... some felt we had adopted a confrontational strategy without taking European interests into account; having done so, we were now unfairly criticizing them for inadequate cooperation and support. There were grounds for the allies' complaint – although I believe they should have given greater consideration to the

need for rapid, decisive actions in the face of the Soviets' blatant aggression.[35]

Europeans wished the détente to continue in Europe, and to avoid provoking the Soviets. They wanted the US to implement deterrence without upsetting European gains in improved relations with Moscow.[36]

At the end of March, NATO delegates gathered to examine the situation and their response strategy. Sir Clive Rose, the UK ambassador in Brussels, made it clear to his counterparts that

[t]he allied policy towards the Soviet Union needed to strike a balance between the extremes of pushing the Soviets into a laager mentality and giving them 'business as usual' ... all governments agreed on the importance of keeping open the dialogue with the Soviet Union.[37]

The Senior Political Committee discussed Afghanistan in the light of Western strategic interests, and produced a summarising paper (which was ultimately declared a 'non-paper', an unofficial study receiving only 'congratulatory unanimity').[38] The paper sought to examine all the possible outcomes of Soviet strategy following the invasion of Afghanistan; it leanted towards the American approach, but stopped short of calling for NATO troops to help in a Southwest Asian confrontation; it was a theoretical exercise in grand strategy, full of 'coulds' and 'mights', and there was no intelligence to support the scenarios. Pessimism overshadowed the analysis: the invasion and the employment of military force 'increased uncertainty about the Kremlin's intentions'. A number of NATO delegates called for a 'prudent' measure, the examination of a 'worst-case scenario' and the alliance's preparedness. Nonetheless, the paper warned:

In the political sphere, Western reactions should be shaped to avoid an escalation of the crisis and include both positive and negative incentives [for the Soviet Union] ... the danger was pointed out that worst-case scenarios would become self-fulfilling if given undue prominence.[39]

As a result, NATO should become more interested in Third World security problems and political instabilities:

> A sustained and harmonized, although not, of course, NATO-labelled, contribution to stabilisation – which should not necessarily be equated with the maintenance of the status quo – should be the central aim of allied efforts to prevent further Soviet encroachment in the critical area and beyond.[40]

This was an abstract concept rather than official NATO policy, which could, however, be transformed into out-of-area operations in the future.

Meanwhile, it became known that East European countries were far from satisfied with Moscow's policy. President Carter, who had been dissuaded from calling a NATO heads-of-state summit on Afghanistan, was informed by Thatcher that a Western summit might give the Soviets the pretext to organise a counter-summit, and thus 'tighten discipline in the opposition camp'. The French, meanwhile, continued their policy of avoiding coordination with Washington and London. There was the possibility that President Valéry Giscard d'Estaing might snub a NATO heads-of-state summit in Washington or Brussels (the British prime minister assuming also that the same possibility existed if such a meeting were to be held in Ankara). Thatcher proposed that Carter should attend the scheduled conference in Vienna (where Giscard would definitely be present) on 22–23 June. Two days later, the NATO foreign ministers' conference in Ankara (25–26 June) would once again demonstrate solidarity; in addition, the foreign ministers, who would meet first in Venice, would contribute to an 'upgraded communiqué' of the Ankara meeting, signalling resolve.[41]

Throughout February–April 1980, Vance sought to initiate a secret dialogue with Moscow. He was in favour of a 'strong, steady, consistent' strategy with 'carrots and sticks' and (by implication) criticised Carter's approach, remarking: '[We] should avoid violent swings between trust and hysteria.'[42] Carter was against military action ('the military option was not advisable') but also against diplomacy. He turned down a proposal from Vance to send a letter to Brezhnev by late January explaining once again the implications of the invasion for US-Soviet relations. But the president cleared a letter (8 February 1980) from Vance to Gromyko, in which the secretary of state warned his Russian counterpart that 'there was a high risk that each might miscalculate the action of the other'. He urged the withdrawal of Soviet troops from Afghanistan as a crucial step towards restoring stability in the region: 'If there was restraint on both sides and respect for the independence and territorial integrity of the states in the region, our respective interests need not lead to confrontation.' Vance 'requested that [Gromyko] indicate to us Soviet intentions in both Afghanistan and the region.'[43]

The president turned down a request for Vance to meet Gromyko in March to restate the February message. A request to send Marshall Shulman as special emissary to Brezhnev was also declined. However, on 21 March Vance met Ambassador Dobrynin, repeating his message that the Soviet Union should understand that Afghanistan was now a key issue in US–Soviet relations. He underlined that the president remained committed to nuclear arms control, and 'did not want to see this essential part of East-West relations destroyed'. He proposed a meeting with Gromyko in April or May.[44]

Eventually, Edmund Muskie, Vance's successor at the State Department, met his Russian counterpart in Vienna on 19 May 1980, the 25th anniversary of the treaty ending the post-war occupation of Austria. *Time* magazine commented:

> Though their meeting is expected to be little more than a polite chat, it has symbolic importance. Not since super-power relations were severely chilled by the Soviet invasion of Afghanistan has there been any high-level contact between Washington and Moscow.[45]

Muskie sounded a pragmatic note, calm but cautious; it seemed that Gromyko, a veteran of dozens of crises and negotiations, could not be frightened by the remarks of an American secretary of state. Muskie repeated the need for 'restraint', and Gromyko claimed that his country had no interest in advancing further towards the oil-producing Middle

East states; each sought to reassure the other that his country had no intention of escalating the crisis.

After the meeting, Muskie commented to NATO ambassadors that he 'was not more pessimistic afterwards than he had been before'.[46] Though he wished to continue with the arms control talks, the Afghanistan question inhibited any negotiations with the Soviets. He assumed that the post-invasion 'building process [of relations with the Soviet Union] would be a slow one'.[47] Gromyko had given him the impression of attempting 'to be relaxed and not to be abrasive'.[48] On substance, Gromyko continued his hard line, 'but he had been ready to smile, something that had not happened when Muskie had seen him a few years ago'.[49] The secretary of state was surprised that Gromyko wished to extend their discussion from two to three hours, but suspected that 'Gromyko's aim had been to test him out, to probe potential soft spots in the US attitude and in the Western alliance'.[50]

Both Muskie and Gromyko admitted that their meeting was necessary, the former expressing the hope that this would be the start of the dialogue to bridge US–Soviet policy differences. Muskie was no hawk, but rather a supporter of détente; he told his counterpart that he wished 'to keep channels of discussion open to the Soviet Union and to convey US concern over Afghanistan'.[51] Early in their discussion Gromyko, in his characteristically aggressive debating style, asked why Washington 'had decided to disrupt détente'.[52] Muskie replied defensively that it was the invasion that had 'brought about a sea change in the US perceptions of how the Soviets regarded détente' – the crisis was inhibiting the improvement of US–Russian relations. Furthermore, the US Senate would refuse to ratify SALT II unless the Soviets changed their policy over Afghanistan. (Muskie did not employ the term 'quid pro quo', but this was effectively what he was offering.) He went on to emphasise that 'US–Soviet relations were central to world peace', Washington respected Russia as a superpower, and there was a need for Moscow to show 'equality, reciprocity and restraint'.[53]

Naturally, Gromyko replied that there was no possibility of any preconditions being acceptable, claiming that the Senate had decided against ratifying the treaty before the crisis, and that NATO member-states had decided to increase their defence spending by 3 per cent, thus proving that they sought superiority over the Warsaw Pact nations. There was also the deployment, already announced, of Pershing II missiles (with nuclear warheads) in Europe. Gromyko stated: 'All these were indications that the US had abandoned the principle of equality and were seeking domination'. Muskie simply replied that it was the expansion – over the past 15 years – of Soviet defence spending that had led to the latest NATO rise in defence expenditure. Similarly, the decision over the Pershings was taken in the light of the Russian deployment in Europe of SS-20 (RSD-10 Pioneer intermediate-range ballistic missiles – designated SS-20 Saber by NATO – armed with nuclear warheads).

Washington remained willing to discuss theatre nuclear forces – weapons not included in the SALT II negotiations – with the Russians; however, as Muskie pointed out: 'The US is still committed to SALT but the calendar was going to be difficult because of Afghanistan.'[54] The discussion turned again to the invasion as such, with Gromyko attempting to justify the Kremlin's decision by referring to the 'continued armed incursions [into Afghanistan] from Pakistan involving Americans and Pakistanis', and claiming that the Soviets had been 'invited' by the Afghan government. This led Muskie to comment sarcastically: 'The man [Amin] who had issued the invitation had not survived the arrival of Soviet troops'.[55] (A similar comment had been made earlier by Carter.)

Gromyko doubted whether the United States would observe the terms of SALT II (though reassuring US government statements had already been issued) without a ratified treaty. Muskie expressed the view that it was 'desirable to keep the prospect of the treaty alive and therefore to exercise restraint. This did not depend upon the treaty.' However, 'Gromyko did not reply to this point but Muskie had the impression that he was unresponsive.'[56]

Gromyko expressed 'concern' at the failed US hostage rescue-mission in Iran, warning that Moscow would oppose US operations against that country, such as the mining of ports and seaways, or a blockade. Muskie then referred to Soviet 'hostile propaganda against Iran' and 'involvement in the internal affairs of Iran through the [communist] Tudeh party.' It was predictable that Gromyko would reject the allegation of Russian collaboration with Tudeh, claiming: 'As regards propaganda this was simply directed against [US] military action and did not compare with Voice of America which would win for the USA a gold medal if the USA were not so against Olympic medals.'[57]

The Soviet Foreign Minister then presented two proposals for the future of Afghanistan, expressing as an 'afterthought' that, given a settlement between Afghanistan, Pakistan and Iran, Russian troop withdrawals could go ahead once 'such a settlement was worked out and when the causes of the intervention had been eliminated.' But, as Muskie pointed out 'no indication had been given of who would judge when the causes had been eliminated';[58] he added that such a settlement would amount to the legitimisation of the invasion and occupation and of Russian support for Karmal's puppet government. However, the Secretary of State assumed that the Soviets were willing to continue discussions with him.

Gromyko did not refer to Afghanistan's neutrality as such, speaking simply of 'non-alignment'. Meanwhile, Muskie considered that 'Gromyko had ridiculed the notion that the Soviets had moved into Afghanistan to control the oil of the Persian Gulf'; 'the Soviets did not need Persian Gulf oil', boasted the Russian.[59] Their discussion was not expanded to include the Western European sanctions against Russia, the US grain embargo, or the Olympics (Muskie assuming merely that they had no time to cover these additional topics). Any prospects of a new meeting went unmentioned.[60]

According to Gromyko's account given to Erich Honecker, Muskie had explicitly asked for Russian help in liberating the hostages in Tehran. Gromyko stated that Moscow condemned the hostage-taking but did not wish to see a US intervention in Iran: 'The US has gathered a large fleet in the Persian Gulf that is not only aimed at Iran and the Arab countries. But we also have a large Soviet fleet.'[61] (Perhaps Gromyko believed that Muskie might blink after this remark; if so, he was mistaken.) In the end, both agreed to keep in contact, though Muskie rebuffed Gromyko's invitation for US athletes to attend the Moscow Olympics. The secretary of state might have assumed that a little self-deprecation could help him to improve relations with the stiff Soviet minister, who quoted Muskie as having stated that he was 'interested in further meetings with such an experienced diplomat as Gromyko. Gromyko had been in diplomacy for 20 years and he only

20 days.' (Perhaps, however, Gromyko was merely seeking to show how highly the Americans regarded him – we cannot be sure that Muskie made this remark.) Finally, Gromyko stated: 'We agree to continue contacts and talks between us.'[62]

The conclusion drawn by R. T. Jackling, head of DS11 (defence relations with non-NATO states) at the FCO, was that there was 'a Soviet effort for a more relaxed dialogue, combined with inflexibility and self-exculpation on the basic issue [of Afghanistan's occupation]'.[63]

Alan Brooke-Turner, the British ambassador in Moscow, considered that the Soviets sought at least a 'polite hearing' in attempting to renew their contacts with the Europeans and Washington. They moved forward in their relations with France: Gromyko paid a visit to Paris; there was a Soviet–French summit in Warsaw in May 1980. Brooke-Turner suspected that Moscow's aim was to reassure its East European allies that they would not be isolated by the West, suffering the politico-diplomatic effects of the Soviet invasion and the possible collapse of the détente. In a bid to improve relations with Europe, Washington and the non-aligned nations, Brezhnev attended Tito's funeral, and the invitation to German Chancellor Schmidt for a visit to Moscow was renewed (it had been postponed the previous January). The Kremlin sought to avoid being portrayed as an outcast, and also invited the Norwegian foreign minister to visit Moscow. The anti-American propaganda remained 'harsh but ha[d] lost some of its ferocity,' remarked Brooke-Turner; the coverage by *Tass* news agency of the Muskie–Gromyko meeting confirmed this. In the ambassador's view, Moscow's objectives in Afghanistan were unchanged, but the Soviets 'were likely embarrassed by the degree of support which has gathered around the idea of boycotting the Olympics'. He did not foresee any further Soviet advance in the region; the Russians had decided 'to sit tight for the time being, while maintaining a façade of benevolent activity'.[64]

In the Moscow corridors of power, both optimistic and pessimistic views of the war were heard, sotto voce. Brezhnev, who had authorised the invasion, sounded a positive note by examining the options of withdrawal and a political agreement – but he did not advance any conclusions, and his mental and physical condition was such that he could be talked round by more forceful Central Committee members, such as Ustinov, Andropov and Gromyko. A glimpse of Brezhnev's evolving views on Afghanistan was provided by an allegation in Valéry Giscard d'Estaing's memoirs (published in 1991, during the post–Cold War spate of such publications). He claimed that, during the meeting with the Soviet chairman in May 1980, the latter had said: 'The world is not in universal agreement [with our actions]. I will make it my personal business to impose [a political] solution. You can count on me!'[65]

In their turn, Thatcher and Carrington met with Harold Brown, the US secretary of defense, who paid a visit to London in June 1980. The British were seeking to accommodate Washington's increasing defence requirements, in the light of possible future operations in Southwest Asia, and a confident prime minister appeared ready enough to work with the Americans.

Brown admitted that while Afghanistan was not crucial per se to his country's interests, if NATO showed insufficient determination the Soviet Union might proceed to further adventurism in future. Since 1970, the Kremlin had been implementing a vigorous programme of arms acquisition, and now regarded Soviet capabilities as equal, or 'even superior' to the US arsenal. Nonetheless, Brown's analysis did not become 'apocalyptical', as US papers circulated in NATO headquarters boasted. He admitted that 'actual military invasions were perhaps unlikely. The greater danger was of the Soviets using their military power as an instrument for political intimidation.'[66]

Thatcher agreed, but replied that world opinion might come to tolerate the occupation of Afghanistan. She pointed out the qualitative improvement in the Soviets' weaponry. Brown claimed that this did not cause him undue worry – the West's military forces were technologically in the lead. The prime minister showed an interest in weapons of mass destruction, questioning Brown on the Soviet chemical and bacteriological weapons programmes. The defense secretary was non-committal:

It was not clear that the Soviets had used nerve gas in Afghanistan, although they might well have enabled the Vietnamese to do so [in their intervention] in Kampuchea. More generally, the Soviet lead in chemical weapons was alarming. The Americans' own capability [of chemical weapons] was obsolete ... [A]s regards bacteriological weapons, his own opinion was that the recent accident in the Soviet Union had probably originated with anthrax bacteria stored for military purposes.[67]

One result of the invasion of Afghanistan was that the Americans were prompted to increase their defence spending, which reached a total of $40 billion over the following five or six years, and funded the development of their rapid-deployment units. As a result, they needed the Europeans to spend more on Europe's defence, and the Japanese to do likewise in the Northeast Asia area. This strategy led Washington to seek an expansion of its facilities on the Indian Ocean island of Diego Garcia (a British possession), where the Americans urgently needed London's permission to continue their building of military installations. Thatcher was ready to agree without going into details, and the scheduled Anglo-American negotiations would proceed.[68] However, she expected domestic and parliamentary reaction to a positive decision on Diego Garcia; and third parties like India would no doubt protest. As she put it, 'The British government's domestic problems over Diego Garcia were perhaps comparable to the United States Government's domestic political problems over the supply of weapons for the Royal Ulster Constabulary.'[69]

However, it was left to Carrington to raise a delicate issue over the Diego Garcia question: 'The negotiations would need to cover not only the physical expansion of United States facilities, but also the arrangements for consultation on their use.'[70] The available minutes show no reply to this remark from either Thatcher or Brown. The foreign secretary, however, was taking a far-sighted view, suspecting that if Anglo-American disagreements over policy or strategy arose in future, the British might feel it behoved them to attempt indirectly to restrain their allies.

The meeting also covered the export of technology to the Soviet Union. Brown favoured the sale of oil-exploration equipment; the West should sell the Soviets the tools, but not the technology to manufacture them, so that as a result their production would depend on the West's 'goodwill'. It was self-evident that exports of computer technology, whether for military or civilian purposes, would have to be severely restricted. In addition, Brown expressed his concerns about improvements in Soviet steel production, which facilitated the building of more armour.[71] The positions taken by the secretary of defense showed once again the contradictory policies of the Carter administration: on the one hand, a grain embargo was to be imposed and exports of technology curtailed, while, on the other, there was manifest eagerness to sell the Russians oil-exploration equipment.

US pressure on the Soviet Union over restrictions on grain exports, however, would have no impact whatsoever, as it was expected that the following year's production in the USSR would increase (Brown had also fallen victim to KGB disinformation – see Chapter 3). Finally, with respect to the Moscow Olympics, Brown stated that the boycott had achieved 'some success'. His government 'understood that the British government had done everything in their power to discourage British participation'.[72]

Meanwhile at the Kremlin, Brezhnev, Andropov, Ustinov, Gromyko and Suslov were consulting on how to proceed with their strategy over Afghanistan. In a rare show of solidarity with Babrak Karmal (and anxious to see for himself the evolving situation) the KGB chairman paid a visit to Kabul in late January 1980. He submitted his observations, but with the usual sycophantic refusal to allow any thought to intrude about questioning the wisdom of Brezhnev's decision to invade. Andropov assumed that Babrak Karmal had understood his 'fundamental tasks' and was working on achieving internal security. For the time being, a month after the coup, the situation looked to have been 'stabilised', but still remained 'complex'.[73] Andropov urged Karmal and his lieutenants to work together, to normalise economic life and to boost the military and the security organisations taking advantage of all the Soviet aid. Ustinov commended the KGB chairman's contribution, but emphasised the question of Soviet troop numbers, which Andropov had not touched upon; no withdrawal of any troops could be scheduled for at least a year and a half. Brezhnev agreed, proposing that they might even increase the deployment; Gromyko concurred.[74]

It took a month or so for the Kremlin to draft its diplomatic strategy (part of which was presented to Muskie, as we have seen). Ustinov, Gromyko, Andropov, Ponomarev and Rakhmanin all agreed that a political settlement over Afghanistan (once internal security was achieved) 'could consist of a complex of bilateral agreements' between the DRA and its neighbouring countries, 'and systems of corresponding guarantees from the USSR, USA and certain other states' (hinting at China, Saudi Arabia and Egypt). The first phase of this strategy would involve direct contact between the Afghan government and those of the neighbouring countries, in a bid to reach an outline accommodation and to convince them not to back the rebels or to interfere in Afghanistan. This would be a quid pro quo for attempting to reach a political settlement. Cuba, as the current chairman of the non-aligned bloc, would be useful in helping to set up such contacts. Pakistan and Iran, in particular, had to be persuaded not to back the rebels, and also to accept verification procedures, while the issue of the Durand line (involving Afghan–Iranian border claims) would be set aside for the sake of achieving an agreement. Afterwards, the Soviet Union, the United States and other third countries would guarantee the bilateral agreements, and the Americans would **agree** not to help the Islamists in any way.[75]

Contacts with the president of Pakistan proved futile. In early April 1980, a Politburo report (signed by Ustinov, Andropov, Gromyko and Zagladin) claimed that the fact of Zia ul-Haq having agreed to talk to Cuba's foreign minister (under its good offices initiative) constituted 'a sign of unwillingness to follow the USA on the Afghan question blindly'.[76] Russian optimism, however, was very soon to evaporate. In July 1980, Zia proposed holding talks with the DRA and Iran, acompanied by Russia in a mediating role. Moscow first consulted Karmal, who wanted to explore this option. Zia's roadmap entailed a foreign ministers' meeting in Moscow in August, and later a heads-of-government summit, though he had yet to discuss the scheme with Iran. Soon, however, Zia backtracked and 'under the guise of additional "explanations" of [the Pakistanis'] proposal', killed any chance of constructive talks. He announced a precondition – that there should be discussions not with

Karmal (whom he wanted replaced) but, instead, with another Afghan leader – adding that his country maintained the Islamic Conference's declaration deploring the invasion and occupation.[77]

Soviet anger was directed against not only Pakistan but also the stance of the Chinese, who declared that the invasion of Afghanistan did not allow for Sino-Soviet political talks to continue as initially scheduled. Soviet ambassadors received detailed instructions from Moscow on its policy towards China and on the strategic assessments of the Politburo's Central Committee. In Russian eyes, the Americans – almost a year before the invasion of Afghanistan – by siding with the Chinese and promising them arms and commercial agreements, had opened the way for the Chinese invasion of Vietnam in 1979. The Central Committee's assessment was also that China was splitting the communist bloc by improving relations with Romania, Yugoslavia and North Korea, 'supporting their nationalistic tendencies in their policies in every possible way'. Pro-Soviet regimes like those in Laos, Vietnam, Cuba and Mongolia were confronting Chinese hostility, resulting from an apparent bid by Beijing to establish an alliance within the communist bloc. In this effort, 'China uses a double-dealing tactic including pressure and promises' with respect to Bulgaria, Hungary, Poland and Czechoslovakia, while 'continuing its gross interference in their internal affairs.' The Chinese leaders were employing 'demagogic and deceptive practices' in trying to persuade the other communist countries that they should not bother with Sino-Soviet quarrels, and that 'China meets their national interests'.[78]

Chinese officials, moreover, seemed to be coordinating their policy of dividing the communist bloc 'all the more closely with imperialist circles, above all with the USA, and their intelligence services'.[79] (In this early period of the Afghan war, the claim that the US and Chinese intelligence services were working together was highly improbable.) In early autumn 1980, Soviet ambassadors received a new set of instructions, similar in content: 'At the present time the partnership between American imperialism and Beijing's hegemonism, which is spreading in the military sphere, is a new negative phenomenon in world politics and dangerous for all of humanity.'[80]

According to military intelligence,

> Beijing has set about manufacturing and experimenting with intercontinental ballistic missiles, capable of carrying nuclear warheads, and is working on the creation of neutron weapons. All this drives the global arms race forward and directly contradicts the interests of détente. This policy of Beijing's seriously threatens everyone, even the USA and Japan and not just the Soviet Union and other socialist states.[81]

The modernisation of its military establishment would turn China into an unpredictable and adventurist power, and the Americans should soon realise that selling 'defensive, non-lethal equipment' to China and their military cooperation with Beijing 'will free up the forces within China and the means necessary for building up its principal strike force – its nuclear capability'.[82]

The Politburo's directive suffered from distortions and hyperbole, as well as from lies which the average diplomat would have little difficulty uncovering. It stated:

> Beijing does not hide the fact that it aims to cause a nuclear conflict between the Soviet Union and the USA, and from its ashes, assume world domination ... Above all China is trying to institute its control over Southeast Asia all the way to the coast of Malacca and the straits of Singapore.[83]

Moscow planned to inform India of the regional consequences of China's arms modernisation and of its siding with Washington, whose support for Pakistan was seen as threatening to Indian national security. The Indian government had to understand that

> Beijing is flooding India's neighbours with arms and, by creating an atmosphere of war psychosis is attempting to maintain in power unpopular regimes such as the current one in Pakistan. Beijing is speeding up its military preparations along

the Chinese–Indian border, constructing missile bases and strategic roads in Tibet, and activating its support for separatist movements in northeast India.[84]

Playing up the Chinese threat to India (citing questionable intelligence) was in effect the main Soviet tactic.

The CIA, for its part, was not so alarmed by the Chinese modernisation programme, noting progress, however, in the development of nuclear-powered submarines, strategic missiles, an experimental fighter, and in planning for the construction of an air-to-air missile. But the overall estimate argued:

> Even with steady improvement in forces and defence industries over the next 15 years ... China will not develop a significant offensive capability against the USSR, largely because of that country's vastly superior industrial base ... China is unlikely to develop forces based on technology rather than manpower or abandon its defensive doctrine of 'People's War under Modern Conditions'.[85]

The Chinese feared the Soviet deployment of superior forces on their frontiers, and 'senior Chinese officials have expressed concern that the PLA might fall so far behind the Soviet military that it could no longer function as an effective deterrent'.[86]

The CIA argued:

> China's appraisal of Soviet intentions and capabilities largely shapes the direction of the defence modernisation effort. The Chinese leadership evidently believes that the Soviet Union's most likely attack would involve heavy armored thrusts, supported by airpower, into Manchuria and possibly Inner Mongolia. The Chinese appear to believe that the Soviets could not effectively employ their naval power against China and that they would refrain from using strategic nuclear weapons because of China's limited but credible retaliatory capability.[87]

In any case, China's early-warning capability had been upgraded through its secret cooperation with Washington. Under Carter, the CIA had been drawing closer to Chinese military intelligence since 1978, in a joint bid to collect data on Soviet ballistic-missile tests. Thus the Americans had a good idea of China's technologies and of attitudes in its armed services. In April 1979, Deng Xiao-ping insisted that the intelligence stations for telemetry, signals and seismic research (in the event of Soviet ballistic missile launches and nuclear tests) should be operated only by Chinese personnel, but accepted that the intelligence product would be shared with the Americans. In January 1980, after the invasion of Afghanistan, the CIA and Beijing agreed that two stations should be built, at Qitai and Korla, in Xianjiang province. Operations commenced late in the same year, with the CIA's Office of Sigint Operations providing equipment and training for the Chinese, and CIA personnel visiting the sites to assist with advice, maintenance and training.[88]

The CIA's military analysis of Chinese intentions and capabilities relevant to the confrontation with Vietnam emphasised the fragile state of the Chinese economy, which directly affected decision-making and strategy. China was in a 'particularly delicate position':

> The Chinese have now concluded that the pace of economic and political reform has been too fast and have begun measures in the past few months to slow down the tempo of change [one and a half lines not declassified] much of the elite and the populace harbors serious misgivings about the changes, but the degree of internal discontent is not clear.[89]

The economy was crippled by inflation, the yuan had been devalued, contracts were cancelled and factories closed; little or no growth was expected in 1981. Government measures aimed mainly to avoid defaulting on international obligations, so as to secure international support for the Chinese economy over the medium term.[90]

It was assumed that at this point the Vietnamese enjoyed an advantage, because the crisis was having a serious impact on the Chinese military: defence-procurement contracts were to be delayed, possibly for a minimum of two years; the armed forces' rank and file was to be reduced. Among the military cadres as well as the peasants (who sought a better life through a military career), resentment was reported at the defence cuts. However,

> China's leaders, of course, could decide to go to war despite the economic crisis. Nonetheless, the costs of a new war [with Vietnam] could have catastrophic consequences for development plans which have now been delayed five or six years, but to which the Chinese remain strongly committed. In practical terms, China probably cannot afford to go to war.[91]

The Chinese and Vietnamese, since the end of their 1979 clash, were in a state of 'no war, no peace', with regular artillery duels in the border areas, and China threatening throughout 1980 that it would teach the Vietnamese a 'second lesson'. The CIA assessment was that the local engagements were 'tailored to the gravity of the provocation and [have] been limited. Neither China or Vietnam seems to want nor are they likely to deliberately initiate a major test of arms for some time.'[92]

By spring 1981, with the Afghanistan campaign in its initial stage, voices in Moscow arguing in favour of making approaches to China were heard more clearly, but it would take until the end of the year for a policy review to be completed. On 30 March 1981, the world (and the ever pessimistic Kremlin) froze, watching the assassination attempt on Ronald Reagan live on television. The president survived, but in the first hours following the event confusion reigned in the cabinet, with Secretary of Defense Caspar Weinberger raising the alert in the Pentagon – though not the Defence Condition level (DEFCON) – and the hawkish Alexander Haig declaring that he was 'in control' in Washington pending the arrival from Texas of Vice-President George Bush. (This controversial statement by the secretary of state, who was only fourth in the line of presidential succession, after the vice-president, the speaker of the house and the president pro tempore of the Senate, was met with fury in the US press, and interpreted nervously by allies and communist countries alike.) Weinberger seemed to fear that a Soviet submarine was close to the east coast, and caused a controversy by telling Haig that he would not raise the alert before the latter's meeting with the press. Haig reassured the journalists that there was no state of alert, only to be informed later by Weinberger that, during his absence, he had received intelligence that led him to the decision to raise the Pentagon alert.[93]

Reagan made a rapid recovery, while the KGB circulated a dossier of reports on him to the GDR's Stasi. Intelligence officers were informed that Reagan was 'a dyed-in-the-wool anti-communist who engaged in a campaign to drive progressive people out of the film industry and the unions'. Later reports described him as 'a firm and unbending politician for whom words and deeds are one and the same', who continually assaulted 'the lack of political freedom, prohibition of free speech, restrictions on religious worship and travel, and economic failures of the socialist countries'.[94]

May 1981, the fifth month of Reagan's presidency, marked the beginnings of panic in the KGB. Reagan's declarations on foreign and defence policy were interpreted in the most distorted way by the Kremlin. The KGB Centre issued urgent intelligence-collection tasks to residencies in Europe, Japan, the Americas and the Middle East for the supposed preparation of a US/NATO surprise nuclear strike against the USSR. This large-scale effort was codenamed 'operation Ryan' (an acronym formed from *raketno yadernoye napadenie*, or 'nuclear missile attack') and absorbed, as a first priority, all available KGB intelligence resources. Though experienced and sober KGB officers in the residencies saw little in Western intentions to concern them, they nonetheless had to carry out their newly assigned intelligence tasks.[95] The Soviet leadership was aware that in 1980 President Carter had signed Presidential Directive 59 addressing the contingency of a protracted nuclear war. Under this directive an explicit decapitation strategy would be implemented against the Soviet leadership and command centres. It was assumed that the weapon to be used by the Americans to destroy the Kremlin would be the Pershing II missiles to be deployed in Europe (though the Russians in fact overestimated their performance).[96]

What the Kremlin did not know, however, was that on 5 May 1982 Reagan had signed National Security Decision Directive 32, under the title 'US National Security Strategy'. This stated that containment was not the only strategy to be followed: the US would take the initiative in making more manifest the shortcomings of the Soviet economy while encouraging 'long term liberalizing and nationalist tendencies within the Soviet Union and allied countries'.[97] In effect it considerably broadened the scope for covert action, as well as for pressing ahead with the arms race – the Soviets would be unable to cope with greater investment in arms, and their economy would collapse.

In public, Reagan boosted the Kremlin's paranoia by presenting, on 23 March 1983, his 'Star Wars' programme – the Strategic Defence Initiative (SDI) – a fortnight after naming the USSR 'the evil empire'.[98] The Star Wars concept was to use both ground- and space-based weapons systems to defend the US from attack by Soviet strategic nuclear ballistic missiles, using laser beams to destroy them in space – a technically infeasible scheme, and far-fetched enough to recall a science-fiction novel or a James Bond film. But it showed the clear intention of the Reagan administration to abandon the Mutual Assured Destruction (MAD) doctrine that, according to veteran Cold Warriors, had kept the fragile peace. The CIA predicted that the likely Soviet response to the Star Wars programme would be increased politico-diplomatic pressure, and, if that failed, a call for negotiations. A 'peace offensive' against the US and the NATO member-states would be the Kremlin's first option; propaganda and disinformation would be directed against European governments, the peace movement, politicians, US public opinion (by spreading claims that the SDI would divert funds from social-security programmes) and the international scientific community. Soviet diplomacy would repeatedly call for the Anti-Ballistic Missile (ABM) treaty, which Washington had signed, to be respected, and blame the Americans for upsetting the balance of power and the SALT II terms of reference. In parallel, the matter would be taken to the UN disarmament committee and the General Assembly. The Soviet military, meanwhile, would turn to the development of counter-measures, together with increased efforts to purchase Western technology and to 'step up their intelligence collection efforts on US plans and intentions'. But according to the CIA, Moscow would be reluctant to invest directly and immediately in new technologies, given the precarious state of its economy.[99] (Later, Soviet Ambassador Anatoly Dobrynin was to admit in his memoirs that the Kremlin, having confidence in America's innovative technology, took SDI as a serious threat.)[100] Ironically, the US was unable at that time to construct such a system; SDI remained a virtual rather than real strategic weapon.

Afghanistan was not the sole preoccupation of the Kremlin. The seriously ill Andropov, now the USSR chairman, forecast a nuclear apocalypse, and pressed the KGB and the GRU for more intelligence, having assumed that Reagan was preparing the American people for the inevitable: a nuclear war. On 28 September 1983, the paranoiac Andropov spoke of 'the outrageous military psychosis' of the Americans, concluding: 'The Reagan administration, in its imperial ambitions, goes so far that one begins to doubt whether Washington has any brakes at all preventing it from crossing the point at which any sober-minded person must stop.'[101]

Earlier, on 1 September 1983, a South Korean airliner had been shot down by Soviet air-defence, pointing to Moscow's fears of a coming US nuclear attack. Nonetheless, throughout 1983 US naval-air exercises, with pilots reaching the limits of Soviet airspace, gave the (false) impression to the KGB and the GRU that these drills were simulated bombing missions – the flight paths and pilots' attitudes showed US intentions, the Soviets claimed. Andropov blamed 'Western special services' for the shooting-down of the airliner, but the CIA and US Navy intelligence concluded that the incident was a Soviet mistake; Soviet air-defence had confused the airliner with an RC-135, which had been on a spying mission the same day. This conclusion was incorporated in the 2 September president's Daily Brief, but failed to catch the attention of the White House. Reagan, Shultz and the rest of the cabinet deplored the murder, and issued statements attacking the amorality of the 'evil empire' – while the Kremlin resorted to lying flatly in public, thus seeming to justify the world's criticism over the incident.[102]

The US invasion of Grenada, on 25 October 1983, further raised Moscow's fear, while the KGB had nothing concrete to report on US preparations for a nuclear strike. From 2 to 11 November 1983, the

NATO command-post exercise 'Able Archer' examined the implementation of the alliance's procedures for the use of nuclear weapons, holding war-simulation consultations with NATO prime ministers, including a unique format of coded communication and radio silences. A simulated DEFCON 1 nuclear alert was also implemented, to provide a more realistic ambience.

Able Archer was seen by the KGB Centre as a cover for an ensuing first strike. Nonetheless, given the paranoia of the Kremlin and the KGB Centre, KGB officers in Western Europe feared not a Western attack but a Soviet pre-emptive strike. Indeed, the Soviets had their nuclear forces and bomber squadrons in East Germany and Poland on high alert. Reagan himself learned in late October (while preoccupied with the terrorist attacks against US marine barracks in Lebanon and with the invasion of Grenada) that the Soviet leadership feared a US nuclear attack, and did not hide his shock at this intelligence. (He might well have learned this from Thatcher herself when they met a few weeks earlier.)[103] The secret source, handled by MI6, was Colonel Oleg Gordievsky of the KGB's London residency, who had passed the information to his handlers as early as February 1983. On 17 February, the KGB residency received a new list of intelligence-collection tasks, and this Gordievski had passed on to MI6.[104]

The KGB raised the alert on 8 and 9 November, on receiving reports of increased security measures at US military bases in West Germany (but this was the result of a US terrorist alert following the attack in Beirut).[105]

The president's justified anxiety at the prospect of a global conflict, with deaths in the millions, shaped his understanding of relations with the Soviet Union, and he sought from now on to increase the pressure on the Kremlin to engage meaningfully in arms negotiations, and to prevent an inadvertent nuclear war.[106] With Schultz, Reagan attempted to open a back-channel to Moscow, sending a message to Andropov while setting up a small team within the National Security Planning Group. On 18 November 1983, the president wrote in his diary:

I feel the Soviets are so defense minded, so paranoid about being attacked that without being in any way soft on them, we ought

to tell them no one here had any intention of doing anything like
that [initiating a nuclear strike].[107]

On 19 December he signed a letter of reassurance to Andropov: 'We
do not seek to challenge the security of the Soviet Union and its
people.'[108]

By the end of 1983, Yevgeny Velikhov, a senior Soviet scientist who
had handled defence projects since the 1960s, was arguing that SDI
would not work, and trying to assuage the Kremlin's fears. Later, in
March 1985, he once again told Gorbachev that he had nothing to fear
from SDI, and should not try to build a Soviet model. (In fact, almost
five years before Reagan's announcement of Star Wars, the Soviets had
experimented with laser beams, and concluded that such a project was
technologically infeasible.)[109]

By 1984 Operation Ryan was being gradually scaled back: no
genuine evidence of a US intention to launch a surprise nuclear attack
was ever found by the KGB or GRU; also, the Kremlin had received
further signals from London and Washington that it should have no
fear of a nuclear war.[110]

On 9 February 1984, Andropov died. He was replaced by Chernenko.
who had sidelined Andropov's protégé, Mikhail Gorbachev, with the
help of Gromyko and Ustinov. The nuclear-alert mentality continued, as Reagan once again showed himself reckless in his statements.
Moscow insisted his intentions were hostile. On 11 August 1984, the
president made a statement in jest, while testing the microphone in
a radio studio: 'My fellow Americans, I am pleased to tell you today
that I've signed legislation that will outlaw Russia forever. We begin
bombing in five minutes.' It soon leaked, and found its way into
media headlines. The Tass news agency deplored the remark as 'un-
precedentedly hostile toward the USSR and dangerous to the cause of
peace'. As for the ever-suspicious KGB Centre working for Operation
Ryan, they must have been terrified; their beliefs about Reagan
seemed to be confirmed. Two days later Secretary of State Shultz, feeling the immediate need to mend fences, convinced Reagan to have
a meeting with Gromyko while the Soviet foreign minister was in

New York for the opening of the UN General Assembly. It would be a hastily arranged meeting, however, with little likelihood of tangible results. On 28 September, Gromyko met Reagan at the White House, each using the occasion to lecture the other – the Soviet minister asking Nancy Reagan at one point if her husband was interested in peace 'at all'.[111]

Meanwhile, the Soviet military continued to upgrade its readiness. On 13 November, a major test of the 'Perimeter' missile-command system was successfully carried out; Perimeter incorporated the 'Dead Hand' procedure, under which, in the event of the Soviet leadership being decapitated and its command-centres destroyed by a US nuclear strike, a retaliatory missile attack would be launched, authorised only by duty officers.[112] The system entered full operational status in 1985, some time after Ustinov's death on 20 December 1984.

The CIA knew nothing of 'Perimeter' or 'Dead Hand', and made no assessment of Soviet anxieties about a potential US nuclear attack. A CIA report issued on 19 May 1984 insisted (inaccurately): 'We believe strongly that Soviet actions are not inspired by, and Soviet leaders do not perceive, a genuine danger of imminent conflict or confrontation with the United States.' The author was aware of the Ryan intelligence provided by Gordievsky, but the report's major flaw remained the paucity of adequate information; the CIA was not even aware of the full extent of the US Navy's provocative tactics in its spring 1983 exercises in the Pacific (involving F-14s flying directly into Soviet airspace). The Navy had failed to disclose its activities in implementing the 'forward strategy' of sailing very close to Soviet territorial waters and airspace, 'keeping the Soviets concerned with threats all around their periphery'. Commanders and pilots turned to 'aggressive defence', a concept promoted by Navy Secretary John Lehman and authorised (as a psychological operation only) by Reagan himself.[113] The CIA report on the Soviet war scare distorted the causes of events, and thus inhibited an understanding of how the Kremlin was interpreting those events, military deployments, incidents and US intentions.[114]

In addition, the August 1984 Special National Intelligence Estimate of Soviet strategy showed that there was a clear Soviet intent to upgrade capabilities and operational readiness. However, the CIA wrongly assumed that Moscow had no fears of an imminent conflict:

> Recent Soviet military and political actions have created concern that the Soviets may be preparing for a major military confrontation with the United States. During the past six months or so the Soviets have pursued a vigorous programme of large scale military exercises, have engaged in anomalous behavior with respect to troop rotation and withdrawn military support for harvest activities, have demonstratively deployed weapons systems in response to NATO's INF [Intermediate-Range Nuclear Forces] deployments ... we strongly believe that Soviet actions are not inspired by, and Soviet leaders do not perceive, a genuine danger of imminent conflict or confrontation with the United States. Also we do not believe that Soviet war talk and other actions 'mask' Soviet preparations for an imminent move toward confrontation on the part of the USSR.[115]

Turning to the estimation of Soviet intentions under Andropov, the CIA concluded in early 1983 that there was no supporting evidence pointing to an aggressive policy in South Asia and the Middle East.[116] The Soviets knew they were bogged down in Afghanistan, and would 'continue to convey the impression of flexibility' over a political settlement.[117] Since Andropov had come to power, the Soviets had played up their intention of seeking a settlement, in a concentrated effort 'to recapture the propaganda initiative', to persuade Zia ul-Haq to talk directly with the Kabul regime, and to extract Pakistan from its close relationship with Washington. In the event, the Soviet diplomats failed to charm their counterparts: 'Little has emerged to lend substance to the early reports of flexibility. When it became apparent that reports of possible Soviet concessions could undermine the position of Afghanistan's Babrak Karmal, the Soviets moved to dampen speculation.'[118]

According to the CIA's estimation, Moscow was 'reluctant' to introduce more forces into Afghanistan, given the political and military costs this would have entailed. There was clearly a stalemate there: 'The USSR is unable to destroy the resistance with the level of force it now has, and the insurgents are too weak and disorganized to defeat major Soviet units.'[119] It was assumed that Andropov wished the talks under UN auspices to continue 'to blunt international criticism', pressing for the Afghan regime to be recognised by the Pakistanis. In short, the Soviets had 'demonstrated no serious interest in making compromises to reach a political settlement'.[120] (The first round of Soviet–Pakistani talks commenced in Geneva on 16 June 1982; the Soviets consulted also with representatives of the Afghan regime, though the latter did not meet their Pakistani counterparts. The talks failed, but the Soviets admitted in private that their merely being held was a very positive outcome.)[121]

Ironically, Andropov was considering progressing towards a withdrawal of Soviet troops from Afghanistan (though he was insecure enough to fear that the USSR would lose face if it implemented the necessarily courageous policy review). The CIA analysis was superficial, concentrating on Soviet official positions and on the declarations and recriminations during Gromyko's meetings with Haig (and later with Shultz).[122] Secret intelligence and analysis did not reveal Andropov's evolving intention to end the occupation and achieve a political resolution. Indeed, Charles Cogan, the chief of the Near East and South Asia division at the CIA Directorate of Operations, later admitted the shortcomings of the reports:

> We never considered that the Soviets would back out of Afghanistan and negotiate their way out. It didn't seem a credible thing for them to do, because we didn't think they were at all predisposed to do that. So naturally when we talked with the Pakistanis we pressed them always to continue the pressure.[123]

The evidence for and indications of the Soviet intention to withdraw from Afghanistan remained sealed in the Kremlin's conference rooms, well away from CIA intelligence assets.

In February 1981, Ustinov himself had sent the Politburo a letter arguing that the occupation should not continue; no military solution being in sight, 'it was necessary to find a political and diplomatic way out'. But his letter was never examined by the Politburo. In autumn 1981, the Ministry of Foreign Affairs had drafted a memorandum,

supported by Andropov and Ustinov, arguing in favour of talks with
Pakistan (at Moscow's invitation) over Afghanistan, in order to arrive
at a settlement that would halt all intervention and allow for the withdrawal of Soviet troops.[124]

On 27 November 1982, senior officers held a meeting, with
Gromyko presiding; he asked them to draft a contingency plan for
the withdrawal of troops.[125] Allegedly, Brezhnev himself had told
Diego Cordovez, the UN mediator, that the key issue was foreign
interference in Afghanistan, implying that he was willing to consider
ordering the Soviet troops home if support for the rebels ceased. (In his
post–Cold War memoir, published in 1997, the former UN Secretary
General Pérez de Cuellar claimed that at Brezhnev's funeral Andropov
had implied that he was interested in finding a political settlement).
Javier Pérez de Cuellar met Andropov again in March 1983, when the
Soviet chairman emphasised the need to seek an agreement on non-
interference in Afghanistan, since this would facilitate the withdrawal
of the occupying forces. According to Georgi Kornienko (Gromyko's
deputy, who attended the meeting, and published his memoirs in
2001), Andropov mentioned the negative impact of the Soviet presence in the country and the resources it was costing.[126]

At the 10 March 1983 Politburo meeting on the possibility of a US
nuclear attack, Andropov admitted that the Soviets were compelled to
follow their existing Afghan policy, not because of Pakistan's intransi-
gence (i.e. its refusal to recognise Babrak Karmal, and Zia's support
for the rebels), but mainly because of their unshakeable belief that
'It [was] American imperialism which well [understood] that in this
part of international politics it [had] lost its positions. That is why we
cannot back off.' But earlier in the same meeting, Gromyko had made
a brave attempt to build an argument on difficulties in the military
field and the slow and difficult negotiations with the Pakistanis
in Geneva: 'This is why we must do everything to find a mutually
acceptable political settlement.' For the time being no set time-frame
for Soviet withdrawal could be presented to Pakistan, but efforts
should continue.[127]

Meanwhile, the CIA (unaware of Moscow's debates or its evolving
intentions on Afghanistan and its fear of a nuclear strike) reported that

Moscow was backing Iraq ('There is good evidence that the two countries signed an arms deal worth an estimated $2 billion in April [1982] – and possibly another arms agreement in December [1982]'), being convinced that, as long as Khomeini ruled in Iran, Soviet influence there would remain at a minimum.[128] The CIA reassuringly claimed that Iran ran no risk of becoming a target for Soviet adventurism:

> It is highly unlikely that the Soviets will intervene militarily in Iran in the next year. Despite their development since 1980 of new strategic concepts for military campaigns in the Persian Gulf region, there are no indications that the Soviets are making any preparations on the ground for such a move.[129]

The increase in Russian troops on the borders of Iran was deemed 'modest', and their operational readiness and activity 'routine'.[130] Nonetheless, the KGB resident in Tehran from 1979 to 1983, Leonid Shebarshin, had received explicit orders to take active measures to 'increase anti-American feeling and soften anti-Soviet feeling'.[131] Throughout the 1980s the KGB had turned its attention to fomenting unrest in Iran. Indeed, an Iranian government representative who met in secret with Colonel Oliver North of the NSC admitted in September 1986 that Tehran was very concerned about Soviet secret operations in the region, and 'in recent months have had their eyes opened by how much effort the Soviets are putting into penetrating and manipulating the Iranian government'.[132]

5

ESPIONAGE AND CLANDESTINE ARMING

The main feature of the Anglo-American covert action in Afghanistan was the delivery of arms to the Mujahedeen. President Carter authorised this type of involvement almost immediately after receiving intelligence of the invasion.[1] Gust Avrakotos, the Greek-American CIA officer who from 1982 onwards was in charge of the clandestine aid operation, commented that the findings signed by the president were

> far and away the most comprehensive lethal findings ever commissioned, the equivalent of a presidential declaration of war ... Carter had no idea he was signing such a blank check. And this would appear to be a reasonable conclusion, given the fact that ultimately the findings authorized operations that helped kill as many as 25,000 Soviet soldiers.[2]

(Avrakotos's figure was inaccurate – the Soviets lost a total of 13,833 men up to 1988.)[3] But the initial CIA aid was kept modest in both quantity and quality; it took until the mid-1980s to upgrade the Mujahedeen's weaponry. In 1981 Robert Gates, then deputy director for intelligence, voiced his scepticism over covert action:

> More often than not, our covert operations are seen as a way to accomplish a policy objective (if there is one) on the cheap, to

cope with a problem where no one has any idea how to obtain
public support for the solution to the problem, or to use covert
action as a short-term tactic to fend off a problem or disaster – a
tactic to be repeated or expanded upon in the absence of the
ingenuity, will or money to come up with a viable long-term
overt option.[4]

In 1980, Prime Minister Thatcher took the covert-operations path.
Indeed, in a letter to Carter she explicitly stated: '[W]e are looking
at a variety of possibilities for covert action'.[5] Thatcher gave MI6 the
green light to come to the aid of the Islamists; but to what extent
she, her cabinet secretaries, the FCO and the MoD judged the secret
arming of the insurgents as successful (or otherwise) cannot be thoroughly assessed given the paucity of documentary evidence. Early on,
MI6 officers established contact with Ahmed Shah Masoud, a Tajik
warlord who was considered a methodical and charismatic leader,
operating in the Panjir valley until his assassination by al-Qaida in
September 2001. In 1982, he was given tactical transmitters; small
MI6 missions also provided limited training for junior commanders.
According to unconfirmed accounts, the SAS trained the Mujahedeen
in mountain warfare in Scotland. Some SAS soldiers accompanied the
rebels in Afghanistan, but after a Russian ambush, a number of British
identity cards were discovered by the Soviets, and this led to a diplomatic incident. Afterwards, the troopers dealing with the Mujahedeen
purportedly left the SAS and acted as mercenaries in a somewhat
implausible attempt at deniability that would hardly have convinced
the KGB.[6] A GRU report in late September 1981 noted the presence of ten British guerrilla-warfare experts in Pakistan to assess the
potential of the Mujahedeen, allegedly compiling a report containing recommendations for British support. In addition, Egypt delivered
stocks of AK-47 Kalashnikov assault rifles to Peshawar in a C-130
transport aircraft, and the ISI held regular meetings with staff of the
US, UK and Egyptian embassies. According to intelligence, Pakistani
security personnel and Afghan nationals were given a six-week guerrilla-
warfare course in the FRG.[7]

Interestingly, the first to refer in public to the arming of the
Mujahedeen, even with anti-aircraft missiles, was Ronald Reagan,

then competing with Carter for the presidency. His first mention of Stinger missiles to be given to the rebels was in a campaign speech in Pensacola, Florida, on 9 January 1980. The *Washington Post* remarked that Reagan 'specifically urged the supplying of US shoulder-launched, heat-seeking missiles that can shoot down Soviet helicopter gunships'.[8] It was an over-eager move to help tribes about whose intentions US intelligence had no clear information, beyond fighting the Soviets. US-made weaponry that inhibited plausible deniability of American involvement was not an option: the CIA, the State Department and the Pentagon all objected. It was to take five years, and pressure from CIA Director William Casey and Congressman Charlie Wilson and others on Capitol Hill, for sufficient momentum to build up for the Islamists to be supplied with this weapon.

In its turn, the ISI remained suspicious of Anglo-American operations, and exerted strong pressure to become the sole channel for aid to the Mujahedeen – an outcome British and American operatives attempted (in vain) to avoid.[9] In Pakistan, the CIA station remained undermanned, with only 25 staff in total – an indication that it was effectively the Pakistanis who were running the Afghan military aid project.[10] Zia obliged the Americans early on to deliver the arms by air to Islamabad or by ship to Karachi; they were then transferred north by the Pakistanis, who distributed them to the Mujahedeen. He did not hold the CIA's paramilitary operations in high regard, remembering the agency's performance during the Vietnam war and the Bay of Pigs fiasco.[11] Zia was cunning enough to take all the credit for the operation, and thus garner the admiration of the Afghan tribes, who had no direct dealings with the Americans – the arms were presented as gifts from Pakistan, thus helping to ensure that the Islamic world would not see the Americans as allies.

In response, the Soviets put strong pressure on the Pakistanis to refrain from helping the Mujahedeen. As soon as 28 January 1980, the Politburo accepted the joint recommendation of Andropov, Gromyko, Ustinov and Ponomarev, who insisted that Moscow should 'constantly exert a restraining influence on the regime of Zia ul-Haq, including via special channels, and ... push him to accept measures to limit the actions of the rebels from Pakistani territory'. In parallel, the Soviets would 'establish contacts and the conducting of negotiations with the leaders and elders of the most warlike tribes [and show] flexibility and a differential approach to various tribes and socio-economic strata'. Moderate clerics would be the priority targets for hearts-and-minds operations.[12]

On 15 November 1982, Zia attended the funeral of Brezhnev and was explicitly warned by Andropov not to help the Afghan guerrillas, otherwise Russia would turn 'against his government' (this suggested active KGB measures against Zia's administration, rather than a threat of invasion). Zia flatly denied that guerrillas were based in his country, or that they had been given aid.[13] In the meantime, Russian artillery and aircraft were pounding the Pakistani border areas where the Mujahedeen were hiding.[14] The Pakistani army had been using Stinger missiles to shoot down the intruders, but Brigadier Mohhamed Yousaf, the ISI Afghan bureau chief in Afghanistan, later admitted that no hits had ever been achieved; some 28 missiles were fired during the course of the war and all had missed.[15]

The KGB was cleared to begin a disinformation campaign in a bid to convince Zia that the Americans wanted to topple him. In February and March 1980, the campaign was launched, with the distribution of leaflets, in Islamabad and Karachi. A key objective was also to convince the ever-suspicious Zia that some of his generals were seeking to oust him. The ISI took this 'information' seriously, and started to investigate. The deputy chief of staff of the army was charged (falsely), and the affair ended up with a reshuffle of the top ranks of the military, with many forced to retire. Two American diplomats (intelligence officers in the US embassy) who remained in contact with some of the generals were declared *personae non gratae*, and had to leave the country. The KGB operatives informed Andropov that Zia (now) believed that the CIA had conspired against him with the help of dissidents in the Pakistani army. The campaign of deception and disinformation touched another of Pakistan's national security concerns – the separatists of Baluchistan. The KGB sparked suspicions of the CIA's role in supporting the separatists.[16] During the first eight months of the war in Afghanistan, the KGB had arranged for 527 disinformation articles to be published in the Pakistani press. But Zia had by now received intelligence, from both the ISI and the CIA, exposing the KGB's unleashing of its campaign of deception.[17] In response, the defiant dictator decided on a mass expulsion of Russian diplomats in August and September 1980, prompting harsh words from the Russians and the restructuring of the KGB apparatus responsible for operations in Pakistan.[18]

At the end of 1980, the KHAD (Afghan Government Intelligence Agency) supplied Baluchistan and Sindh separatists with arms, under the KGB's direction. By April 1982, the KHAD had opened new camps for training the separatists, and together with the KGB had infiltrated agents via the mass waves of refugees reaching Pakistan. According to unconfirmed – and possibly inflated – KGB statistics, 26 KHAD agents had access to the Mujahedeen leaders' headquarters, and 15 were serving in the ISI, in Pakistan's armed forces or in its bureaucracy. Among the tasks of these agents was to heighten distrust among the Afghan resistance groups, so as to diminish their potential for joint action.[19]

New KGB operations against Zia ul-Haq began in April 1981. The key task was to convince Muslims that the dictator was a traitor to Islam. Once more, leaflets were distributed purporting to come from an armed group (which did not in fact exist), and to voice Khomeini's strong 'criticism' of Zia's policies.[20] Meanwhile, Murtaza Bhutto (the elder son of the former prime minister, whom Zia had executed) maintained contact with KHAD and coordinated attempts against the dictator's life. In early 1982, two attempts to bring down Zia's jet with an SA-7 missile failed at the last minute.[21] The KGB disinformation operations continued, with allegations that American scientists had established a biological-warfare facility in Lahore (under the guise of a local medical centre) and were using Pakistanis in their experiments. Outbreaks of bowel disease in the neighbouring areas of Lishin, Surkhab and Muslim Bag, as well as epidemics and animal deaths in Punjab, Haryana, Jammu, Kashmir and Rajasthan, seemed to provide confirmation; local communities grew restless. Zia was alerted, and in February 1982 ordered the deportation of the chief American scientist. Andropov seemed very happy at the outcome of this operation, commending the KGB resident in Pakistan.[22] The following

May, the KGB caused panic within the Indian government with disinformation to the effect that US armed forces had stockpiled chemical and biological weapons in Pakistan.[23]

Meanwhile, the CIA bureaucracy was hesitant in moving on Carter's finding that the Mujahedeen should be helped with arms. Stansfield Turner, the then CIA Director, confided, in January 1980,

> We could not get [the CIA bureaucracy] interested in this. I was mad. I wanted to show we could react. They [the Russian-made arms to be supplied to the Afghans] were still in Texas or someplace, and I couldn't get these people to move them off, so I set a deadline myself. [The CIA bureaucrats] didn't really appreciate that Turner and Carter would back this thing. They figured we'd get [the Mujahedeen] started and then leave them hanging down there. Personally, I had to beat people over the head to get the programme moving.[24]

In January 1980, the CIA eventually cleared the shipment of Russian-made light weaponry and ammunition (enough for 1,000 men) to Pakistan, for the ISI to distribute to the tribes. CIA analysts of course understood that assault rifles were no match for Russian armour and attack helicopters, but for the time being this remained the only offer. The CIA saw this arms programme as a unique opportunity for the US to be viewed as a friend of the Islamic world, as well as a signal to Russia not to advance into Pakistan or the Gulf.[25] The programme of aid to the Mujahedeen, code-named 'Operation Cyclone', continued until the demise of the Soviet Union in 1991.

Brzezinski, meanwhile, had yet to appreciate the full repercussions of the war in Afghanistan; in a 17 January 1980 meeting with Vance and Brown he sounded a cautious note: 'A massive insurgency at present is probably not in our best interest. Rather a low-level and enduring insurgency is essential to keep the Islamic states mobilized against the Soviets in Afghanistan.'[26] Brzezinski paid a visit to Anwar Sadat, who agreed to facilitate the secret arms transfer to Pakistan; secular Egypt thus joined in the operation to arm the Islamists.[27]

To what extent the CIA geared up throughout 1980–81 for the arming of the Mujahedeen would remain undocumented for years to come. An interesting glimpse of early attitudes in the CIA is provided by the comments of Joanne Herring (a wealthy anti-communist Texan, who enlisted Congressman Charlie Wilson in the campaign to aid Zia, with whom Herring maintained direct communication). She visited Pakistan in 1980, and complained that the US consul she met 'was a kind of apologist for the Soviets'; she believed at the time that the CIA was playing 'a fake game'.[28]

Nonetheless, in early 1980 a CIA operation was mounted to establish whether the Soviets had been employing chemical-warfare agents in Afghanistan. This involved the physical collection of environmental samples and of Soviet military equipment, as well as testimony and medical data provided by casualties. The first sample taken was a rocket tube and warhead fragments found in Konarha province. By 1982 a total of 14 objects (from victims' clothes to used gas masks) had been brought to the CIA laboratories for analysis. The chemicals used against the rebels mainly included irritants, incapacitating substances, nerve agents, phosgene oxime and perhaps trichothecene toxins, mustard, lewisite and unidentified toxic smoke.[29]

A number of secret sources reported incidents and storage locations involving chemical agents. One incident, never adequately explained, entailed three dead Mujahedeen fighters who were found in firing positions and still holding their rifles; it was an indication, concluded the CIA, that 'the attacker had used an extremely rapid-acting lethal chemical that is not detectable by normal senses and apparently causes no external physiological responses before death'.[30] Secret sources provided reliable intelligence to the effect that a variety of chemical-warfare agents were stored in Soviet army and air bases. A former ordnance officer in the Afghan army claimed that a large number of artillery shells and grenades filled with sarin, soman, phosgene and diphosgene were held in Kabul, in Bala Hissar (in an underground storage depot at the airport site known as Khafaramanag), in the Khair Khana district military depot near Kandahar, at the airbases of Shindand and Jalalabad, and near Herat. It was confirmed that chemical-warfare troops, with reconnaissance and decontamination units, were based at Kabul, Shindand and Chaghasaray airbases.[31]

One secret source reported that, in May 1979, chemical agents had been used against insurgents in Herat, and another told the CIA that, on 21 August 1980, Soviet aircraft had twice released chemical bombs on a village near Herat, killing a total of 300 people. A further source

confirmed the use of chemical munitions by the Soviets against the Mujahedeen. These reports [this one, and all those mentioned above] neither confirm nor refute the use of lethal chemical agents. One report [one line not declassified] indicated that Afghan and Soviet units used helicopters to disseminate 'poisonous gas causing many deaths'.[32]

Additional intelligence over the period 1979–82 showed that the Soviets had initially taken into Afghanistan what were possibly organic arsenical compounds, but soon withdrew them. Chemicals were used to compel Mujahedeen guerrillas to leave caves in which they were sheltered. It was mentioned that, in April 1980, Colonel-General V K. Pikalov, the officer in charge of Soviet chemical-warfare troops, and 20 expert officers visited a location attacked by chemicals. Notably, intelligence revealed that the Soviet units stationed in Mazar-e Sharif lacked an adequate supply of sodium hydroxide, a potent chemical-warfare decontaminant, and had asked for an immediate supply.[33]

The CIA emphasised that most reports of heavy casualties caused by chemical agents had come in the first three months of 1980 in north-eastern Afghanistan. 'In 1981 more evidence on chemical attacks became available and there are indications that chemical agents will continue to be used.'[34] One report claimed that, in the week 13–19 January 1980, chemical bombs had been dropped against rebels in Jalalabad and near Feyzabad, in the Hazarajet area of Bamian province and in Takhar province (eastern Afghanistan). The bombs exploded in mid-air, releasing a 'vapor' that 'felt damp on the skin. Inhalation of the vapor is said to have caused difficulty in breathing, nasal excretions, vomiting, blindness, paralysis and death. These symptoms are associated with nerve agent poisoning.'[35]

Other reports in the same mid-January week described Soviet fighters and helicopters attacking remote areas in north-eastern Afghanistan (among others, in Badakhshan province), releasing bombs which dispersed gas causing 'blindness, paralysis and death'. In February 1980, a US official who visited refugees of different ethnicities (possibly located in Pakistan) recorded descriptions of chemical attacks in several provinces.[36]

Further intelligence was secured from an Afghan army officer who had been trained in chemical warfare in the Soviet Union. He claimed that the incapacitating and blister agents in munitions were effective within a 50-metre radius, and caused 'unconsciousness for varying periods'.[37]

Meanwhile, disinformation was continuing to spread. On 25 March 1980, the Afghan regime accused the US of supplying the Mujahedeen with chemical agents, in the form of 'lethal US grenades' (which in reality were US-made police riot-grenades, available commercially). 'According to a reliable source, however, the Soviets used lethal agents near Herat in March and placed the blame for the incident on US-provided chemical weapons' used by the rebels.[38]

Foreign journalists also helped in filling in the intelligence picture. A Dutch war correspondent reported that he had been an eyewitness to two chemical attacks near Jalalabad on 15 and 21 June 1980, and had managed to film an Mi-24 gunship releasing canisters 'that produced a gray-white cloud. A victim with blackened skin was photographed in the village five hours after the attack.' The reporter was himself exposed to the agent, and suffered blisters on his hands and 'a swollen and itchy face'. It took him some ten days to recover from skin lesions, nausea, diarrhoea and stomach cramps. The CIA analysis commented that the Dutch journalist's story was 'one of the best first-hand accounts available from Afghanistan. The agent has not been identified, but it could be a mixture containing phosgene oxime or hydrogen sulphide along with other components.'[39] A US journalist provided similar intelligence from other attacks, claiming that canisters, containing 'a yellow-green gas' and an incapacitating substance were 18 inches long and eight inches in diameter. Indeed, 'we had heard reports about a lethal gas that causes unconsciousness and then death'.[40]

In August 1980, an air-raid with chemical weapons left 300 dead in Sya Wusan village (30 kilometres south-east of Herat). The Afghan military authorities simply told the population that victims could not be treated, and medical facilities were closed (possibly to protect local authorities and medical personnel). The CIA report remarked, 'it was in this time frame that the chemical battalion at Sindand set up an operational decontamination station'.[41]

In April 1981, chemical attacks were reported east and west of Kabul, in the Konar valley and north of Kandahar. An account was given by an Afghan helicopter pilot who had defected to Pakistan, and who claimed that there had been chemical attacks in the provinces of Badakhshan, Qonduz and Konarha, the canisters being simply thrown out of the helicopter by the crew. He also claimed, 'There was a specific gas that is absorbed by the body and leaves the skin soft so that one can pierce it with the finger.' He described an incident when a change in the wind moved the gas in the direction of Soviet and Afghan troops, causing casualties among them. In July 1981, a US doctor of Afghan origin visited refugees and treated victims of chemical attacks. In the Konar valley the rebels received advance warning from an Afghan officer of a coming Russian operation; he told them that the Soviets held four types of chemical agents, but would use only the incapacitating one. The advice offered was for the rebels to use wet rags over their faces. Indeed, during the operation Soviet helicopters dropped gas canisters in 25 different areas. The results caused fighters to lose consciousness; some later recovered, but others died, their unprotected skin turning dark green or blue-green.[42]

US embassy personnel visited a hospital in Karachi where a wounded Mujahedeen guerrilla was being treated. He described gas attacks with irritants (a hallucinogenic gas) and an apparent nerve gas. Canisters filled with the green-yellow gas were captured by the Mujahedeen based in Pakistan, and the CIA initiated talks to get hold of these items.[43]

While the KGB and GRU had no difficulty in discovering the arming of the rebels, Ustinov's reports to the Central Committee were not always accurate; on 2 October 1980 he alleged that 'American instructors [were] taking an active part in the training of rebels' in Pakistan:

> The instructors have come mainly from the Washington-based International Police Academy and the Texas-based school of

subversion. In March and April of this year alone the USA sent 100 instructors through Karachi into the regions of Pakistan bordering on the DRA. Some of these instructors directly organized the operation of rebel units on the territory of Afghanistan. The USA is providing shipments of weapons to the Afghan rebels mainly through third countries (Egypt and Saudi Arabia).[44]

He also claimed that Egyptians and Chinese, together with Pakistani instructors, were training the rebels. The aim of the Carter administration, meanwhile, was to unite the rebels; that this was the American policy was disclosed by B. King, the head of mission in Islamabad, in a communication to the secretary of the Ministry of Defence, Lieutenant-General Khan. US consulates in Peshawar and Karachi were working to that end, and 'an Afghan section that has been created in the USA consulate in Karachi is supervising rebel operations and providing them with weapons and equipment'. Most importantly:

> The American CIA has devised special recommendations for the use of religious movements and groups in the struggle against the spread of Communist influence ... agents from the American special services in Pakistan are carrying out vigorous work among the Pushtun (Pashtun) and Beluga tribes, provoking them to carry out anti-government acts in Afghanistan.[45]

All these activities, coupled with propaganda abroad by CIA-backed Afghan émigré groups, inhibited any progress towards internal security in the country.[46] It is obvious that Ustinov played up CIA involvement at a time when American support for the rebels was slow in starting, but it was untrue that American instructors were involved directly in the training of Islamists. Under Zia, it was Pakistan which maintained contact with and trained the guerrillas, pressing them to unite under seven main groups.

Meanwhile, credible intelligence of Russian casualties was hard to find. In September, a Russian soldier defected to the US embassy in Kabul, and was interrogated with the help of a British diplomat (though it was somewhat embarrassing for the Americans to admit tacitly that they needed help merely to interrogate a defector). He claimed that the Soviets were winning, but had already suffered casualties reaching 15,000; this was discounted by British intelligence.[47] In the cabinet, the Lord Privy Seal spoke of approximately 2,000–3,000 dead and 5,000 wounded.[48]

Initially, the arms sent to the guerrillas via Pakistan were mainly vintage .303-calibre Lee-Enfields (which had been the Afghan family and tribal weapon for decades); the CIA shipped more than 100,000 of these rifles. Nonetheless, in the early period of the war it was discovered that the price for the obsolete ammunition had soared in the black market, and the CIA had to pay a higher price, reaching 18 cents per round (supply-and-demand economics doing no favours to covert operations). However, Avrakotos received information from former allies in Greek military intelligence that the Yugoslavs retained stocks of Lee-Enfields, together with their ammunition, which Belgrade obligingly agreed to sell for 7 cents per round.[49] The Turkish military were also approached, and offered rifles of 1940–42 vintage, with some 100 million rounds.[50]

In contrast to the aspirations of Avrakotos, Herring, Wilson and their close ally Zia, US aid to the Afghans, under William Casey, the free-wheeling CIA director (who held cabinet rank in the Reagan administration) remained cautious during the early 1980s. Later, however, he keenly endorsed the waging of a clandestine war against the Soviets in Afghanistan. Casey (who was also Reagan's campaign manager) had served in the OSS during the Second World War, and retained his high-risk spirit in dealing with politics and finance. Gates remarked:

Actually for the first several years, it was something of an adventure to work for him, because he would pick up the phone and punch a button without much concern for who was at the other end of the line and start shouting instructions ... I don't think he would have recognized the CIA organization chart the first several years he was there, if a lot depended on it ...[51]

Gates reflected further: 'He [Casey] would demand something be done immediately which the agency no longer had the capability to do.'[52] (This showed that the director had no real grasp of the agency's capabilities.) Casey quarrelled intensively with the Directorate of Operations, showed contempt for Congress and attracted criticism from the press.[53]

Casey entertained romantic notions of freedom fighters, believing in the need for a crusade against the Soviet Union, 'the evil empire' (as Reagan had described it). He was fascinated by covert action and spy-craft, which – as an amateur – captured his imagination; perhaps this was the key reason he was on bad terms with the Directorate of Operations. In addition, he tended to mumble (perhaps due to old age), and this inhibited communication with the president. During a cabinet meeting early in his presidency, Reagan discreetly asked Vice-President George Bush: 'Did you understand a word he [Casey] said?' Later the president admitted to the conservative author and commentator William F. Buckley:

My problem with Bill was that I didn't understand him at meetings. Now you can ask a person to repeat himself once. You can ask him twice. But you can't ask him a third time ... so I'd just nod my head, but I didn't know what he was actually saying.[54]

Eventually, Casey left the CIA with its morale lowered, attracting adverse comments from both Congress and the press.[55] Besides, it was all too easy for the ruthless Zia to take advantage of over-eager American spy chiefs like Casey and his close entourage, and of politicians like Wilson (and earlier Carter and Brzezinski), and to fund the ISI and its policy over Afghanistan at the expense of the US taxpayer.

Meanwhile, it was revealed that China and Egypt had supplied the Mujahedeen with light arms, ammunition and light anti-tank weaponry. In June 1980, the US defense attaché in Kabul discovered that two ships from China and Egypt had unloaded their cargoes in Karachi, transferring to the Pakistanis an undisclosed number of light infantry and anti-tank weapons, as well as Russian-made SA-7 anti-aircraft missiles, for onward transit to the Mujahedeen. Secret intelligence also indicated that in north-east Afghanistan the Chinese had transferred weapons directly to the Islamist rebels, having been in communication with them.[56] China joined the clandestine arming operation in 1980 (probably without Washington's knowledge) to support the Islamists against Russia – and not in the mid-1980s, as has previously assumed by researchers. According to another account, Beijing dispatched Uyghur Muslims from Xijiang via the Wakhan Strip to join the Mujahedeen.[57] In fact, the Chinese Premier Zhao Zi-yang stated openly during his 3 June 1981 visit to Islamabad that his government would 'provide active support – political, moral and material – to all who fight the hegemonic policy of the USSR in Afghanistan'. In addition, the KGB reports spoke of secret operations – Chinese military instructors training Mujahedeen in Pakistan (in Peshawar, Chintral, Badzhaur, Miramshakh and Quetta). In Peshawar there was 'a group of Chinese working in counterintelligence, helping to reorganize the counterintelligence apparatus of the northwest province of Pakistan, smoking out agents from among the Afghan refugees'. On 12 May 1982, the Politburo was given a memorandum listing the arms the Chinese had given to the rebels. This emphasised that training bases were established in Xinjiang-Uyghur and in the town of Linzhou in Tibet. In the last of these locations, it was alleged, more than 3,000 fighters had already received training, while 'separate Chinese instructors act directly in Afghanistan'. As for the Chinese embassy in Kabul, it was deemed an epicentre of espionage, keeping in contact with the rebels and urging Afghan citizens to join the resistance. Embassy personnel (presumably intelligence officers) met with their American, British, West German and Italian counterparts on a weekly basis, 'to trade information of a political intelligence nature.'[58]

It seemed that armed Islamists would continue to haunt their erstwhile benefactors. In April 1990 Beijing would face uprisings in Xinjiang-Uyghur; throughout the 1990s the danger of Islamic terrorism was emphasised by the Chinese authorities, while the Uyghur minority suffered a crackdown on their aspirations for democracy. In January 2002, the Information Office of the PRC State Council condemned bin Laden's backing for his 'jihad in Xianjiang'.[59] The history of covert action is a saga of ironies: in the late 1960s the Politburo authorised the KGB in Kazakhstan to foment unrest in China by giving arms and propaganda material to minorities in Xuan province, including the Uyghur, urging them 'to unite against Chinese chauvinism' and to fight for self-determination. Soviet propaganda was also broadcast in Uighur. The Uyghur had suffered tremendously during the persecutions of the Cultural Revolution, but the KGB was somewhat premature in assuming that they could be employed against Beijing's rule.[60]

In 1981–82, Casey's CIA was far from eager to give more help to the Afghans in dealing with the Mil Mi-24 (Hind) attack-helicopters which dominated the skies of Afghanistan, launching ferocious rocket attacks. In April 1982, Zia met Casey and admitted, 'The Pathans [Pashutn] are great fighters but shit-scared when it comes to air power.'[61] Meanwhile, a high-ranking CIA officer briefing Congressman Wilson insisted that the Russian-made DshK heavy machine gun (on offer from the US via the covert channels) was the best available for the guerrillas' air defence.[62] Congress authorised no more than $15 million for aid to the Mujahedeen in 1983 (the amount being hidden within an air-force appropriation). Saudi Arabia handed over another $15 million, this being the general financing agreed with the Saudis. (At then-current prices, for $30 million the Pentagon could have bought two F-15s or six Blackhawk helicopters.)[63]

Meanwhile, the CIA eagerly invested in a scheme to stir up the Muslim populations of the Soviet Union. In 1982, in collaboration with the ISI, the agency commenced supplying Islamist pamphlets for the Pakistanis and the Mujahedeen to take to the USSR. Casey, an inveterate optimist, assumed that the Muslims of Central Asia 'could do a lot of damage to the Soviet Union'. Additionally, some 10,000 Uzbek-language Korans were dispatched, to be followed by books describing Russian atrocities against the Uzbeks. In the summer of 1984, the Mujahedeen smuggled large numbers of Korans to Uzbekistan. However, the CIA scheme could not be kept secret from the Kremlin. A 1981 resolution of the Central Committee had already authorised measures to counter the Islamist threat within the USSR, and as the war dragged on the CIA reported Soviet Muslims' resentment at the occupation of Afghanistan; there were reports of troubles and demonstrations, though not on a large scale. One such

report estimated that support for the war among Muslims in the
USSR had

> increased markedly, while opposition has only grown marginally
> ... support for the war presumably strongest among various
> local elites ... Although nationality and religious differences
> persist, many believe the Soviet system is carrying out modern-
> ization that is desirable, and they fear what might happen if
> religious fanatics replaced the present government [in
> Afghanistan]. There people clearly are repulsed by the violence
> of religious fundamentalists in Iran and among the Afghan
> insurgents.[64]

A secret source was mentioned (whose name has not been declassified –
probably a dissident) as 'implicitly endorsing this view'.[65]

However, in effect the CIA had to admit that the scheme had
failed. Muslim soldiers did not defect en masse to the Mujahedeen; in
fact many wished to serve in Afghanistan to take advantage of loot-
ing opportunities. A large majority of Soviet Muslims viewed the war
consistantly with the Kremlin's official position, and had no wish to
confront the Soviet social order. Besides, there was already a degree of
tolerance towards Islam in the Soviet republics – this meant that the
sending of Korans was not a factor that could have ignited armed protest and serious trouble. Finally, research into the declassified Politburo
minutes for the period 1980–86 has shown that the top leadership was
not preoccupied with an Islamist threat within the USSR.[66] Casey
too readily assumed that Soviet Muslims viewed the Afghans as their
brothers, and that they would be ready to jeopardise their own standing in the Soviet republics.

During his consultations with US officials, Zia insisted on the concept of 'making the pot boil for the Soviets but not so much that it
boils over onto Pakistan'. He exerted pressure for Pakistan's new F-16s
to be equipped with the same radar as Israel's (a policy Wilson ar-
dently supported).[67] In early 1983, the Mujahedeen's weaponry was further enhanced by the acquisition of more Soviet-made SA-7s, secured
through the CIA's collaboration with a Polish general.[68] However, this

did not represent a CIA policy of escalation, but merely a successful collateral operation that paid some dividends for the arms supply to Afghanistan.

Meanwhile, Zia was playing with fire by holding Russian prisoners captured by the Mujahedeen near Peshawar. In 1984 two of these men escaped; armed, they locked themselves in a house and demanded to be released into the custody of the Russian embassy. A Mujahedeen fighter fired a rocket into the building, but succeeded in also blowing up a nearby ammunition store, killing the two Soviets. The Russian press then got wind of the incident, praising the prisoners' heroic bid for freedom.[69]

The Saudi General Intelligence Directorate (GID) worked with the Pakistanis in financing madrassas and arming recruits in refugee camps, in parallel with CIA joint operations. Safe houses were set up in Peshawar with stocks of war materiel. The GID was against the Americans having direct contact with the guerrillas, hand-picking and then funding Afghan warlords without informing the Pakistanis.[70]

In their turn, the Soviets included Iran in their area of operations. In April 1982, 25 Mi-8 helicopters carrying Spetsnaz troops launched a devastating assault against a village on Iranian soil, mistakenly believing (due to an error in the coordinates provided by an over-flying Tupolev) that it was a Mujahedeen base. After the bombing, the Spetsnaz descended to collect intelligence, but two Iranian F-4s soon appeared over the horizon. The Soviet helicopters took off with the troops, but one was hit by an Iranian rocket and crashed. The rest returned home realising that the base was nearby (by that time the rebels had fled). Eventually, the F-4s withdrew, once MIGs appeared on the scene to support the Spetsnaz (though they had not in fact been given clearance to fire at the Iranian aircraft).[71]

In July 1982, while some CIA officers of the Operations Directorate showed themselves willing to back an expansion of covert operations, the Directorate of Intelligence analysts took a pessimistic view, citing the vastness of Russian resources. The Soviets could increase the cost of resistance to the extent that it would become 'too high for the insurgents to bear'. Casey concurred; nonetheless, he was gradually focusing his plans on escalating the secret war in Afghanistan.[72]

Back in Washington, the DIA confirmed Iranian backing for Shiite groups in Afghanistan in the shape of M-1 rifles and G-3 assault rifles, as well as the dispatch of Revolutionary Guard members on training assignments. The Pentagon valued this confirmation highly, seeing (rather prematurely) an expansion of Iranian influence among the Afghan resistance. The Mujahedeen also received land mines, antitank rockets, heavy machine guns, uniforms and boots. The main group supplied was the Hesbe Islami, led by the notorious Hekmatyar, operating in south and east Afghanistan against the Soviets and Afghan warlords. (Hekmatyar had commenced his war against Masoud as early as August 1981.)[73] Other recipients of aid were the Harakat'e Islami ('Islamic movement') and Shiite groups in the Hazarajat region of central Afghanistan, fighters who found themselves in conflict with Western-backed Sunni groups. Since mid-1983, Iran had remained in contact only with Shiite groups, and by the end of the year its military aid programme was being reduced, due to shortages encountered by the Iranian military as a consequence of the Iran–Iraq war.[74] During the early years of the war, however, Moscow had provided arms to Iran, despite Khomeini's polemics against the Soviet occupation of Afghanistan. According to the CIA, the Soviets provided spare parts and artillery pieces worth some $350 million, and East European states, with the Kremlin's concurrence, furnished ammunition and light weapons; 'to our knowledge, the last direct transfer of weapons from the USSR to Iran occurred in 1984', remarked a DIA report. The Soviets under Andropov and Chernenko ceased to support Iran because they feared that the balance of power with Iraq would be upset. Besides, the Gulf states were complaining about the Iranian threat. The CIA did not consider that Afghanistan had been a factor leading to the curtailment of Soviet arms supplies to Tehran.[75]

The same year, Avrakotos discussed Afghanistan with MI6 in London. He was impressed by the British tactic of maintaining direct contact with Masoud, thus avoiding the Pakistani channel. But the Afghan warlord was the not content with the support he received; he held secret negotiations with Soviets, and in 1981–83 ceased to confront them. In autumn 1982, after a devastating Russian raid into the Panjir Valley, Masoud bypassed the Jamiat-i-Islami group he belonged to, and asked for international humanitarian aid. The CIA reported: 'In the past Masoud has sometimes exaggerated his problems in an effort to obtain more help ... Masoud's direct appeal is a further indication that insurgent commanders are gaining prestige at the expense of the Peshawar exiles.'[76]

In January 1983, Masoud met Colonel Anatoly Tkachev of the GRU, presenting himself as 'not an adversary of the Soviet Union and the Soviet people', according to the colonel's later report. The warlord concluded deals with the Soviets guaranteeing that the villages under his protection in Panjir would not be attacked. In turn the population would offer food, and he would not obstruct the creation of an Afghan army base at the southern end of the valley. The deals enraged other, ISI-backed warlords. Masoud took advantage of the truce to organise an army of 5,000 fighters, with 200 heavy anti-aircraft machine-guns, 120mm howitzers and two ex-Soviet tanks, in preparation for a new confrontation with the Soviets and rival rebel groups.[77]

By spring 1984, the secret deals had eventually fallen apart and the Soviets launched a combined attack, codenamed Panjshir-7. After a pre-emptive strike, Masoud and his fighters retreated to the mountain areas, and Kabul radio boasted of the warlord's defeat. Meanwhile, the Soviets attempted to kill him – an Afghan spy opening fire at a range of 30 feet, but missing his target. Masoud discovered two other spies in his entourage, one of whom was his cousin, and a unit commander.[78]

On 18 May 1984, the GRU achieved a coup: rebel correspondence found in Panjir revealed a spy network in Kabul. This actionable intelligence led to the demise of the network, whose tentacles extended into the Communist Party, the police, the administration, the Ministry of Defence, the KHAD and regional administrative authorities.[79]

Efforts to clinch secret deals with warlords continued. In 1985 Valeri Mitochin, a KGB adviser to the KHAD (where the Parham faction dominated), worked to persuade a rebel commander and his 300 fighters not to oppose the regime, their reward being that they would keep their arms and be provided with housing and employment. But, this effort stalled because the local Afghan governor – who belonged to the Khalq faction and thus opposed Babrak Karmal – refused to provide housing, and because the local military commander wanted to confiscate some of the weaponry to be sent to Kabul. In addition, the KGB failed to win the support of the Soviet Communist Party adviser, who had no wish to mediate between the local governor and the KHAD. Similar difficulties faced advisers on many other occasions.[80]

Masoud was a Tajik, and Avrakotos was frustrated by the fact that the Pakistanis were funnelling aid to Pashtun groups – seven in all, artificially put together as an arbitrary Pakistani method of keeping the rebels under some sort of control by Zia.[81] Avrakotos discussed the problem with an SAS officer who since 1980 had been secretly infiltrating the Panjir Valley on reconnaissance missions; Avrakotos aspired to establish his own channel to Masoud.[82] The CIA officer remarked of MI6's attitude: 'They had a willingness to do jobs I could not touch. They basically took care of the "How to kill people Department".' MI6 lacked money, but Avrakotos showed himself a willing financier on behalf of the CIA, so long as he was never informed of what MI6 had done.[83] He met with Masoud's brother, and in 1984 Sibghatullah Mojaddedi, a fellow professor-turned-warlord, and was introduced to Casey by Congressman Wilson at the latter's office in the Old Executive building next to the White House. Wilson pressed the CIA hard to buy the Swiss-made Oerlikon light anti-aircraft gun, and to pass it on to the Afghans. Mojaddedi, together with another Afghan, described the ferocity of the raids by Russian Hind helicopters against Afghan villagers. Still Casey remained unmoved; he told Wilson that a mere anti-aircraft weapon like the 20mm Oerlikon was not the silver bullet for Afghanistan. But the congressman insisted.[84]

In early 1984, Casey changed his stance over Afghanistan, pressing the Pakistanis hard to arrange a visit with the Mujahedeen being funded by the CIA. Though Zia, fearing a Russian raid on the border camps, was against the CIA director's having direct contact with the Mujahedeen, he eventually concurred. In collaboration with the CIA station in Islamabad, the ISI rushed to set up a safe camp near Islamabad for Casey to greet his freedom fighters. Essentially, it was a bid to deceive the American visitor; tired after a long and circuitous drive, he reached the camp to greet the Afghans (hand-picked by the ISI) and their Pakistani instructors, and observed a drill exhibition.[85]

The CIA had no wish to see Western-made weaponry in Afghanistan, but Wilson again stepped up the pressure, disclosing a parallel offer by Egypt to sell the CIA more SA-7s for Afghanistan.[86] The CIA was still seeking to maintain plausible deniability, despite President Reagan having publicly admitted that Washington was helping the guerrillas. Wilson was defiant, and to the surprise of the CIA leadership (who had not asked for more money) managed to increase the 1984 appropriation for the secret war in Afghanistan to $40 million. But his condition was that the CIA must buy the Oerlikon.[87]

Howard Hart, the CIA station chief in Islamabad, was growing anxious. Wilson's initiatives threatened the peculiar unwritten rules of engagement between the CIA and the KGB, and Hart feared that if Moscow – which already knew that the Americans were supplying low-tech arms to the Mujahedeen – realised that they were now equipping the guerrillas with latest-technology weapons, the Soviets would escalate, further upsetting the balance of power in Central Asia. For all his experience, Hart was unable to deal with the eccentric Wilson, who seemed able to direct CIA operations deep within Afghanistan. While Casey appeared adventurist in Afghanistan, he was in fact focusing most of his attention on Latin America and the Contras. Hart (who was aware of the deep divisions among the Afghan tribes) saw Afghanistan as a point where the Russians could haemorrhage in a contest that might last for decades of indecisive battles and ambushes. He did not believe in the possibility of the superpower's defeat and withdrawal, which Wilson hoped for.[88] Eventually, the station chief failed to convince Wilson that the Russian-made 12.7mm DshKs were appropriate for the guerrillas.[89]

The Pentagon, meanwhile, was more than happy for the Afghans to seize any Russian military technology they could and pass it on to the Americans for close examination. The defection of Afghan pilots provided the CIA and the Pentagon with an intact Mil Mi-8 in the early 1980s, a Mil Mi-24 (Hind), after a defection in mid-1985, and an SU-22; these were great opportunities to study Soviet technology.[90]

In 1984 the Reagan administration – although it had decided on the Star Wars programme, invaded Grenada, described the USSR as 'the Evil Empire', and implicated itself in the Iran-Contra scandal – did not take a hawkish stance over Afghanistan, and abstained from supplying the Mujahedeen with sophisticated weaponry. Wilson had spotted this policy contradiction, and after lengthy debates convinced the Senate Intelligence Committee to back him against the hesitant CIA.[91]

Meanwhile, secret sources reported the views of the Soviet military: in August 1984,

> [a] [not declassified] officer told [half-line not declassified] that the Soviet military was increasingly concerned about the situation in Afghanistan, did not believe it could defeat the resistance with current troop strengths, and feared it could even lose ground.[92]

Another secret source 'has claimed that, while many officers see the war as an opportunity for personal advancement, a number of lieutenant-colonels and colonels see it as disastrous for the USSR on strategic, economic and moral grounds'. Additionally, a Soviet military document captured by a 'Mujahedeen commando' in early 1985 advised Moscow 'to either pull out or to drastically increase troop strength, because of military low morale, high casualties and the unreliability of the Afghan army'.[93] This intelligence showed that the Kremlin was about to reach a decision to increase troop levels. It was a logical response in political as well as military terms: an expansion of operations would boost the Soviet position in negotiations under UN auspices. The problem was not a paucity of secret intelligence but how to assess true Soviet intentions (which involved disengagement without loss of face, as we will explore in Chapter 7). And this was difficult for the CIA bureaucracy, as we have seen, because no one argued that Moscow seriously intended to negotiate the end of the occupation.

Meanwhile, Casey recommended that the CIA buy some Oerlikons, in a bid to ease pressure from Wilson; it was a manoeuvre Avrakotos knew about; it would take more than a year to have the weapons ready.[94] Nonetheless, in April 1984 Wilson and Avrakotos commenced their secret partnership for increasing aid to the Afghans,[95] while Casey still strongly believed that Nicaragua and not Afghanistan was the place to defeat the Soviets and their surrogates.[96]

Given Wilson's appetite for Western-made anti-aircraft weapons, as well as his ability to channel Congress appropriations to finance new arms procurement for the Islamists, it was only a matter of time before he and Avrakotos again involved the British. Avrakotos's associates discovered that the $44 million the Saudis had been contributing was not restricted by US legislation to foreign arms purchases, and they diverted this sum to buy British-made Blowpipe missiles; these weapons had appeared to perform well during the 1982 Falklands War.[97] However, the Blowpipe option was strongly opposed by the ISI's Afghan Bureau head, who dismissed reports of its performance, and later claimed in his memoirs that the purchase had only been cleared on political grounds: '[Zia] took the political view that acceptance of the Blowpipe would involve the UK directly as a supporter of the Jihad, and thus the Mujahedeen cause would gain internationally'.[98]

In parallel, Wilson and Avrakotos visited Egypt to inspect the 800 SA-7s readied for sale by the Egyptian government; the purchase was not concluded because of the bad condition of the missiles. Nonetheless, Avrakotos explored and implemented, with the help of the Egyptians, the construction of Katyusha rockets for the Afghans. By the end of 1985 he had ordered 7,000 on behalf of the CIA, and the Mujahedeen had launched some of them against Kabul airport, penetrating the outer defence perimeter.[99]

At about the same period, the CIA station chief in Beijing aired the idea of buying arms for the rebels directly from China. The Chinese were more than happy to sell the CIA AK-47s, DshKs and RPGs. Essentially, Beijing saved the CIA considerable funds, since the black-market prices fell dramatically after the massive secret entry of the Chinese. Indicative was the price for an AK-47: initially reaching $299, it went down to $133 (after the secret Egyptian arms sales); the Chinese sold it for less than $100. In late 1984, Chinese cargo ships sailed from Shanghai to Karachi; out of the $50 million Wilson had appropriated for Afghanistan in 1984, the Chinese received $38 million.[100] Peter Tomsen, the deputy chief of the US diplomatic mission in Beijing (1985–89), was involved in the secret agreements with the Chinese.

Later he would also hint at the corruption among the Chinese generals, remarking: 'Whole factories owned and run by the Chinese military switched over to producing Soviet-style AK-47s, PRGs and 122mm and 144mm rocket launchers to be shipped to Karachi. Chinese generals happily pocketed the fat CIA checks, approximately $100 million a year to spend on their weapons programs.'[101] It was an irony stemming from over-eager covert action: Washington was helping to finance a communist state, the second such to attain great-power status. Given the antagonism with the Soviet Union and its alliance with Pakistan, China would have provided the Mujahedeen with arms even without American involvement. In effect, Washington paid China to follow its own policy of support to the rebels.

Generally, the high cost of the arming of the Mujahedeen included transportation by truck and mule from Karachi and Islamabad to the Afghan border, and even beyond. Brigadier Yousaf wrote: 'The cost of moving a mortar from the Pakistan border to the Mazar-i-Sharif area was approximately USD 1,100, while just one bomb cost around USD 65. Little wonder that the monthly expenditure by the parties on transport and allied expenses was USD 1.5 million.'[102] In addition, he admitted that some weapons were diverted to the Pakistani Army border units, listing some 200 14.5mm heavy machine guns, plus unspecified numbers of RPG-7s and SA-7s.[103]

Despite the close US–Pakistani relationship, Zia had his own agenda – the development of a nuclear weapon. Vernon Walters, former CIA deputy director and UN ambassador in the Reagan administration, paid him a visit to ask if he had a continuing interest in nuclear weapons, whereupon Zia took refuge in a flat lie, telling him that his regime had no such ambitions. Secret intelligence, meanwhile, revealed the contrary. In 1985, it was discovered that a Pakistani agent had attempted in the US to buy krytron high-speed triggers, the switching devices for detonating nuclear weapons. A tsunami of media leaks ensued, but Islamabad could count on Wilson to argue Pakistan's case in Congress, reminding politicians of India's nuclear weapons programme. Wilson was also informed that the CIA was running a successful penetration operation that had produced incriminating intelligence on the Pakistani programme.[104]

Eventually, Wilson and his supporters in both Houses of Congress saved the day, leaving Pakistan to go nuclear and managing to drive the Afghanistan budget up to $250 million, with the Saudis providing a further $250 million. All this money was to be spent on weapons, the programme of psychological operations being modest in cost.[105]

Meanwhile, plans for establishing an Afghan route for mass Russian defections were debated, but discounted as unrealistic. The Islamists tortured and killed all their prisoners; Casey himself remarked that no Russian 'would like to defect to those animals.'[106]

CIA funding of its involvement in Afghanistan increased in 1985 to 50 per cent of the entire CIA operations budget, reaching almost 70 per cent the following year (it was a time when strong criticism of the Iran-Contra scheme had seen its funding drastically reduced). Nonetheless, in the Senate, ultra-right-wing criticism of the CIA's performance in Afghanistan executed pressure to increase expenditure even further.[107]

In the meantime, Zia was being closely watched by the Kremlin. On 11 March 1985, only three hours after the death of his predecessor Konstantin Chernenko, Michail Gorbatchev was elected chairman of the USSR. At Chernenko's funeral, which Zia attended, the new chairman explicitly threatened him, saying that he would 'destroy his country' if Pakistan continued to back the guerrillas (in fact Pakistani special forces had been operating with them, in addition to providing arms and other supplies; Zia once again denied giving the rebels any support).[108]

By April 1985, the CIA estimated that the war had resulted in the deaths of 8,000 Russian troops and the shooting down of more than 600 helicopters and fixed-wing aircraft, while the rebels' casualties had reached some 40,000 and the Afghan army's 67,000. The latter force suffered from desertion, and its dismal combat performance compelled the Soviets themselves to take on front-line operations. The CIA's conclusion was that the Soviets had so far 'shown little imagination in developing counter-insurgency tactics and they have relied mainly on stereotyped search and destroy operations that often give the insurgents advance warning of an assault'. On the other hand, the Islamists suffered from chronic and lethal divisions among their tribes and their leaders, as well as from a lack of training and of war materiel. Indeed, 'guerrilla bands show little expertise in small-unit operations',[109] (Some of the CIA's statistics cited above were quite wrong: by 1988, 118 Soviet jet fighters and 333 helicopters had been destroyed, mainly on the ground.)[110]

The war would soon escalate further, with the better-armed Afghans and the more aggressive Russian commanders, operating near the borders with Pakistan and Iran, attempting to block any infiltration. The dispatch of up to 10,000 fresh Russian troops, including special forces, was thought to be a possibility; meanwhile, 'war weariness does not appear to present a problem to either side', concluded the CIA.[111]

As far as the deployment of Russian fighter aircraft in Afghanistan was concerned, the CIA noted a gradual increase in 1984; in January 1984 a total of 72 were operating in Afghanistan, among them 12 of the latest SU-25s based at Bagram, and 15 SU-17s at Shindand; by the end of that month the total number had risen to 87. In March, 15 Mig-21s of the reconnaissance squadron stationed at Bagram were replaced by SU-25s, and in June 30 Mig-21s based at Bagram and Shindand were replaced by Mig-23s. By the end of the summer, the total number of Soviet fixed-wing aircraft had reached 102 (15 Mig-23s arriving in Kandahar from Russia), and in September another 12 SU-25s were deployed at Bagram.[112]

Nonetheless, this CIA report on tactics made no reference to deceptive Soviet methods, which had been employed as early as 1980. In fact the KGB, the GRU and their surrogate, the KHAD, had established pseudo-Mujahedeen groups, composed of Russian special forces. These groups engaged tribes, fomenting dissent and internal strife among the Afghan warlords. Under the codename 'Cascade', each KGB unit operated with no more than 145 men. In early 1981, a Cascade unit managed to come into contact with Khoja Shir-Aga Chungara, a Tajik warlord with a force of 250 men and control over some 48 villages. KGB agents succeeded in turning him against other tribes, and he subsequently took part in 21 major joint operations with Cascade units; he himself set 40 ambushes, killing a total of 31 Mujahedeen leaders, and his forces increased to a total of 900 men. In 1982, other Cascade units turned another four Islamist groups, and by 1983 there were 86 'false bands' operating in

Afghanistan.[113] In parallel, agents were spreading disinformation. For example, at the end of 1980 a letter forged by the KGB, purportedly written by a fighter under the fundamentalist warlord Hekmatyar, was placed in the headquarters of another leader, Muhammed Nabi Muhammadi, 'warning' him that Hekmatyar was planning to kill him. Meanwhile, bogus pamphlets denouncing Hekmatyar were spread among the refugee camps of Peshawar. Hekmatyar had built a reputation as a ferocious, unscrupulous leader who fought other tribes as well as the Soviets. Even Zia tried to reason with him, stating: 'It was Pakistan who made him an Afghan leader and it is Pakistan who can equally destroy him if he continues to misbehave.'[114] Nonetheless, the ISI Afghan bureau chief admitted that Hekmatyar received more aid because his anti-Soviet operations were deemed more efficient. Brigadier Yousaf stated in his memoirs: 'The fundamentalists came out on top with 67–73% [of military aid] much to the CIA's chagrin, but using strictly military criteria it would never be otherwise'.[115] This claim, however, is not supported by hard evidence; Peter Bergen, CNN's terrorism expert, argues persuasively that

> Hekmatyar's party had the dubious distinction of never winning a significant battle during the war, training a variety of militant Islamists from around the world, killing significant numbers of mujahedeen from other parties, and taking a virulently anti-Western line. In addition to hundreds of millions of dollars of American aid, Hekmatyar also received the lion's share of aid from the Saudis.[116]

According to Graham Fuller (the CIA station chief in Kabul until 1978, and later head of the CIA's long-range forecasting bureau), Hekmatyar worked for the ISI in the late 1960s, and received more aid since Zia considered him a Pakistani asset in the war against Russia. Suspicions that Hekmatyar was a Russian spy (given his fights with other Mujahedeen groups) were also aired by some CIA officials.[117] To the KGB and the GRU, Hekmatyar was a person 'inclined to extremist actions, imperiousness, great ambition and eccentricity'; he once declared himself a fanatical Pashtun first, and a Muslim second. As the owner of 'enterprises that produce narcotics' and the operator of laboratories turning opium into heroin in the Northwest Frontier province of Pakistan, he was heavily involved in the drug trade. Letters from Hekmatyar found by the KGB revealed that 'toxic chemical agents' had been given to him by 'international friends'.[118]

Meanwhile, sceptics in the CIA were assuming that Washington's alliance with Pakistan would not run as smoothly in the long term as in the current phase of arms transfers. Top CIA intelligence officers considered that Pakistanis like Yousaf (the head of the ISI Afghan bureau) were fundamentalists who feared that the CIA would foment trouble for Islamabad, and plan to undermine Islam.[119] Eventually, new talks on aid to the Afghans, in the form of light weaponry, led the CIA to pay Islamabad $8 million to start the production of cartridges for .303-calibre Lee-Enfield rifles[120] – a very profitable deal for the Pakistanis. Meanwhile, donkeys were badly needed for the transport of weapons and ammunition, and a number of secret deals with donkey owners in Egypt, China and Tennessee were concluded, the unfortunate animals ending up in a war zone with somewhat less attentive owners.[121]

It seems that Senate criticism of CIA policy on Afghanistan, Casey's evolving stance towards the Mujahedeen, the Avrakotos-Wilson partnership and the dramatic increase in the budget for Afghanistan together created such momentum that on 27 March 1985 Reagan signed National Security Decision Directive 166, authorising the CIA to confront the Soviets 'by all means possible'.[122] This was a landmark blank cheque, which opened the way for the supply of latest-technology weaponry to the Islamists. The gloves were now clearly off – plausible deniability no longer restrained the Islamists' supporters.

Given Wilson's obsession with providing anti-aircraft weapons to the Afghan rebels, it was only a matter of time before he turned to the Stinger missile, the most up-to-date anti-aircraft weapon General Dynamics had to offer. However in the autumn of 1985, the CIA was continuing to block the dispatch of Stingers, insiders arguing that the weapon could well end up in the wrong hands – for example, those of Iranian terrorists, who would gain the capability to shoot down Western airliners. (Terrorism was rife in the Middle East at this time: only two years earlier, in October 1983, the US Marine and French barracks in Beirut had been blasted by terrorists, killing 299 troops and compelling Reagan, the following February, to withdraw from Lebanon.) Besides, sceptics argued that the employment of Stingers would confirm, in an almost boastful way, US intelligence involvement in the Afghanistan war.[123]

Unfortunately for the reluctant CIA officers, by the end of the year Wilson had discovered a $300 million Pentagon appropriation that was due to be returned unspent to the Treasury in January 1986. The congressman was willing to 're-programme' the money for the Stingers; in addition, the Saudis could back him with another $300 million. The budget for Afghanistan for 1986 had now reached immense proportions.[124] Those CIA officers who feared that the Soviets would be provoked into invading Pakistan if the Stinger was deployed were silenced, after repeated arguments from Avrakotos, who insisted that the Soviets had for years been well aware of the secret arms shipments through Pakistan; had they wished, they could have invaded earlier.[125] By spring 1986, General Dynamics was processing the order for Stingers for Afghanistan;[126] the first consignment of 200 missiles reached Pakistan in July 1986.

A few months later, Colonel Oliver North of the National Security Council met an Iranian government representative who admitted that Iran was providing support to the rebels; the Iranians now sought to 'cooperate' with the Americans in this policy. For years they had been operating a logistics and training base near the Afghan border, where they had been attempting to show the Mujahedeen that the Russian Mi-24 gunship was vulnerable to surface-to-air missiles; they claimed to have already shot down Mi-24s with Red Eye missiles. The rebels, however, remained wary of the Iranians.[127] (It should be noted that MI6 had discovered the secret US strategy to free the hostages held in Lebanon by cooperating with Iran, the source being a Middle East agent.)[128] The Iranians told North that a rebel had disabled a T-72 main battle-tank by firing a rocket-propelled grenade from a range of 80 metres.

However, Soviet special forces remained a nightmare for the rebels: 'the Spetsnaz were' very effective. The only battle with Spetsnaz which the Mujahedeen won was recently one near Herat where they also took a couple of Spetsnaz prisoners.'[129] Already in March 1986, two

Spetsnaz battalions, having received intelligence from an agent in the Mujahedeen, attacked a rebel base depot in Krer, Pakistan, and after a fierce battle were extracted by helicopter, while gunships provided covering fire. A similar raid took place in December 1987.[130]

On Christmas day 1987, in 'Operation Magistral', Soviet paratroopers engaged a force they assumed to be Pakistani special forces: their opponents' uniforms, tactics and coordination led the members of the 9th Company of the 345th Airborne Regiment (engaged in a fierce defence of Hill 3234 near the Mujahedeen base of Sarani, which had been successfully raided two days earlier) to assume they were confronting the Pakistani army's 'Black Storks'. Confirmation came from the interception of tactical communications offering (premature) congratulations to the Pakistani commander for taking the hill – which eventually, in fact, would remain in Russian hands – as well as from observation of Pakistani army helicopters landing close by to evacuate their casualties. The raid on the Sarani base had been a bonus for the GRU. Franz Klintsevich, the head of the Spetsprop (intelligence and psychological operations) detachment of the 345th Regiment, found valuable documents there, later stating:

> There was a surprising amount of paperwork, including plans
> and records, maps, photographs and a lot of passports and other
> documents, many of them false ... There were sacks and sacks
> full of documents which I removed and then sifted through.[131]

Earlier, in an October 1987 meeting with Robert Gates, the CIA deputy director, Zia asked for tactical intelligence on India's large-scale military manoeuvres, disclosing his apprehension at New Delhi's intentions. However, Gates refused to cooperate, saying that 'friends do not discuss friends with friends', and that Zia should not ask for more help.[132]

The Pentagon, meanwhile, was hesitating at the prospect of transferring Stingers to the Mujahedeen. Caspar Weinberger, the secretary of defense, sided with those who argued that this latest technology might fall into terrorist hands or reach the Soviets. There were also serious worries about decreasing the US Army's Stinger stockpile by donating some of it to the rebels; Fred Ikle, the undersecretary of defense, described the JCS's concerns as 'huge'. Finally, the generals warned that accountability was non-existent, since the weapons delivered to the ISI by the CIA were distributed as the Pakistanis saw fit. Soon, however, the tide turned: some CIA officials pointed out that the Stinger technology was already compromised by a leak, in Greece, of information on design and components. In 1985 a Russian double agent revealed that Greek spies for the GRU had stolen more classified information. Indeed, in November the same year the Soviets went on to publish a detailed report on the Stinger's performance. Furthermore, it was claimed, the US Army stockpiles would not decrease because General Dynamics had already started producing Stinger-POST, an upgraded version of the original model (and, in any case, the Mujahedeen could not be supplied only with the original version because the company had focused its production resources on the new version).[133] As for what might happen to the missiles, besides being employed against Russian aircraft, some Afghans admitted to the Americans that they were occasionally selling the weaponry they were receiving.

The outcome was that the secretary of defense and George Shultz, the secretary of state, concurred on supplying Stingers to the Mujahedeen,[134] and in April 1986 Reagan signed the relevant authorisation (though a last-ditch effort by the CIA bureaucracy, citing information that the Soviets were developing new anti-missile defences and that there was a resulting need for this to be studied further, delayed the transfer of the first 50 missiles and their launchers to the Pakistanis).[135]

Retrospective accounts, from 1992 and 1995, argue that the decision to give Stingers to the Afghan rebels was based on top secret 'highly specific' intelligence received in 1984 and 1985 indicating that the Kremlin had opted to escalate the war.[136]

In the autumn of 1986, the Mujahedeen began to employ the Stinger, with considerable success, shooting down three Hind helicopters on its first outing;[137] the CIA confirmed this the same day (25 September), having redirected the latest-technology Keyhole KH-11 satellite. The Stinger sidelined the other missiles the Mujahedeen had had at their disposal, namely the SA-7, the Milan and the British Blowpipe (the last of these not having been credited with even a single hit).[138] But a few days later, in early October, GRU agents operating within the Mujahedeen stole two Stingers.[139] Raids against the rebels' supply lines by the Spetsnaz and their Afghan allies resulted in the seizure of a number of other Stingers, while more were acquired by bribery.[140] Masoud conceded as early as 1984 that 'their commandos [the Spetsnaz] have learned a great deal about mountain guerrilla-warfare and are fighting much better than before'.[141] In early 1987, a Spetsnaz group, in an airborne assault supported by a gunship, trapped a Mujahedeen party near Kandahar and seized their three Stinger launchers; a few months later the Iranians managed to buy four Stinger launchers and 16 missiles from the Mujahedeen.[142]

The Soviets were not slow to devise effective counter-measures against the Stinger. They installed in their bombers upgraded anti-missile radar systems, upgraded flares, infrared beacons, and baffles on the exhausts to impede the locking-on of the heat-seeking missile. Pilots of fixed-wing aircraft flew at higher altitudes, beyond the three-mile range of the missile (the Russian ground troops mocked them as 'cosmonauts'), while helicopter pilots flew very low to hide from the Stinger, which needed a 'hot' target against the 'cold' background of the sky. Though low flying exposed the helicopters to small-arms fire, their armour plate provided adequate protection. In addition, night flying enhanced Russian air superiority, since the Mujahedeen lacked night-vision equipment. A high-risk tactic entailed flying at the edge of the three-mile range to lure the rebels into firing a missile, thus disclosing their position for a rocket attack.[143]

In July 1987, another Pakistani agent was arrested in the Philippines after attempting to buy 25 tons of a special steel alloy vital for the construction of nuclear weapons; fortunately for Zia and Wilson, however, the aid programme for Pakistan had already been approved by Congress. Again, Wilson rode the tide and defended Zia against his critics – only to learn the following year that Zia had been killed, together with the US ambassador, in a suspicious air crash.[144] Immediately after the incident became known, Leonid Shebarshin, head of the KGB First Chief Directorate, sent assurances to Islamabad that neither his agency nor KHAD had any involvement in Zia's de-mise. He believed that Pakistani feuds were to be blamed – Zia had after all executed former Prime Minister Bhutto in 1979, and the latter's faction were still after his blood.[145]

The escalation of the war entailed two scenarios: Afghan raids into the USSR, and the assassination of Russian military personnel, especially those of high rank. The KGB and the CIA had reached an unwritten agreement not to target each other's personnel, and the CIA bureaucracy feared for the safety of their staff in stations all over the world. They also urged the Mujahedeen not to target KGB or Russian officers. Congressmen like Gordon Humphrey, however, pushed for the killing of senior Soviet officers in Afghanistan, with the ISI supplying special explosives for car-bomb attacks and Casey himself endorsing the targeting of Russians.[146] Eventually, the CIA devised a tactic of supplying the ISI with sniper rifles to be passed to the Afghans, but with no night-vision goggles or scopes. In add-ition, the CIA withheld any information on the residences of Russian officers or on their security perimeter, emphasising to the Pakistanis that these long-range rifles were for anti-materiel purposes, targeting vehicle tyres and armoured personnel carriers from a distance.[147]

According to a later account by Brigadier Yousaf, the head of the ISI's Afghan bureau who organised the incursions into the USSR, the first rebel reconnaissance missions took place in 1984.[148] While the CIA financed the distribution of Korans in the Soviet republics, it was against further escalation, and the intelligence it passed on to the Mujahedeen did not include topographical or any other information that could be of value in supporting attacks within Soviet territory. Nonetheless, the brigadier commented: 'The CIA, and others, gave us every encouragement unofficially to take the war into the Soviet Union, but they were careful not to provide anything that might be traceable to the US.'[149] Planning for the destruction of the 1,000-metre-long steel bridge over the Amu (Oxus) river commenced in early 1985, with the knowledge of the CIA, which provided some technical data – recommending suitable explosive charges – but avoided giving current intelligence on the bridge's security.[150] However, by late 1985 Zia himself had ordered the abandonment of any such endeavour; he feared the Russians might retaliate by blowing up bridges in Pakistan. Nonetheless, attacks against Russian barges on the Amu were facilitated by MI6. Yousaf wrote:

We required limpet mines that a small recce boat or a swimmer could carry, which could be clamped to the side of the [target] boat just below the water line. For these we turned to the British, via MI6. They obliged, and it was the UK's small, but effective, contribution to destroying a number of loaded barges on the Soviet side of the Amu river throughout 1986. Others were sunk by recoilless rifle fire from positions in the reeds and swamps near the south bank'.[151]

The same year raids within the USSR aiming at the derailment of freight trains (on the Samarkand–Termez–Amu line) were organised. However, 'two large-scale operations failed when the Soviets reacted quickly to cut off the invaders. I am certain they had been forewarned.'[152] Operations to lay mines between Russian border posts were coupled with another operation in December 1986: 30 Mujahedeen crossed the border river near Wakhan, in rubber boats, and attacked the security posts of two hydroelectric power stations in Tajikistan. On another occasion the town of Pyandzh came under rocket attack, together with the small airfield nearby:[153]

These cross-border strikes were at their peak during 1986. Scores of attacks were made across the Amu from Jozjan to Badakshan provinces ... That we were hitting a sore spot was confirmed by the ferocity of the Soviets' reaction. Virtually every incursion provoked massive aerial bombing and gunship attacks on all villages south of the river in the vicinity of our strike'.[154]

The Soviet army had realised that they could do nothing to stop the infiltration of the Mujahedeen from Pakistan, nor to block their access to weaponry. The operations planners were growing more desperate, to the extent that in the Central Committee session of 13 November 1986 the then deputy minister of defence, Field Marshal Akhromeev, proposed a dangerous idea to Gromyko: 'We must go to Pakistan', he urged, assuming that only an invasion could deal effectively with the issue at hand. But Gorbachev's chairmanship ensured that such a course of action – a major Soviet escalation of the war – was not discussed.[155]

In April 1987, however, the ISI's Afghan bureau did organise a further escalation: the Mujahedeen, armed by the Pakistanis, launched raids within the Soviet Union. It remains debatable to what extent the head of the bureau, Brigadier Yousaf, acted without the explicit authorisation of the usually very careful Zia. The first group attacked an airfield near Termez in Uzbekistan with rockets (striking over a period of ten days), the second launched road ambushes against Russian military convoys, and the third used rockets to attack a factory located ten miles inside Russian territory. At about the same time, the CIA (unaware of these Pakistani-supported operations) circulated satellite photographs among top decision-makers in Washington that showed Muslim demonstrations in Alma-Ata (Almaty), the capital of Soviet Central Asia; this may have indicated fertile ground for the fomenting of troubles within the USSR.[156] Once information on the Mujahedeen strikes within the USSR had been disclosed, the chief of the CIA's Directorate of Operations telephoned the station chief in Islamabad asking him if there had been any agency involvement. (If the CIA had had any connection with these attacks, US law would have been broken – these actions having surpassed the authority of the CIA as defined by presidential findings and National Security Policy Decisions.)[157]

The Soviets threatened Zia: this kind of action put 'the security and integrity of Pakistan' in great danger. This was a blunt reference to invasion, and the Reagan administration scrambled to reassure the Soviets that there was no American involvement in it. Zia was put under strong pressure to order Yousaf to stop, but the latter needed some time to relay the message, because his Mujahedeen did not maintain radio contact (and besides, they were hardly the most disciplined of militias).[158]

Throughout the war, the CIA recruited 'HUMINT' (clandestine human intelligence sources) to report on hostilities. Usually, Europeans posing as journalists and photographers travelled to Afghanistan

together with ISI-backed Mujahedeen. Some were veterans of the
French Foreign Legion; the majority were simply adventure-seeking
characters whose compensation for working with the CIA was modest,
reaching no more than $1,000 per month. The recruitment of these
amateur spies was facilitated by a former CIA station chief in Paris
who now worked in Pakistan. Some were provided with communications equipment, but most had only cameras and notebooks.[159] Beyond
these spy-travellers, the CIA managed to evade the ISI and establish
secret contact with some Mujahedeen commanders, among them
Masoud, who in 1984 received his first money from the Americans.
Other CIA-financed commanders were paid between $20,000 and
$100,000 per month (the upper figure if they enjoyed influence in
more than one province). This CIA-financed network, kept secret from
the ISI, included about 50 regional commanders and agents but possibly excluded the Western spy-travellers.[160] For the delivery of cash,
the Muslim *hawala* system was employed. The Afghan spies were
occupied with reporting on battles, the impact of the insurgency,
the stance of other warlords, the performance of the Stinger missile,
the coming of Sunni Arab volunteers, and the financial and material
support received from the ISI, Saudi intelligence and rich Saudis like
Osama bin Laden, who was known as a financier.[161] Erroneously, and
in hindsight ironically, senior CIA officials and Arab specialists at
the State Department did not view bin Laden as anti-American, and
tried to find ways of boosting the number of Arab volunteers moving into Afghanistan. Milt Bearden of the CIA station in Islamabad
commented: 'Actually [bin Laden] did some very good things ... he
put a lot of money in a lot of right places in Afghanistan.'[162] In the
mid-1980s, at a time of repeated terrorist incidents in the Middle East,
the CIA was so absorbed by its deals with Saudi Arabia and Pakistan
on funding the Afghans and their Arab allies that their predominant
anti-Americanism was simply forgotten.

By mid-1988, a total of 900 Stingers had been shipped to Pakistan
and Afghanistan, and according to US statistics they were responsible
for the loss of some 269 Russian helicopters and fixed-wing aircraft.[163]
The Americans' fear of losing track of the missiles did not diminish,
and the CIA paid close attention to the Stinger's battery inventory – not

least because prolonged storage in an environment subject to tempera-
ture changes could result in deterioration of the battery, thus making
the missile useless. In 1988, a Stinger was discovered on an Iranian
boat, and examination showed that its battery had indeed run down.
Also, the heat-seeking device installed in the missile's tip was considered too sensitive to operate after prolonged mishandling. One CIA
official argued that, while the weapon had a shelf-life of one year,
interested parties who had managed to get hold of a Stinger could
themselves devise a battery to power it. A 1987 Central Command
(CENTCOM) study, however, put the battery's shelf-life at a minimum of ten years.[164] Later CIA estimates put the number of Stingers
acquired by the Iranians at up to 100.[165] (Given that there was no terrorist attack by Iranians or their surrogates using the Stinger, we are
led to believe that Tehran had no intention of using it, merely wishing
to retain the ability to do so.)

According to a CIA officer involved in the later programme of
buying back Stingers, the estimate that the missile had a limited shelf-
life was a ploy to lower the price in the black market.[166] We should
note, though, that since the Pakistani Army held Stinger launchers
and missiles, and the ISI always backed the Mujahedeen and later
the Taleban, it would not be too difficult for the insurgents to secure spare parts to make the launchers function, or to obtain more
missiles.

Nonetheless, in a better-safe-than-sorry bid, the CIA launched a
$100-million programme to buy back the approximately 200 Stinger
missiles (with their launchers) that remained in Mujahedeen hands
after the Soviet withdrawal from Afghanistan, though of course not
all were recovered.[167] Episodic and fragmentary testimonies indicated attempts to employ them: two Stinger launchers, for example,
were intercepted when al-Qaida members attempted to transfer them
from Pakistan to Sudan in 1993. In 1995, a cameraman on a Western
journalist's mission to Kabul saw three Stingers for sale. In 1998,
Osama bin Laden admitted at a conference that some al-Qaida members had tried to transfer a Stinger launcher to Saudi Arabia, but had
been arrested. Peter Bergen saw a Taleban team carrying two Stinger
launchers at Kandahar airport in December 1999. The same year,

Masoud's followers claimed to have shot down a Taleban aircraft with a Stinger.[168] We should note that Stingers were not employed against coalition aircraft during 'Operation Enduring Freedom', or later in counter-insurgency operations. In November 2002, however, al-Qaida attempted to shoot down an Israeli airliner near Nairobi airport, but the weapon misfired.

The Stinger saga, which commenced in 1986 with the first introduction of the weapon, continues to this day; fears that the missile would be widely used in terrorist attacks have not been realised. Despite the number of Stingers that went missing during the Afghan war, plus a marginal number that could have been obtained from other sources (for example, Pakistani army depots), and the fanatical determination of al-Qaida and other terrorist groups to carry out spectacular attacks, the weapon has yet to be used. Perhaps the Stinger (or at least the version of it provided to the Mujahedeen) did indeed have a shelf-life limited by sensitive technology unable to cope with extreme weather conditions or mishandling.

Soviet Foreign Minister Edward Shevardnadze claimed after the war that the Stinger missile 'definitely prolonged our stay ... It made our military men, our hawks, much more determined than ever not to withdraw, not to appear to be giving in under duress.' Field Marshal Akhromeev concurred, as did George Kennan, the architect of containment.[169] Nonetheless, these were post–Cold War claims. The Stinger was not a decisive weapon that compelled Russia to withdraw from Afghanistan. Gorbachev had decided to end the conflict well before the introduction of the missile in Afghanistan, as will be explored in Chapter 7.

6

DISCOVERING CHINESE INTENTIONS

The Sino-American collaboration under Carter culminated in intelligence-sharing with respect to the deployment of the Vietnamese military in Cambodia and on the borders with China during the 1979 Sino-Vietnamese conflict. A high-ranking Chinese diplomat who acted as an intelligence courier confirmed the secret partnership. In parallel, the Chinese scaled down their support for regional communist insurgencies: in December 1980, Deng Xiao-ping informed the secretary-general of the Malayan Communist Party that its China-based radio broadcasts would cease; the Burmese party was also warned that Chinese support would be wound up in five years' time. Meanwhile, Deng's commitment to domestic reform resulted in a reduction in the scope of declarations promoting revolution and class struggle.[1]

Despite the new warmth in Sino-American relations (and the continued Chinese participation in the secret arming of the Mujahedeen), the CIA described Beijing's gradual cooling towards Washington. In early 1981, the proposal of a US arms sale to Taiwan brought to the fore, in the corridors of power within the Chinese government, questions as to the usefulness of siding with the Americans. In October, China called for the Americans to agree on a date for terminating the supply of arms to Taiwan (a step Washington would never have contemplated undertaking). A year later, on 17 August 1982, a Sino-American joint communiqué set aside the subject of the date; objections from nationalists in Beijing became increasingly less muted. In addition, the passing of the Taiwan Relations Act by the US Congress provoked Chinese charges to the effect that it was 'inconsistent' with the spirit of post-1979 Sino-American relations. Another key foreign-policy issue was the sale of advanced US technology to Beijing: China wanted more, but Washington imposed restrictions, which in turn led to complaints – just as in the 1950s the Chinese had objected to the USSR's reluctance to meet all their demands, so they now blamed the US for not giving them more help in the modernisation of their industry.[2]

Tensions heightened with the defection of the Chinese tennis player Hu Na, to which Beijing responded by cancelling the remaining Sino-US cultural and sports exchanges and events, as well as the visit of a US legal delegation, scheduled for 1983.[3] Chinese propaganda started referring to the United States as 'a hegemonist power', like the USSR.

Meanwhile, Beijing's strategists reviewed their policy towards the Soviet Union. It was not only a matter of reducing tensions, and thus the possibility of war with the Soviets, but also (as the CIA noted) the policy review was a 'useful reminder' to Washington that China has other options in its foreign policy. It was evident that the Chinese had reassessed their relations strategy towards Washington:

> China has shown little interest [since the 17 August 1982 communiqué] in exploring an arms supply relationship with the United States and has also played down strategic cooperation as a basis for developing bilateral ties. Still, China has clearly not written off its relations with the United States. Despite its diminished emphasis on a strategic relationship and its pursuit of a more independent foreign policy, Beijing continues to seek US technology and to evince an interest in developing economic and commercial ties with Washington.[4]

By late 1981, Beijing had concluded that the Soviets were serious about working to improve bilateral relations, given the severe economic problems they were encountering; this was also the CIA's initial conclusion. Within the Chinese leadership, some argued that reducing tensions with Moscow could effectively save resources for the modernisation of industry and of the defence establishment (as well as helping in general with the ailing Chinese economy). Some of the governing elite also voiced fears that close cooperation with Washington could cost China its image as an independent actor in world politics, especially in the eyes of the Third World. The Chinese assumed that, by playing up their rapprochement with Moscow, they would upgrade their negotiating position vis-à-vis the United States. The Reagan-administration policy of supporting Taiwan militarily disappointed supporters of Deng Xiao-ping, who had assumed (prematurely) that the Americans' cooperation with Beijing indicated they were no longer interested in Taiwan. The CIA's estimate was that 'Beijing's current tactics are intended in part to gain stronger commitment of support from the United States', in the shape of new agreements on the transfer of advanced technology.[5]

In addition:

> The domestic priorities of the Dengists – which include reducing the influence of the military, preparing the ground for a major party purge, and managing criticism of the social effects of China's opening to the West – also probably reinforced the leadership's inclination to pursue a more cautious foreign policy.[6]

According to a secret source (the name remains classified), there was a consensus among Chinese leaders for 'a cautious, sceptical approach toward both Washington and Moscow', though China had no intention of isolating itself. In any event, the CIA assumed that the Chinese, in their meetings with the Soviets, did not have clear-cut long-term expectations; they continued to regard the Soviet Union as the main threat to their national security, and to be angered by its arming of Vietnam and occupation of Afghanistan.[7]

China could not play an equal role in a triumvirate, but a secret source (the name remains classified) indicated that 'the Chinese want to protect and enhance' their bilateral relations with Washington.[8] However, they showed themselves willing to keep the Americans guessing as to the nature and extent of their rapprochement with the USSR.[9]

The Chinese had in fact misunderstood US intentions, wrongly assuming that Washington was seeking a security relationship with Beijing (by providing defence equipment) in a bid to enhance Chinese security vis-à-vis the USSR. In return, the Americans (from the Chinese viewpoint) wanted Beijing to refrain from protesting at the arming of Taiwan.[10] It was this misunderstanding, at the top level of government, that ignited the fierce foreign-policy debate which in turn led to the new 'independent' foreign policy, with Chinese propaganda blaming US' hegemonism.[11]

Nationalist sentiment gave way to pragmatism, however, when dealing with businessmen and US officials over technology transfer. Indeed, 'Chinese officials went out of their way to assure US officials and businessmen that trade should not be affected by the tensions in other aspects of the relationship.'[12] The CIA was confident that China would not jeopardise its relations with Washington, since this would also affect its relations with its other major commercial partner (in addition to Hong Kong) – Japan. 'Chinese leaders understand that China's ability to acquire high technology from Japan could be complicated by a serious downturn in Sino-US relations', stated the CIA's analysis.[13] Sober assessments of how relations with the Americans would evolve now characterised Chinese thinking: 'Clearly the Chinese have reduced – to a more realistic level – their expectations about the degree to which the United States and China are likely to cooperate in any military sense against the USSR.'[14]

In the meantime, the Soviets developed further formidable capabilities, which shadowed China's defence modernisation. The CIA estimated that,

> [W]hile the Chinese behave as if they do not expect the Soviets to mount an attack on China unless there is a severe provocation, we believe China's strategy and military modernization are proceeding on the assumption that Soviet capabilities will continue

to improve – a trend that can only widen the gap between the quality of the two forces.[15]

China employed the tactics of a street-trader to make the United States and the Soviet Union assume that it was not eager to improve relations with either, but it was evident that its priority was to conclude profitable deals with Washington rather than Moscow. The CIA analysed the tactics thus:

> Knowing that the Soviet proposal in September 1981 to reopen border talks was timed to exploit Sino-US differences, Chinese officials deferred response, while informing the United States of the offer as a reminder that Beijing had other options. As Moscow pressed Beijing with new overtures, Beijing delayed resumption of political talks until after the August [1982] communiqué had eased the Sino-US crisis. This reduced the potential for negative effects on Sino-US relations and at the same time allowed Beijing to address Moscow from a strengthened position, enhancing prospects for exacting concessions.[16]

In their talks with the Soviets scheduled for 1983, the Chinese were interested in improving bilateral relations, and, if some meaningful results could be achieved, would not press immediately for changes in Russian policy on Indochina or Afghanistan.[17] The CIA was clear:

> China does not expect the Soviets to negotiate seriously about their presence in Afghanistan. Beijing knows that the Soviets do not regard China's position as a decisive factor in the situation, that Moscow has demonstrated it is engaged in an extended anti-insurgency effort, and that China can use its opposition to the Soviet presence to good effect in its anti-hegemony effort in the Third World.[18]

Brezhnev made a hesitant bid to approach the Chinese, but without reducing his doctrinal criticism of Chinese communism. In a March 1982 speech in Tashkent, the Soviet leader acknowledged 'the existence of a socialist system in China', and played down any threat the Soviet Union might pose for Beijing. He hoped for an improvement in relations, delinking the process from Afghanistan, Cambodia and the border dispute. The Chinese replied that the normalisation of relations had a precondition: a change in Soviet policy on the three issues known as the 'three obstacles'. It was assumed that Brezhnev, now very ill, had left the speech to Andropov, who was preparing his candidacy for the chairmanship and exploring subtle ways of changing Soviet policy on China.[19]

In its turn, China assumed that Brezhnev's friendly overtures resulted from a US resolve to stand up to Soviet aggression in Afghanistan and elsewhere, as well as from the Soviets' realisation of their own vulnerability. In the summer of 1982, a secret policy review was underway in Beijing. Deng Xiao-ping (at that time chairman of the People's Political Consultative Conference) argued in favour of 'a big move' towards improving relations, but without changing Chinese positions. Indeed, he had already foreseen a quid pro quo: before any normalisation, Moscow would have to show good faith by resolving one of the 'three obstacles'. Indeed, on 10 August 1982, a high-level official of the Chinese Foreign Ministry left for Moscow to convey Deng's proposal. The reply received was laconic, but hopeful: the Soviets were prepared to talk 'at any time, at any venue, and at any level [in order] to remove the obstacles for normalisation of relations'. Deng realised that the reference to 'removing the obstacles' meant the Kremlin was serious, and Brezhnev himself stated, in a speech in Baku in September, that the normalisation of relations was 'an important matter'. Already, before the opening of the Chinese Communist Party congress in the same month, Deng had agreed to resume the political consultations at vice-foreign-ministerial level.[20]

Upon his election as Soviet chairman, Andropov showed his clear intention to change policy on China. At Brezhnev's funeral, he held a long conversation with Huang Hua, the Chinese foreign minister, and in 1983 Deputy Foreign Minister Mikhail Kapitsa was duly invited for talks in Beijing.[21]

Reagan seemed distinctly eager to upgrade cooperation with China: going beyond military programmes, he announced a policy of peaceful nuclear cooperation with Beijing, signing National Security Decision

Directive 76 on 18 January 1983. Defense Secretary Weinberger, meanwhile, remained an ardent supporter of the policy of arming China, increasing budget resources for 1984.[22]

Soon afterwards, in the Kremlin, Defence Minister Ustinov blocked Andropov's strategy of scaling down tensions with China. At the 31 May 1983 Politburo meeting, the Soviet chairman presented positive prospects for economic collaboration with Beijing, the Chinese having already offered an agreement. Gromyko, who was suspicious that the Chinese would not go farther than a trade agreement since they had not changed the preconditions for normalisation, asked Ustinov if there could be a withdrawal of troops from Mongolia and the Sino-Soviet borders, to show good faith. Ustinov insisted forcefully:

> Regarding Mongolia, it must be said that if we withdraw the Soviet forces located there to our territory, then we will lose a good base, we will deprive ourselves of a forward defence area. Indeed, everything is built for use there. Therefore there is no sense in making any moves back to the Soviet border. Regarding Cambodia and Vietnam, we have discussed this many times. I suggest that we shouldn't lose the achievements of these military bases; we need to hold positions gained there.[23]

Nonetheless, the Soviet Foreign Ministry several times proposed a discussion of confidence-building measures, but the Chinese wanted to resolve the border dispute first. Ustinov himself had Politburo backing for a plan to speed up the deployment of SS-20s in Siberia in 1982–83 – which of course made the Chinese nervous; they soon lodged complaints. Andropov preferred not to disagree with Ustinov on this.[24] (Perhaps the deployment was connected to Andropov's view of contingencies – as we saw in Chapter 4, he feared a US surprise nuclear attack at that time.)

During roughly the same period, senior Soviet military officers appeared unconcerned about Beijing's intentions. China's defeat in the 1979 war with Vietnam was noted as a proof of the low performance of its troops and equipment. Thus, even if a Western-backed modernisation programme was implemented, the Chinese would struggle to make up ten to fifteen years of technological backwardness in engine construction and navigation systems, as well as in the recruitment and training of qualified cadres.[25] In April 1983, meanwhile, two Sino-Soviet border-trade agreements were signed, keeping hopes alive.[26]

In mid-1983, a CIA analysis reported on the development of China's nuclear and conventional capabilities, but was reassuring as to its continuing amicable intentions: 'They may have become more independent in rhetoric while remaining close [to the US] in substance.'[27] Indeed, 'The lengths to which they have gone to preserve the substance of relations with the United States in trade, training and technology transfer, despite serious strains over the Taiwan issue, indicate the importance they attach to those relations.'[28] Continuing to view the USSR as the main threat and to seek more US technology, as well as opposing the Soviets' occupation of Afghanistan and their support of Vietnam, Chinese policy would 'provide a basis, albeit limited, for strategic collaboration with the United States in the form of consultation on strategic questions and parallel foreign policy actions'.[29] Indeed, one 'parallel foreign policy action' was selling the CIA Chinese-made weapons to arm the Mujahedeen, as noted in the previous chapter. (However, there was a flaw in the CIA's analysis: the Chinese did not seek strategic collaboration with Washington, since they had no wish to sacrifice their status as an independent power. They simply wanted technology and trade agreements, so their exports could become more competitive.) In addition, the Sino-Soviet rapprochement put in doubt Soviet veracity on the part of the always-suspicious Vietnamese leadership.[30]

For the time being, China had only one nuclear missile system, the CSS-4, able to reach targets either in Alaska or Hawaii. Two silos for the CSS-4 were operational, and at least four others were under construction (though these would not become operational before 1986).[31] Older-generation missiles, the CSS-1 and CSS-2, were also operational; the intelligence estimate put the total of these two types between 60 and 115. The CIA also estimated that China maintained approximately 150 nuclear bombs and some 50 nuclear detonators.[32] Thus China retained some deterrence over the Soviet Union, not because of their small number of nuclear weapons – in comparison to the Soviet arsenal – but because the Soviet leaders feared Chinese capability. It was remarked: 'The deterrent effect is also heightened by the Soviet view of China as the most threatening of the third-country nuclear powers and the assumption in Moscow that the Soviet capital remains the target of highest priority for the Chinese missiles.'[33]

Beijing maintained an 'ambivalent' stance towards the gradual arming of Japan, believing that the US–Japanese defence agreements counter-balanced the potential of the Soviet presence in the Far East.[34] The hunt for advanced technology was a key foreign-policy aim for China, which concluded research and scientific agreements with European countries, purchasing military equipment directly and boosting academic exchanges in the fields of engineering, chemistry and physics. Meanwhile, the Chinese operated 'a small but growing programme to acquire advanced technology and technical data through covert means, particularly aimed at obtaining restricted US, West German and Japanese technologies having direct military application'.[35]

President Reagan led from the front on China, confidently engaging its leaders. Once he had arrived in Beijing (on 26 April 1984), however, he sounded so anti-communist that the Chinese censored reports of his speeches; they remained negative regarding the prospects of a strategic partnership with Washington, and had no wish to be carried away by Reagan's anti-Soviet stance, nor to get embroiled in his confrontation with Moscow.[36]

Soviet propaganda and media attacked China throughout May 1984, and on the 9th of that month First Deputy Premier Arkhipov cancelled his planned visit to Beijing. In late June, the Soviets opened an exhibition in Moscow of propaganda photographs on Chinese 'aggressive activity' in the Sino-Vietnamese border area. The KGB was one of the organisations, which also included the Foreign Ministry, that remained hostile to Beijing. Indeed, secret sources were too scarce for the KGB to assess Chinese developments since the mayhem of the Cultural Revolution. In early 1984, Vladimir Kryuchkov, the head of the First Chief- Foreign Intelligence- Directorate (FCD) and KGB chairman in 1988–91, insisted that, in the late 1970s,

Beijing [was] blocking normalisation of Sino-Soviet relations …
[It was] counting on deriving political advantages for itself by

manoeuvring between the West and the socialist countries, and trying to blackmail the West with the prospect of an improvement of relations with the Soviet Union.[37]

He remained critical of the performance of the KGB residencies, noting the lack of secret sources:

The [FCD] has achieved some useful results over the past two years in its work against China, but the successes have been in general in the nature of isolated episodes. Many residencies are still slow in dealing with the specific tasks posed by [agent] recruitment. Insufficient attention is being given to promising categories of Chinese nationals abroad, such as specialists, students and trainees. Little effort is being made to select agents for prolonged periods in the PRC or in Hong Kong or Taiwan.

Residencies must step up their endeavour to achieve solid results in recruiting Chinese nationals. The most highly trained officers and experienced agents must be directed into this work. We must not let slip the opportunities created by the changeover in personnel in the Chinese state's administration, the process of discrediting Maoist ideology and the purge carried out in the Party.

Nowhere more than in working against China do we require circumspection, patience, endurance and accurate appreciation of the particular characteristics of the Chinese.[38]

In the same year (1984), the FCD authorised a plan of active measures aimed at helping to undermine Sino-US relations, in order 'to counter the military and political rapprochement between the PRC and the USA and other imperialist countries on an anti-Soviet basis'. In this set of active measures was included a plan to disrupt the Sino-UK talks on the hand over of Hong Kong.[39] The Directorate T (Scientific and Technological Espionage) of the FCD was spared harsh criticism. However, an April 1985 report berated the 'negligence' of the heads of the residencies who lacked Chinese contacts, 'a source of great anxiety' for the Kremlin, which under Gorbachev intended to boost relations with Beijing. After the end of the Cold War an FCD official admitted: 'We had an unbridgeable gap in our information sources on China.'[40]

Beijing remained calm, interpreting all Soviet polemics as the consequence of domestic infighting and Soviet anger over the Reagan visit. On 30 June 1984, Vice-Foreign Minister Qian Qichen, the top Chinese expert on Russia, visited Moscow to meet Deputy Foreign Minister Kapitsa in a bid to keep high-level Sino-Soviet channels open. Nonetheless, by 10 July Beijing was attacking Chernenko's foreign policy in public, calling it 'a destructive force slowing the course of Sino-Soviet normalisation and derailing US-Soviet arms talks'. By 21 September 1984, however, the situation was showing signs of improvement: Gromyko and Foreign Minister Wu Xue-qian had a calm, though 'not substantive', meeting during the UN General Assembly. On 18 October, a fifth round of Sino-Soviet talks was convened in Moscow, but no meaningful results were achieved, with the Russian media sniping at Chinese foreign policy.[41] One bilateral commerce agreement was signed in November, and three in December, marking a slow change in Sino-Soviet relations. Arkhipov visited Beijing in the spotlight of positive publicity. Afterwards, the Chinese made it clear, however, that no 'breakthrough' had been reached; hostile propaganda and polemics, with reference to clashes at Sino-Vietnamese borders and doctrinal criticism, resurfaced from January 1984 until Chernenko's death in March 1985. In a show of solidarity with the Vietnamese, the aircraft-carrier *Minsk* and the amphibious assault vessel *Ivan Rogov* sailed to the Gulf of Tonkin.[42] The Chinese military noted the Soviet naval presence and its implied message. In any case, throughout the 1980s Deng Xiao-ping was ready to play up the confrontation with Vietnam in state propaganda so as to mobilise support among ordinary Chinese, who were suffering stark income inequalities as a consequence of his reforms.[43]

Meanwhile, China was boosting its contacts with Washington. On 12 January 1985, General John W. Vessey, the JCS chairman, arrived in Beijing, to which *Izvestiya* responded by criticising Chinese policy. The ailing Chernenko, in a 22 February speech, sounded positive about working to improve relations with Beijing. From 3 to 24 March 1985, a delegation from the Chinese National People's Congress

visited Moscow; it was the first parliamentary exchange in two decades, noted the CIA. The death of Chernenko on 10 March, and the
advent of Gorbachev, marked a new dynamic in Sino-Soviet relations.
It was a time for symbolic gestures, with the Chinese dispatching a
top-ranking delegation, under Vice-Premier Li Peng, to attend the
funeral of the Soviet leader, and Gorbachev responding by emphasising his intention to improve relations with Beijing.[44] A sixth round of
political consultations commenced on 9 April 1985, and a week later
Deng referred explicitly to the three obstacles (Afghanistan, Indochina
and the Sino-Soviet border dispute) blocking an improvement in relations, calling Russian support for Vietnam's operations in Cambodia
'the easiest one' for the Soviets to remedy. At the Central Committee
plenum on 24 April, Gorbachev spoke of reciprocity in relations with
China.[45]

By summer 1985, Deng and his supporters had assessed Gorbachev
as a 'flexible' leader who would need at least two years to master
the Kremlin, influence the Politburo and select a foreign and defence
apparatus to serve his policy line. Thus major changes and initiatives
in Soviet policy should not be anticipated before 1987.[46] (This was
a perceptive forecast: in September 1988 Gorbachev made a speech
in Krasnoyarsk in which he declared his intention to work towards
building Sino-Soviet confidence, and to hold discussions with Beijing
on outstanding territorial and military issues.)[47]

The Sino-Soviet rapprochement surprised Washington, to the
extent that the CIA admitted its previous analyses had been too
pessimistic:

The level of hostility between Moscow and Beijing will decrease,
and there will be additional agreements on trade and economic
[issues] and other such secondary matters. These changes have
come, however, a little more quickly and have gone a little further
that the Estimate a year ago held likely. Both Beijing and Moscow
probably genuinely desire a way to lower tensions for a variety of
domestic political and economic reasons. Each side appears to be
testing the other's flexibility and intentions to determine whether
something substantial can be attained at low cost.[48]

In any event,

> [China] would like to obtain greater room for manoeuvring
> between the United States and the USSR, while in the long run
> establishing itself as the swing partner in the triangular relation-
> ship. Beijing does not want to appear to be standing still in the
> triangular relationship while the other two sides negotiate.[49]

Indeed, Beijing sent Moscow positive signals which the CIA had to
piece together to build even a vague picture of Chinese intentions. But
the analysts always had to take into account the fact that Soviet and
Chinese propaganda operated in parallel in the conclusion of agreements, high-ranking official visits and gestures by top leaders.

The Chinese remained silent (a non-event noted by the CIA) on
the occasion of the fifth anniversary of the Afghanistan invasion, and
briefly reduced troop numbers on the Sino-Vietnamese border, while
Gorbachev, in his inaugural speech as chairman of the USSR, made no
reference to any serious differences with China. It seemed that Beijing
had understood: the standing chairman of the Chinese National
People's Congress, Peng Zhen, called Gorbachev 'comrade'. There was
a private Chinese request for Gorbachev to meet Vice-Premier Li Peng,
in which the Chinese official passed on the congratulations of General
Secretary Hu Yao-bang on the new Soviet chairman's election. It was
the first party-to-party exchange of messages in 18 years.[50]

But the Americans remained perplexed, the CIA admitting, 'we
have little reporting about either side's motives and calculations in
this latest round of symbolic gestures. We believe that both sides
probably have been engaged in tactical manoeuvring ...'[51] The Soviets
and Chinese showed an interest in influencing the Reagan administration, knowing that the Americans were keenly observing their evolving
approach. The CIA analysts were confident on one point:

> We strongly believe [that] no specifically pro-Soviet factions exist
> in the Chinese leadership. Debates in Beijing probably focus on
> the degree of 'tilt' toward the United States or the USSR and on
> how to find a balance that best serves Chinese interests.[52]

However, there remained a lack of intelligence on Soviet intentions:

> We have little hard evidence concerning Gorbachev's foreign policy agenda. [Nonetheless] at the same time, we have good reporting that the Gorbachev leadership wants to establish an image of toughness and immunity to pressure toward all the USSR's adversaries, clients and allies.[53]

According to US embassy reports, top Soviet officials were optimistic about a warming of relations with China, but still feared that Beijing might not change its position towards the Soviet Union.[54]

Security on the Sino-Soviet border now became a subject for consultation, demonstrating each side's intention to bring about an essential improvement in relations; the CIA reported to policy-makers Chinese agreement to discuss the subject: 'Therefore, we now judge that it is more probable than the [previous] Estimate predicted that the border talks on territorial issues will resume.' The talks might lead to confidence-building measures, but the current stalemate might continue for the next two years.[55] However, a shadow would be cast over the security talks by China's military support for the Mujahedeen, and by the Soviets' occupation of Afghanistan, as well as their support for Vietnam: neither China nor the Soviet Union would change its policies on these issues.[56]

In a March 1985 speech, Deng Xiao-ping (then the chairman of the Central Military Commission) called the socio-economic and political reforms since 1978 a 'second revolution', that was 'an unprecedented thing in China's history of thousands of years'.[57] The Chinese refurbished their ideological arsenal and their government and party institutions, and were seriously inclined to let the power of the market, rather than central planning, influence economic activity. The results of the experiment of special economic zones (SEZs) in Xiamen, Shantou, Shenzhen and Zhuhai (the last two bordering on Hong Kong and Macao, respectively), which had boosted foreign trade and foreign investment in industry, were praised by Deng himself in 1984. But, by mid-1985 he had become more cautious about the heavy concentration of investment in SEZ construction projects, referring to them as 'experimental', and thus hinting that he could shut them down. In the event, he focused production on upgrading technology in major industrial centres seeking joint ventures with foreign investors. The SEZs would gradually compete with other centres in China.[58]

Reform was also to be seen in the military establishment, which sought the development of professional and better-armed cadres; the military's role in party politics, however, was to be limited.[59] The CIA was impressed by the intention to institute reforms, though not by Deng's ability to impose them. The Chinese leader and his supporters would always have to ensure that reforms would not erode their own position – loosening state controls might lead to loosening their hold on party and personal power.[60] Besides, 'sharp differences' were reported among top officials with respect to the planned reforms – the traditional and endemic system of *guanxi* (networks of personal relationships) fiercely resisting any change.[61]

Meanwhile, China no longer seemed to fear the Soviet Union. In the framework of Beijing's relations with the US, Japan and the USSR, 'the Chinese will continue to perceive that they are not threatened by the Soviet Union', focusing on modernisation and seeking as much US and Western advanced technology as they were allowed to obtain.[62] Taiwan, however, would remain a thorny issue, and the Chinese might even 'escalate pressure' for Washington to cut down arms sales to the island.[63]

Meanwhile, in Moscow reform-minded advisers on Sino-Soviet relations, brought in by Andropov and continuing to serve under Gorbachev, were confronting the Byzantine intrigue of the anti-Chinese league of ideologues in the Politburo and the Foreign Ministry. At the Central Committee's Department for Liaison with Socialist Countries, long-serving officials like Vladimir Rakhmanin, the first deputy head, who had built his career on Sino-Soviet antagonism and the ideological critique of Mao's policies, continuously resisted any policy review. In fact, he gave instructions to report on Chinese claims to Soviet territory; when no such claim was found in the archives, his department doctored Chinese statements and maps from the 1960s to show to the rest of the Central Committee that the Chinese retained hostile intentions.[64]

While Gorbachev sought to boost Sino-Soviet relations, he had no wish to accept Chinese preconditions. In mid-November 1987, he gave an interview to the Chinese weekly *Liaowang* – it was the first time in 30 years that the chairman of the CPSU had granted an interview to a Chinese newspaper – and called for a summit to be a 'logical component' in the contacts and talks between the two communist states. Beijing was in no hurry to reply.[65]

By 1988 no Sino-Soviet deal had been reached on the border dispute, but the CIA noted that 'some Soviet troops have left Mongolia and there may also have been other reduction in Soviet troops facing China'. Moscow withdrew one of its five divisions from Mongolia, and China acknowledged the Russian troop reduction on its borders. The Chinese had reduced their military forces by a million men, and Moscow agreed to disband the SS-20 missile group deployed in Asia (though this was done to conclude the INF treaty with Washington signed in December 1987).[66] Contemporary sources estimated the number of Soviet troops deployed in Mongolia at 0.5 million, facing 1.6 million Chinese – 55 versus 81 divisions. From March 1985 onwards, there was a steady upgrade of the total Soviet force in terms of both equipment and manpower. Two divisions had been moved 'to active status, albeit at low readiness levels'. The 55 Soviet divisions maintained 'a considerable edge in mobility and firepower', being 'capable of stopping a Chinese attack into the USSR and of mounting a quick counterattack. They are also capable of mounting a limited offensive into north-eastern China.' Nonetheless, in the event of war, Moscow was 'highly reluctant' to employ nuclear weapons to achieve limited territorial objectives, fearing retaliation.[67]

Chinese leaders, meanwhile, would always have to bear Vietnam in mind. Since 1981 the Soviets had been expanding their base in Cam Ranh Bay, which hosted 16 Tu-16s (deployed, possibly due to the war scare, in November 1983 and available in the event of war to bomb US and Chinese targets), eight Tu-95s and Tu-142 long-range reconnaissance and anti-submarine aircraft, as well as a squadron of Mig-23s, plus nuclear-powered submarines. If war came, southern China would be at the mercy of the bombers, which carried nuclear munitions that could obliterate towns, military bases and industrial centres.[68] The CIA was also aware that, near the base, the Soviets operated a signals-intelligence facility to provide early warning. Deputy Director Gates claimed that 'this SIGINT facility, paralleled worldwide only by the Soviet SIGINT facility at Lourdes, Cuba, substantially improved Soviet intelligence capabilities' in Southeast Asia, covering Chinese and US Navy deployments in the western Pacific.[69]

The Soviets were certainly seeking better relations with Beijing; they were also confident that their immense capabilities confirmed their superpower status in the Far East. They countered China by demonstrating their growing influence over North Korea, to which Deputy Foreign Minister Kapitsa paid a visit in November 1984 and, according to reports cited by the CIA, signed a military agreement which

> was followed by unprecedented joint reconnaissance collection missions by Soviet aircraft ... Closer ties with Pyongyang serve to remind the Chinese of Moscow's determination to have a say in the future of the Peninsula, and give the Soviets valuable opportunities to collect intelligence over the Yellow Sea.[70]

The Soviet Pacific fleet had received much attention from Soviet strategists who deployed a second Kiev-class aircraft carrier. In 1982 two Y-class nuclear-powered ballistic-missile submarines patrolled the Sea of Japan; they were ordered to test the limits of US reactions in response to the Americans' deployment of Pershing II missiles in Europe. The Soviet submarines operating in the Sea of Japan could quickly be turned against Chinese and US targets, while two regiments of naval Tu-22 Backfire bombers (a total of 40 aircraft) deployed in the Far East could confront US aircraft-carrier groups. The new D-class submarines could launch ballistic missiles at the United States from positions in the north-west Pacific and the Sea of Okhotsk. Since 1981 the Soviets had installed 72 new SS-20 launchers in the Far East; this force now comprised 162 launchers, capable of releasing 486 nuclear warheads: 'These launchers enable the Soviets to threaten more of the growing numbers of sensitive military targets in China [two lines not declassified].' Another 40 Tu-22s Backfires were based near the Sino-Soviet border. The CIA claimed that the upgrade of Soviet anti-aircraft units since 1983 was aimed at overall defence of the Pacific coast, rather than simply the border with China.[71]

Since 1985 the Chinese, in their turn, had been establishing 24 combined forces, or 'group armies', to reinforce the 15 border divisions already in place. While the Soviets offered an agreement on confidence-building measures, the non-use of force, and arms reduction, Beijing showed no willingness to proceed, seeking first to reach agreement on the border dispute.[72] The Soviets offered a non-aggression pact in 1987. Beijing also rejected this, aiming confidently at the political normalisation of Sino-Soviet relations through the removal of the 'three obstacles'.[73] Nonetheless, the CIA received reports of weekly meetings between officers from the two nations' border units; it was thought that Sino-Soviet military contacts would proceed in parallel with the political dialogue, and that China would continue purchasing dual-use equipment on a limited basis. Beijing was not looking for a significant purchase of Soviet arms or technology-transfer, seeking rather to upgrade Chinese capabilities by acquiring US technology, and to strengthen ties with Washington. There would not be 'genuine military cooperation' between China and the Soviet Union, according to the CIA's assessment.[74]

The planned withdrawal of the Soviets from Afghanistan had an impact on Sino-Soviet relations. The CIA noted:

> The beginning of Soviet withdrawals probably helped convince the Chinese that the Soviets were, as they claimed, really pressing Vietnam to resolve the Cambodian problem. Completion of the withdrawal may encourage China to further upgrade the Sino-Soviet political dialogue.[75]

Gorbachev's reform programme and Deng Xiao-ping's modernisations seemed to create a momentum for upgrading Sino-Soviet relations: 'new thinking' was becoming more influential among the leaders of China and the USSR. By the mid-1980s the standard, vociferous quarrels about socialist doctrine had waned. In any event, since the time of Andropov the official Soviet line on the Chinese threat and the Chinese military had changed, to the extent that no articles were now to be found in the military journal *Voennaia Mysl*, which in the 1970s had published the most pessimistic military analyses. The significant reduction – of one million men – in China's military convinced Soviet academics and military strategists that no Chinese menace was lurking over the horizon. Furthermore, China was showing an increasing interest in development projects, industry and trade.[76]

During roughly the same period, the Chinese acquired defensive weaponry from the United States, and Washington cleared the sale of high-tech electronics for the Chinese F-8 fighter. Other sales in 1986 included the modernisation of a large-calibre artillery plant, torpedoes, and four artillery radars (though not all these items had been delivered before Washington suspended the programme after the Tiananmen massacre in June 1989).[77] The intelligence liaison, however, continued: US intelligence personnel were allowed to observe Soviet nuclear tests from Chinese facilities.[78] Most importantly, Gorbachev and his reform-minded Politburo members and deputies did not understand Sino-American military collaboration to be a threat to the Soviet Union, as Brezhnev and his Sinologists had.[79]

According to the CIA, Gorbachev privately expressed 'considerable suspicion' of Chinese foreign-policy motives, but worked hard to improve Sino-Soviet relations, knowing that defence cuts contributed to the survival of the Soviet economy. He increased pressure on Vietnam to withdraw its forces from Cambodia, decreased the number of Soviet troops in Mongolia and left Afghanistan, while calling repeatedly for a Sino-Soviet summit. On 18 January 1989, he announced that 75 per cent of the Soviet forces in Mongolia would be redeployed in the USSR, and in an earlier speech (on 7 December 1988) had hinted that ground forces in the Far East would be reduced by some 250,000 troops.[80]

Eventually, on 15–18 May 1989, the Sino-Soviet summit took place. Gorbachev, whose reforms attracted the applause of Chinese students, demonstrated his charisma. At the same time Deng Xiao-ping invited three US warships to visit Shanghai to remind Gorbachev of the growing Sino-American collaboration. The rift between the communist parties of China and the Soviet Union vanished, with Gorbachev and Deng Xiao-ping shaking hands. The Cambodia question was not fully resolved, but left to the foreign ministries to discuss.[81]

The CIA maintained from the eve of the summit that both parties had been struggling to find an accommodation over the final communiqué:

> A variety of reports indicate that the two sides are still trying to work out differences on communiqué language especially dealing with a Cambodian settlement and that Soviet Deputy Foreign Minister Rogachev may have arrived early to iron out a compromise.[82]

A secret source (the name remains classified) 'expressed concern recently that Chinese student demonstration would distract attention from summit and that Chinese officials may even partially blame Moscow for exacerbating the problem because students view Gorbachev as a hero of political reform'.[83] On Sino-Soviet relations at the military level, the CIA, the NSA and the DIA all agreed that

> Moscow's decision to allow a permanent Chinese presence in Khabarovsk – its Far East Military District headquarters – is a major sign of reduced tensions and may lead to progress on settling the border demarcation dispute over the islands opposite the city.[84]

In addition, 'Special intelligence suggests the Soviet defence industry has been investigating the feasibility of co-producing an export model of the T-72 tank with Beijing.' In early February 1989, the Soviet Nizhniy Tagil Tank Plant drafted a list of components for the T-72M1 that could be produced in China. The Soviet army maintained only 1,000 of this advanced model in the Far East. In any case, the Chinese, argued the CIA, would continue to purchase Western-made defence systems.[85] There was also some suspicion of a Sino-Soviet intelligence-sharing scheme: 'The Chinese and Soviet military establishments may also begin a dialogue on regional affairs and limited intelligence exchanges – areas which Beijing had in the past refused to consider [rest of paragraph, some seven more lines, not declassified].'[86]

As for the reaction to the student protests, the fact that the ceremony venue was moved and that the main body of students were not

expelled was interpreted as a 'temporary consensus' among Chinese
leaders, who were still debating the issue:

> [source not declassified] told [source not declassified] late last week
> several hardliners within the Politburo as well as middle ranking
> cadres in Beijing and Shanghai oppose General Secretary Zhao's
> conciliatory approach ... Deng Xiao-ping has become increas-
> ingly disengaged from the debate.[87]

Meanwhile, GCHQ was intercepting communications of military units
deployed in Beijing, informing Whitehall in time that the Chinese
intention was clearly to crush the students; no Chinese military
echelon was to question the orders it was given.[88]

The demise of communism in Eastern Europe and the student
unrest in China had a short-term effect on Sino-Soviet relations. Beijing
leaked to the press a classified Central Committee paper criticizing
the Soviet Union for the events in Eastern Europe, and in early 1990
the official criticism became more intense. But Moscow responded
calmly. Deputy Foreign Minister Rogachev flew to Beijing to reassure
the Chinese leaders, but mainly to show the intent to continue with the
improvement in their countries' relations.[89] The Chinese showed themselves realists. Li Peng, now premier, visited Moscow as planned in April
1990 and signed an agreement on guiding principles of mutual and
balanced force reductions and confidence-building measures. Military
collaboration increased to the extent that, in 1991, Beijing purchased a
squadron of Su-27s.[90]

In May 1991, during Jiang Zemin's visit to Moscow, an agreement
was signed on the eastern part of their borders that included one river
island. Damanskii/Zhenbao island, the location of the 1969 war, was
transferred to Chinese sovereignty. The other islands still claimed
by China (Bolshoi Ussuriiskii/Heixiazi and Tarabarov/Yinlong)
were conveniently omitted from the document.[91] On the eve of the
1989 summit, the CIA informed the White House that Damanskii
had already been transferred to China, and that unarmed Chinese
soldiers were patrolling there; this 'could be a signal to Moscow that
China will not place major military installations on Heixiazi island if

it is [also] returned'.[92] In any event, China approached the territorial dispute with caution in a bid to avoid any precedent-setting, keeping in mind its disputes with India over its borders and the Spratly islands. The CIA's assessment with reference to an intention on Gorbachev's part to hand back Heixiazi, meanwhile, turned out to be mistaken.[93]

As for Pakistan, China increased its arms sales, by the mid-1980s surpassing the amount of US-made weaponry delivered to Islamabad. By the autumn of 1992, the CIA had calculated that 75 per cent of Pakistan's armour and more than 50 per cent of its aircraft were provided by China, which also played a major role in the maintenance of the equipment. After the suspension of US foreign aid to Pakistan, decided upon by the Bush administration in June 1989 in the light of Islamabad's obduracy in pursuing its nuclear programme, China became the primary arms supplier to Islamabad. Sino-Pakistani collaboration might also have had a nuclear or secret intelligence role; this can be inferred from the CIA assessment:

> Chinese support continues to include joint projects, such as the Sandak copper mine; financial and military aid, including [half line not declassified], cultural and technical exchanges; cooperation in defence and space technology, such as the launch of the first Pakistani meteorological satellite; and high level visits.[94]

Counterbalancing India was a strategic aim for the Chinese. As early as January 1990, the CIA noted: 'If New Delhi decided to escalate its production of nuclear weapons, Beijing's response would seek to preserve Chinese nuclear superiority and protect Pakistani sovereignty.'[95]

7

THE CIA AND GORBACHEV

Upon becoming secretary-general of the CPSU, Mikhail Gorbachev captured the full attention of the CIA and the rest of the Anglo-American intelligence community. Robert Gates, then deputy director of the CIA, later commented that the 'CIA had been enthusiastic about Gorbachev since he emerged as Andropov's protégé early in 1983. We knew a lot about him.'[1]

This chapter, being based on contemporary reports, will outline the flaws in predicting Gorbachev's intentions. The Soviet leader had already been noted as a protégé of Andropov and Suslov, and during his December 1984 visit to London he seized the media spotlight. The CIA assessment commented: 'Accompanied by his chic wife, he demonstrated a sense of humor, mercurial intelligence and sophisticated style that made him an instant media sensation.' Prime Minister Thatcher did not hide her favourable impression of Gorbachev: 'I like Mr Gorbachev. We can do business together.'[2] Thatcher and Gorbachev had received briefings on each other from Oleg Gordievsky, a key KGB officer in London recruited by MI6. Nonetheless, Gordievsky was wrong when he argued that Gorbachev was 'just another Soviet apparatchik'.[3] Thatcher was not carried away by the judgement of her spy.

The prime minister informed Reagan about her good impressions of Gorbachev, as well as passing on her misgivings about the SDI (though in her memoirs she later applauded the programme).[4] In any event, Gorbachev was considered a leader who lacked the 'killer instinct' of former Soviet leaders; hard work and powerful patrons had led him to be elected, not purges, coups or military achievements: 'He has a self-confidence and freedom from paranoia noticeably lacking in the old guard.'[5] However, Gates admitted that 'much of what CIA knew in 1985 about Gorbachev's personality and style was from his visit to Canada in 1983 and his visit to Britain.'[6] Indeed, Secretary Shultz complained about the CIA's 'thin knowledge' on the eve of Gorbachev's election.[7]

The CIA's rank and file struggled to identify his exact intentions (the patience shown by Beijing, in waiting through the first two years of Gorbachev's term in office for Soviet policies to emerge, was not a characteristic of the American mindset). The main thesis of their estimates was notoriously flawed, although based on accurate factual intelligence from official statements, propaganda and the monitoring of troop deployments. CIA Director Casey, his deputy Gates and the rest of the CIA Sovietologists in the Directorates of Intelligence and of Operations agreed on the premise that Gorbachev *had* to be a hard-liner, having enjoyed the backing of Andropov and Suslov in his fast-track ascent to the Politburo. The first CIA assessment of the secretary-general (under the title 'Gorbachev, the new broom', dated 27 June 1985) was dispatched to the White House. The Soviet leader was focusing on the fight against corruption, it said, but would not seek radical reform in foreign and domestic policy. Gorbachev was 'the most aggressive and activist Soviet leader since Khrushchev', it was remarked.[8] (Comparisons with Khrushchev increased US angst about a Soviet adventurist style similar to that which had caused the 1962 Cuban missile crisis.) Reagan needed no further convincing as to the aspirations and personality traits of his opponent. On 7 April he rejected, as mere propaganda ploys, the Soviet leader's proposals for a halt to the deployment of SS-20s, Pershing II and cruise missiles in Europe, and on 17 April for a moratorium on nuclear tests. Thatcher (mistakenly) agreed with Reagan.[9]

In addition, the president received intelligence under the ultra-secret classification 'Veil': a secret source disclosed top-level consultations in the Kremlin that concluded with Gorbachev deciding to escalate the war in Afghanistan by giving the Red Army another chance to win. A surge of forces had been deployed; operations had been underway in 1984–85. (Later it emerged that the Veil intelligence was accurate but misleading; a retrospective critique found that CIA analysts had sided with Director Casey's understanding and views of hostile Soviet intentions, his assumption being that the Soviets had no plans to negotiate or to withdraw from Afghanistan.)[10]

The Veil intelligence was indeed a coup in 1985, but the surge in Soviet forces (which had been decided by the Politburo in Chernenko's time – Gorbachev merely saw it through) should have been assessed in a comparative perspective. After all, the war in Indochina was for the CIA the recent past,[11] and there was an analogy with US strategy over Vietnam: Washington escalated the war with the invasion of Cambodia (April/May 1970) and the mining of North Vietnamese harbours (1972) to secure advantages in the evolving talks with Hanoi. Gorbachev acted in the same way as Nixon had with his 'Vietnamisation' bid. The Soviet leader backed his new Afghan protégé Muhammad 'Najib' Najibullah, the ruthless head of the KHAD who, as president of the Republic of Afghanistan (declared in November 1987), implemented a 'national reconciliation programme' aiming to curb the resistance without sharing power with the Soviet forces or easing their burden. He went on to change the constitution in 1988, and managed to get the Loya Jirga to accept it.

Since 1981, the CIA had been missing a piece of vital intelligence – the Kremlin was in fact serious in seeking to negotiate its way out of Afghanistan. Bearden, the CIA station chief in Islamabad, wrote in his memoirs (published in 2003): 'Though it was not known at the time, Gorbachev took over in the Kremlin with a single, unencumbered goal in Afghanistan: to get out.'[12] Nonetheless, at the end of March 1985 a CIA analysis argued that Gorbachev 'does not seem to have an immediate interest in seeking to revise Soviet goals and strategy' over Afghanistan, and that, in any case, the Soviet Union maintained the economic and military resources to cope with the escalation of the war; the number of its troops and the supplies of war materiel for the Najibullah regime could be increased at will. It was mentioned that the 'inevitable sluggishness and unevenness of the resistance logistic network, shortages in many needed items, food problems and the fragmented nature of the war will probably cause [an increase in] resistance effectiveness only gradually'.[13] The Soviets, confidently, 'have signalled that more outside support will not dissuade them from pursuing their objective of full control over the country'.[14] Most significantly: 'We see no signs that Moscow is now prepared to seek a genuine political solution that requires abandoning Soviet objectives and withdrawing from Afghanistan.' Moscow sought to destabilise the Zia regime in Pakistan, 'but apparently lack[ed] adequate means' to do so.[15]

> For the time being, however, we believe that Moscow prefers to avoid the military costs and risks of a major troop increase. Logistic preparations for an increase of 50,000 troops, for example, would require several months and would probably not decisively affect the course of the war.[16]

The estimate pointed the way to arming the Islamists more effectively. Reagan did not spend much time in debate; on 27 March he readily signed National Security Decision Directive 166 (which remains classified), unleashing the arming of the Mujahedeen as well as support for CIA covert action.[17] The president had already been informed of a lethal incident in East Germany: on 24 March, 80 miles north-west of Berlin, Lieutenant-Colonel Arthur D. Nicholson of the Military Liaison Mission was shot dead by a sentry while on a mission to photograph a storage depot for Soviet tanks. This the Soviets declared was off-limits for the liaison missions; Washington deplored the murder, but did not escalate tensions. (It was not until May 1988 that Dmitri Yazov, the Soviet defence minister, offered a formal apology to Frank Carlucci, his US counterpart.)[18]

Gorbachev knew very well that he would have to rely on the KGB to secure his position and to implement his evolving domestic and foreign-policy agenda. Unknown to the Americans, Gorbachev had criticised the KGB's political reporting once he had entered office. In December 1985, the head of the KGB, Viktor Chebrikov, was called in to a discussion with Gorbachev and other Politburo members, during which the Soviet chairman deplored the 'distortions of the factual state of affairs in messages and informational reports sent to the Central Committee of the CPSU and other ruling bodies'. The meeting concluded with a consensus that all should observe 'the Leninist requirement that we need only the whole truth'.[19]

It was only later realised by the CIA that KGB officers who had supported the invasion in 1981–82 had altered their views, and were now seeking to end the occupation. A 1988 CIA report claimed:

> [one line not declassified] even officers in the KGB who had initially favored intervention began to have doubts by the winter of 1981–82, reporting that 'a majority of KGB officers felt that it was time to close the matter of Afghanistan because the Soviets had become too involved there'; [not declassified, but probably a KGB source] noted that after the election of Gorbachev this sentiment became more pronounced within the KGB.[20]

April 1985 was a very good month for KGB recruitment: a CIA counter-intelligence officer, Aldrich Ames, 'walked in' to the Soviet embassy in Washington, offering to spy for the Kremlin. His offer was gratefully accepted, and within weeks Ames had provided intelligence pinpointing CIA spies in the Soviet military establishment. GRU General Oleg Penkov, KGB officer Oleg Gordievsky and at least 12 other spies within the KGB and GRU were discovered; the majority were executed, though Gordievsky, with the help of MI6, managed to escape to Britain.[21] In addition, the US embassy in Moscow was penetrated throughout the 1980s by informers and signals-intelligence operations, disclosing among much else diplomats' estimates of the war in Afghanistan.[22]

In its May 1985 intelligence assessment, the CIA repeated that 'war weariness does not appear to present a problem' for either the Russians or the Mujahedeen.[23] As for the increase in Soviet forces:

> In our opinion, tactical force adjustments have so far been implemented on only a limited basis, and have not materially improved the security situation. The Soviets have not been willing to

adopt the aggressive, potentially costly tactics – for example low-altitude bombing and helicopter attacks – that could increase their effectiveness against the insurgents.[24]

This was written well before the introduction of the Stinger missile. (In 1984, under Chernenko, 4,000 troops had already been introduced, taking the total up to 110,000, and there was a notable military effort on the borders with Iran and Pakistan. The GRU apparatus was reinforced with a new photo-mapping unit deployed in Kabul, as well as an army-level radio-interception unit with the task of pinpointing the location of rebel transmitters in the mountains.)[25]

In the summer of 1985, General Zaitsev was dispatched to Afghanistan to examine the potential for military victory; he came back with a single suggestion: to seal the borders with Iran and Pakistan – an unattainable goal.[26] In October, Gorbachev invited Karmal to Moscow, urging him to moderate his socio-economic reforms so as not to upset Afghan Islamic customs. He then shocked the Afghan leader by telling him that, by the following summer, the Soviet troops would withdraw and allow the regime to deal alone with the Mujahedeen. The head of the KHAD, Najibullah, attended this meeting, and witnessed Karmal's surprise and consternation.

At a Politburo meeting on 17 October, Gorbachev remarked that Karmal had wrongly assumed that Moscow was more interested in Afghanistan than he was, and thus he expected a continuous Soviet military presence there. Gorbachev urged the other Politburo members to agree to the withdrawal of the occupation force in such a way that the Soviet Union would not lose credibility and status in the eyes of either allies or opponents. In the Politburo's tradition of sycophancy, silence implied concurrence. Ambassador Dobrynin remarked later: 'There was no objection and no strong endorsement, but rather reluctant silent agreement.'[27] Vitaly Chernayev, the foreign-affairs advisor to Gorbachev who attended the meeting, remarked in his diary:

Gorbachev has finally made up his mind to put an end to it ... Marshal Sokolov took the floor twice, and it was obvious that he was ready to pull out of there and had no plans for giving Karmal any indulgences.[28]

Nonetheless, from March 1985 up to February–March 1986 Gorbachev, in public, followed the propaganda rhetoric of Brezhnev, confirming in the CIA's eyes that he was also intransigent.[29] Without access to the minutes of the meeting or to a talkative participant, the CIA was quite unable to discover the 'silent agreement' of the Politburo members; thus its analysis focused on official statements, propaganda and the profiling of Gorbachev as a protégé of Andropov and Suslov.

Gorbachev now opted to oust Karmal (who had after all been deemed inefficient by the KGB as early as 1982–83) and to replace him with Najibullah. The GRU considered the latter a Pashtun nationalist, 'an intelligent, clever and vicious politician' with no alcohol vice like Karmal, determined that the regime should do more to defeat the rebels.[30]

President Reagan was informed of Afghan policy on the eve of his meeting with Gorbachev. The CIA, in its 6 November 1985 assessment, put the Soviet troop increases for 1984–85 at up to 7,500 men, remarking on 'more forceful measures to suppress the insurrection's growing capabilities'.[31] (This contradicted the May 1985 analysis mentioned above, which had discounted the possibility of a more aggressive effort by the Soviet forces.)

On 14 August 1986, a CIA estimate argued that Moscow was continuing to avoid matters of substance in US–Soviet talks on Afghanistan. There was a consensus among the Directorate of Intelligence analysts that, while the Soviets exhibited a certain willingness to talk with the Americans on regional conflicts involving communist regimes (such as in Afghanistan), this was merely part of a strategy to mount pressure against the Reagan doctrine from his critics in Congress. By the same CIA reasoning, Moscow was assumed to be trying to link regional conflicts with US–Soviet arms-control talks, 'generating a further incentive to pressure the [US] administration to hold back'.[32] In the analysts' eyes, Gorbachev and his reform-minded officials were attempting to show 'statesmanship' by avoiding mention of the US as a power implicated in 'neoglobalism' and 'state terrorism'; but they remained firm in 'not necessarily' wanting to boost regional conflict resolution and arms talks. So far, the Soviet representation in the talks was confined to mid-level officials with no policy-making authority.[33] 'Almost certainly' the Soviets were not willing to negotiate with Washington to resolve the conflicts in Afghanistan, Nicaragua, Angola or Cambodia, but 'they might see the talks as a means of smoking out US intentions', remarked the authors of the estimate.[34]

In September 1986, SNIE 11-9-86 warned (mistakenly) that Gorbachev wanted US–Soviet relations to return to a détente-like framework, in a bid to appear flexible before the American and European elite and public audiences on arms-reduction talks, again so as to increase pressure on the Reagan administration and to assess to what extent he could secure real concessions, the chief aim of which was to constrain SDI and other US defence programmes.[35] (Indeed, the October 1986 Reykjavik summit collapsed because the development of the much-feared SDI could not be stopped, as Gorbachev had repeatedly asked.)[36]

At the 13 November 1986 Central Committee meeting, Gorbachev was clear: Moscow had to finish the war within a year or, at a maximum, two years.[37] Reinvigorating the talks with Pakistan was of major importance for a regional accord. Gorbachev and Marshal Akromeev (who made a proposal to take over operations in Pakistan) sounded sure that a Soviet withdrawal from Afghanistan would not mean US military deployment in the country: [The Americans] are not going to go into Afghanistan with armed forces', remarked the Marshal. The Central Committee again agreed with Gorbachev's recommendation – to plan for withdrawal, to allow Najibullah to take the initiative in national reconciliation, and to approach Pakistan.[38]

On 27 February 1987, Gorbachev met Italian Minister of Foreign Affairs Giulio Andreotti. The Soviet leader made obvious his intention to negotiate an end to the war. He emphasised that, according to 'very reliable sources', the Americans intended to set obstacles in the way of a settlement 'by any means', knowing that if Moscow succeeded they would lose in their propaganda war to cast the Soviets in a bad light. Andreotti replied that he was aware of this information from Pakistani diplomats. Gorbachev continued: 'We follow US policy very closely and respond to signals which come from reasonable, realistic circles ... we have a positive frame of mind but not everything depends on us.'[39]

By August 1987 the CIA, in assessing Gorbachev's foreign-policy apparatus, claimed that the secretary-general of the CPSU had indeed 'moved systematically to overhaul all key foreign policy making bodies [and had] made himself the final arbiter of these [inter-service] differences, enhancing his power over the decision making process'. The military's recommendations faced more challenges from the Politburo than earlier; Gorbachev continued to use flexible tactics rather than to seek the resolution of all disputes with the United States.[40]

In a 20 September 1987 report entitled 'Moscow's Afghan Quagmire: no end in sight after eight years', the CIA insisted that Gorbachev was showing flexibility, but had no intention of resolving the Afghan question. Gorbachev might have called Afghanistan 'a bleeding wound' in his February 1986 speech to the CPSU Congress, withdrawing six regiments in the autumn of 1986 and raising the issue of a timetable for withdrawal at the Geneva talks, but 'these signals and gestures appear to have been primarily propaganda tools designed to put Islamabad and Washington on the defensive in the hope of securing "reciprocal" concessions'.[41] By early 1987, Moscow had signalled its intention of withdrawing, and of persuading Pakistan to accept an agreement, but there were no changes in the substance of Soviet positions. The Soviets, in parallel with their diplomacy, took the war to Pakistan not only through cross-border raids but also by staging terrorist attacks to foment rebellion against the Zia regime. Gorbachev had no wish to abandon Najibullah, insisting that the PDPA should dominate the future government.[42] The Soviet chairman had to deal with evolving criticism directed at his handling of the Afghan situation and his socio-economic reforms; 'his political vulnerability was underlined by the recent demotion of his ally, Moscow party chief Yeltsin', remarked the analysis.[43] If Gorbachev agreed to accept less in Afghanistan (i.e. by withdrawing the occupation force and accepting a non-PDPA regime), this, together with the side-effects of his reforms, could bring about his downfall.[44]

The analyses of the Directorate of Intelligence were repetitive, establishing a biased thesis that could not be shaken by Secretary of State George Shultz, who believed in Gorbachev's good faith. The Directorate claimed that Gorbachev, with the Afghan reconciliation programme under Najibullah, was simply playing for time and following a general strategy of international public relations. This strategy was coupled with a bombing campaign within Pakistan to convince

Zia to seriously consider an accommodation over Afghanistan. The Afghan regime needed as much support as it could get, and thus a viable withdrawal timetable could not be offered by Moscow. In any case, despite the supply of sophisticated US-made weaponry and increases in casualties among the Soviet military, an October 1987 CIA estimate claimed: 'There is no indication that Moscow has concluded that the war has taken a decisive turn for the worse requiring fundamental revision of their goals.'[45] Analysts got it wrong largely because they did not look back 15 years to Nixon's strategy for ending US involvement in Vietnam by 'Vietnamising' the war, without overtly abandoning Saigon. Gorbachev followed the same strategy: like Nixon, he clearly intended to withdraw and simply struggled to maintain surrogates in place in a bid to save face. The national reconciliation programme was Gorbachev's and Najibullah's own version of 'Afghanising' the war.

Gates followed the same pattern as the CIA in his assessments of Gorbachev and arms development. Two weeks before the Soviet leader arrived in Washington for the December 1987 summit, the CIA deputy director warned that there was

a continuing extraordinary scope and sweep of Soviet military modernization and weapons research development ... we see no lessening of their weapons production. And further, Soviet research on new exotic weapons such as lasers and their own version of SDI continues apace.[46]

The DIA readily agreed with this analysis; despite the INF agreement (under which it was agreed to eliminate 1,846 Soviet Pioneer missiles in return for the destruction of 846 Pershing IIs) and the evident intent of Gorbachev to reach an agreement on nuclear weapons, the Pentagon insisted: 'All evidence points to continuity in the Soviet Union's military policy.'[47] The CIA suspected Gorbachev regarding Afghanistan and nuclear weapons; there also remained the lethal problem of Russian biological weapons. Clearly, the agency lacked secret intelligence; two years later the British would offer essential help. In 1989 MI6 benefited from the defection of a director of Biopreparat, the Soviet organisation responsible for the development of biological weapons (euphemistically called 'work in special problems' by the Soviets). He disclosed a programme for the development of strategic and tactical biological agents resistant to antibiotics; massive quantities had already been weaponised. He assumed that, since Shevardnadze had been informed, Gorbachev was also in the know.[48]

With respect to Afghanistan, Gorbachev led the way. The State Department had received (and believed) his clear back-channel messages. Indeed, on 2 February 1988, Bearden, the CIA chief in Islamabad, was told by the US embassy in Islamabad that, in a week, Gorbachev would announce the start of the withdrawal.[49] Since mid-1987, the Soviets had used Shevardnadze to reiterate their intention of withdrawing troops (though the CIA rank and file could still not be induced to believe it). Shultz was told by Shevardnadze on 16 September 1987 that Moscow intended to leave Afghanistan in 1988: 'We will leave Afghanistan. It may be in five months or a year, but it is not a question of its happening in the remote future.'[50] Bearden claims that Shultz did not reveal this to William Webster, the new CIA director, until November 1987. In any event, the CIA continued to cast doubts on Soviet good faith, with Deputy Director Gates betting that the Soviets would not pull out during the Reagan presidency.[51] Gates himself had dinner with the new KGB chairman, Vladimir Khryuchkov, who referred to the need for a political settlement and mentioned the intention to withdraw.[52] But he was not as unambiguous as Sheverdnadze had sounded to Shultz.

On 8 February 1988, the Soviet chairman made a statement on Soviet television, reprinted in *Pravda* and *Izvestia*, announcing the start of the withdrawal on 15 May, as long as an agreement was reached in Geneva by 15 March. He committed himself to withdrawing a large proportion of the forces in the first half of the process (this was a US–Pakistani demand aired in the talks); the withdrawal was not linked to the formation of a national coalition government in Kabul. The US administration had been calling for a fixed date for starting the withdrawal, but Gorbachev's initiative took them by surprise. In addition, the chairman did not address directly the thorny issue of putting a stop to both the US and USSR providing arms to the rebels and the regime, respectively. Washington's assessment was that Moscow sought simply to leave Afghanistan, and thus Reagan had no good reason to cease arming the Mujahedeen. In vain, Shevardnadze offered a time-table for the withdrawal, attempting to convince Shultz that Najibullah was working for the formation of a national coalition government, and that the Americans should therefore cease arming the insurgents.[53]

The announcement of the withdrawal was a bold and statesmanlike move by Gorbachev, not foreseen by the Anglo-American intelligence community, which for the past three years had put more weight on Soviet propaganda and official positions than on the evolving attitudes of Gorbachev, whose real intentions had always remained secret.

The thesis that Gorbachev was playing for time collapsed, and the CIA rushed to change its assessment. In March 1988, SNIE 11/37-88 was circulated. Up to the present, only the key judgments have been declassified, and no further intelligence or discussion is available. Nonetheless, the phrasing of these judgments shows that there was a reappraisal of existing information, perhaps coupled with favourable analysis of Gorbachev's and his diplomats' latest statements; there was no new intelligence. (In his turn, Secretary of State Shultz must have felt vindicated when the CIA changed its estimation of Gorbachev.) Now the CIA was claiming that the Kremlin had made 'a firm de-cision' to cease the occupation of the country; Gorbachev had built 'a leadership consensus' for withdrawal, but was aware of how slim Najibillah's chances of survival had become. But some unjustified sus-picions, however, remained:

> The Soviets want to withdraw under the cover of the Geneva accords. We believe they would prefer to withdraw without an agreement, however, rather than sign one that formally restricts their right to provide aid and further undermines the legitimacy of the Kabul regime.[54]

However, Gorbachev, like his predecessors, had been working for years to reach an agreement with Washington and Pakistan; the Soviets had no motive to abandon this effort. The estimate claimed that even stalled talks in Geneva would not inhibit the Soviet troops from returning home, while the Mujahedeen would prevail in post-occupation Afghanistan despite their in-fighting. The new regime, controlling only Kabul and the tribal leaders' areas, would be

> Islamic—possibly strongly fundamentalist, but not as extreme as Iran. While anti-Soviet, it will eventually establish 'correct'—not friendly—ties to the USSR. We cannot be confident of the new government's orientation toward the West; at best it will be ambivalent and at worst it may be actively hostile, especially toward the United States.[55]

Sunni fundamentalism was wrongly considered milder than the Shiite version that ruled in Iran. CIA analysts foresaw the anti-American feelings and intentions of the Mujahedeen, but did not alter the policy of the agency, which eventually backed the Islamists in the siege of Jalalabad in 1989 (see below). Ironically, the scenario the CIA judged much less likely pictured the future accurately: 'We also cannot rule out a scenario in which the Kabul regime manages to survive for a protracted period after withdrawal, due to an increasingly divided resistance. The odds of this outcome, in our view, are very small.'[56]

The Geneva Accords (a set of instruments) were concluded on 14 April 1988; the signatories were the United States, the Soviet Union, Pakistan and Afghanistan, but not the Mujahedeen. Non-interference in Afghanistan was agreed upon:

> (3) to refrain from the threat or use of force in any form whatsoever so as not to violate the boundaries of each other, to disrupt the political, social or economic order of the other High Contracting Party, to overthrow or change the political system of the other High Contracting Party or its Government, or to cause tension between the High Contracting Parties;
>
> (4) to ensure that its territory is not used in any manner which would violate the sovereignty, political independence, territorial integrity and national unity or disrupt the political, economic and social stability of the other High Contracting Party;
>
> (5) to refrain from armed intervention, subversion, military occupation or any other form of intervention and interference,

overt or covert, directed at the other High Contracting Party, or any act of military, political or economic interference in the internal affairs of the other High Contracting Party, including acts of reprisal involving the use of force;

(6) to refrain from any action or attempt in whatsoever form or under whatever pretext to destabilize or to undermine the stability of the other High Contracting Party or any of its institutions.[57]

Nonetheless, no signatory government appeared willing to keep its word: the issue of arming the regime and the rebels was not resolved. The United States made a key statement showing its intention:

The obligations undertaken by the guarantors are symmetrical. In this regard, the United State has advised the Soviet Union that the United States retains the right, consistent with its obligations as guarantor, to provide military assistance to parties in Afghanistan. Should the Soviet Union exercise restraint in providing military assistance to parties in Afghanistan, the United States similarly will exercise restraint.[58]

The agreement could be seen as a framework for diplomats who sought to resolve the issue or as a facade for cynical intelligence officers. It enabled the orderly withdrawal cedilla to c (see p. 28) of the Soviets; though it did not serve Moscow's position in the region, the lives of thousands of soldiers were saved. Shevardnadze employed all his diplomatic skill to persuade Najibullah and Abdul Wakil, the latter's foreign minister, to sign the agreement, reassuring them of Moscow's constant support for the regime – which in fact contradicted the Geneva Accords' terms of reference.[59]

Diplomats and intelligence officers did not approach the agreement in a relaxed manner. On 10 April, four days before the conclusion of the Accords, the Ojhri camp near Rawalpindi in Pakistan, the main logistics facility for the arming of the Mujahedeen, was destroyed by a munitions explosion, leaving more than 100 dead and more than 1,000 wounded. Shrapnel from 10,000 tons of munitions was scattered over a 12km radius. The event triggered conspiracy theories implicating the KGB and KHAD in an act of revenge, suggesting the CIA would cease its support for the Mujahedeen while the Russians were leaving, even claiming that the Pakistani military had mounted a cover-up operation to conceal the fact that they held the Stinger missiles which were unaccounted for. Only a week afterwards, the Pentagon spoke of sabotage instigated by the KHAD, while some experts in the CIA hinted at a mere accident; in any event no conclusive proof emerged regarding the cause of the explosions. One Defense Department official claimed that they seemed to belong to a pattern of attacks over the weekend that included an attempted rocket attack on an oil-storage installation in Peshawar, a fire at an ordnance factory in Lahore, and a bomb discovered and defused in Islamabad. At the outset, Zia cautiously referred to 'an extraordinary accident', but a few days later he too blamed sabotage.[60] To this day, the causes of the explosion have not been thoroughly researched. Nonetheless, the Ojhri episode considerably depleted the war-materiel stocks held by the rebels, who had planned with mounting confidence to take over a city once the Soviets had left Afghanistan. Mohammad Yousaf, the head of the Afghan bureau of the ISI until 1987, commented in his memoirs that, after the destruction of the camp, the CIA declined to move swiftly to replace the losses in ammunition and weaponry. Indeed,

> The explosion was followed by the cutback in [the CIA's] shipment of arms. Had they really wanted to, I feel sure that strenuous efforts would have been made to replenish the Ojhri camp. No such efforts materialized; in fact it was not until the following December that further supplies arrived. The CIA knew that delivering arms at that time of the year effectively meant nothing would reach the Mujahedeen for a further three months, by which time the Soviets had gone.[61]

Meanwhile Najibullah was provided with whatever war materiel he asked for, strengthening his defences; he even ended up with Scud missiles. In addition, after the Ojhri incident the ISI was in a state of confusion, which was intensified after the killing of Zia and the ISI head in a helicopter crash in August 1988. The severe depletion of the Mujahedeens' arms stocks – together with a lack of tactical intelligence, of thorough planning and of force coordination – was considered a key factor leading to their defeat in the battle of Jalalabad in March–June 1989. While the CIA had endorsed the attempt to take Jalalabad, Yousaf complained bitterly that 'the US shipments were still substantially less than necessary, the reserve stocks had never been built up again after the Ojhri camp disaster, and there had been little forward planning or dumping of available stocks prior to the battle'.[62]

Meanwhile, the CIA concluded an analysis on the apparent and growing tension between Gorbachev and the KGB. Socio-economic and legal reforms challenged its authority to guarantee internal security, while Gorbachev had stepped up party oversight of its workings. No doubt 'many in the KGB hierarchy' had assumed back in 1984 that Gorbachev was the ideological successor of Andropov, and regretted the appointment of Chernenko; nonetheless they continued to believe in Gorbachev, considering him a man of change. In his turn, Gorbachev, according to a secret source, 'held the foreign intelligence capabilities of the KGB in high regard'.[63] Indeed, in the first plenum, the secretary-general oversaw the election of the KGB chairman, Chebrikov, as a full member of the Politburo. But their relations would be overshadowed by differing views on *glasnost* and *perestroika*. According to a secret source in the autumn of 1986, Chebrikov voiced his criticism of a wide array of the reforms that had been undertaken: 'Since then there [had] been persistent reports by a wide range of sources that Gorbachev intends to replace Chebrikov' to increase his personal control over the KGB.[64] In September 1987, the KGB chief went a step further, openly criticising the reforms in a speech to mark the 110th anniversary of the birth of Felix Dzerzinski, the first head of the Cheka; he claimed they had brought 'undesirable consequences'. Some of his audience – the intelligence rank and file – began to fear that reform might cost them their privileged position in Soviet society.[65] Chebrikov warned repeatedly that *glasnost* enabled foreign intelligence services to spy more easily. In an April 1988 speech he failed to support openness, blaming 'poor' ideological education and Western propaganda for the rise of nationalism in the Caucasus.[66]

The CIA, meanwhile, maintained only limited information on the KGB's attitudes towards economic reform. A secret source 'suggests that while many senior KGB officials welcomed such administrative measures in 1985 ... they became concerned that economic reform would reduce their role in managing sensitive industries in the defence-industrial sector'.[67]

The KGB was leaking rumours on Soviet leaders, noted the CIA: back in 1982 the KGB under Andropov had leaked damaging rumours, both in Moscow and abroad, about Brezhnev and his family; the KGB chairman, it was thought, was seeking to boost his candidacy for the supreme post of secretary-general of the CPSU. In addition, 'Gorbachev's association with KGB officials allowed him to utilize confidential information against his rivals in the struggle for succession in early 1985'. But now it seemed that elements of the KGB had turned against him; rumours were circulating of failed attempts against his life. A secret source 'reported that he was shot in 1986, the target of a bomb attack by Latvian dissidents in April 1987 and poisoned in August 1987'. In addition, 'some reporting also indicates that lower level KGB officials in some areas have been involved in "plotting" against Gorbachev'.[68] A secret source 'reported that he met with individual army commanders to ask their support should the KGB join a political coup, although there is no other reporting to this effect. It is not plausible', remarked the CIA analyst.[69] Over the previous two years KGB officials, siding with conservative, anti-reform Politburo members, had leaked rumours portraying Gorbachev as 'a weak embattled leader and his wife Raisa as pushy, ambitious and a political profligate spender'.[70]

Gorbachev, according to the CIA report, was now aware of the shortcomings of the KGB and its level of nepotism, as revealed by a number of reports. He was also angry that he had received no warning of the rise of nationalism in the Caucasus. In addition, he was critical of the KGB because of the slow reaction of the Ninth Guards Directorate when a West German pilot had landed with his Cessna on Red Square – it had taken the KGB over 30 minutes to arrive at the scene. Secret sources had reported that, in March 1988, Gorbachev had replaced his KGB bodyguards with paratroopers. The CIA commented: 'We have no other information to confirm this claim, however, which appears to reflect popular perceptions of sharp differences between the Secretary General and the KGB.'[71] Meanwhile, Yeltsin and Chebrikov quarrelled, with the former urging reform to curtail the authority of the KGB and the latter blaming him for 'seeing too many foreigners and talking too freely to them'.[72] The CIA estimated that Gorbachev and the KGB had now reached a stand-off.[73] Only if he moved further towards reform of the intelligence services and the legal system would a clash become more visible (and destabilising). The estimate did not name the withdrawal in Afghanistan as a factor that could have inflamed Gorbachev's relations with his spies; in fact, the KGB had backed Gorbachev's agenda (though it seems the CIA was unaware of this). Throughout the summer and autumn of 1988, in heated debates in the Kremlin, the Soviet military, backed by Georgi Kornienko (the deputy foreign minister), argued for reaching an agreement with Masoud and boosting Tanai (the Afghan minister of defence). Shevardnadze joined with Najibullah.[74] Gorbachev skilfully employed Shevardnadze and the KGB to silence the arguments of the military, who wanted to de-escalate combat operations. The Soviet chairman sounded an authoritarian note in the Politburo meeting of 18 September 1988, demanding an end to quarrelling: 'We must carry out the line of the Politburo and not adapt it to individuals in the General Staff or the working group.'[75] (Perhaps the military's strategy was more rational, and could have saved more Soviet soldiers' lives – while simultaneously dividing the Mujahedeen – but Gorbachev had identified the retention of Najibullah after the withdrawal as face-saving.)

During the same period, the British intelligence community remained sceptical of Gorbachev's intentions, even though Reagan appeared more confident and optimistic about reaching an agreement with Moscow. Sir Percy Cradock (the UK ambassador in China during the invasion of Afghanistan, and now the head of the JIC) held firmly to a pessimistic line, claiming (mistakenly) that Gorbachev's decision to leave Afghanistan and to agree to arms cuts was merely

a tactical move on the part of a devoted communist seeking to boost
the Soviet economy. The MoD followed Cradock's logic, pre-empting
any proposal to reduce UK defence spending. For her part, Prime
Minister Thatcher was sounding optimistic by the spring of 1988,
welcoming the scheduled withdrawal of the Soviets from Afghanistan
and the signing of the INF treaty.[76] Meanwhile, Sir Anthony Buff, the
director-general of MI5, retained a more sober and accurate understanding of Soviet intentions, remarking in a post–Cold War interview: 'JIC assessments were maintaining that nothing [in the Kremlin]
had changed, and that it was extremely unlikely that it would change.
I did not agree with this and said so.'[77]

The Soviet withdrawal was an orderly operation that concentrated
on two main routes: from Kandahar, via Laskhar Gah, Farabrud and
Herat, to Kushka, in the USSR (the western route), and from Ghazni
and Gardez, via Kabul, Bagram and Puli Khumri, to Termez, also in
the USSR (the eastern route). The first phase took place between 15
May and 15 August 1988, with 50,000 troops returning home safely;
the second phase was between 15 November 1988 and 18 February
1989. Gorbachev kept to this strict timetable, despite the operational
disadvantages it caused. The Kremlin was mainly interested in showing the White House that there was no question of failing to adhere to
the Geneva Accords. Garrison facilities and war materiel were transferred, following all the necessary procedures, to the Afghan army. The
Mujahedeen attacked and held Konduz briefly, before being expelled
by the Afghan army and Soviet airpower. The final withdrawals were
secured by corridors of steel – armoured vehicles and main battle tanks
moving to cover the rest of the vehicles, providing security on both
sides of the main road.[78] Masoud had been persuaded not to attack the
Soviet forces, and local arrangements for safe passage were facilitated
with the usual bribes and secret deals. But Najibullah (who was preparing to deal unaided with all the Mujahedeen once the Soviets had
left) pressed the Kremlin hard, and eventually Shevardnadze argued
in favour of an operation against Masoud that would break the cease-
fire. The senior officers of the 40th Army had no wish to confront
Masoud, but had no option other than to obey their orders. 'Operation
Typhoon' was launched on 23–25 January 1989 on the southern

approaches to the Salang tunnel. Full air and artillery cover was
provided, and the Mujahedeen were taken by surprise: they had
allowed their presence to become visible, believing that no assault would
take place under the deal agreed with Masoud. According to the Soviet
post-battle damage assessment, 600 rebels were killed; 32 mortars,
15 rocket launchers, 46 heavy machine-guns, ten supply dumps, 36
strong points and 15 trucks were destroyed. Masoud bitterly deplored
the operation in a letter to Soviet Ambassador Vorontsov dated 26
January 1989. (Curiously, the ambassador had given the Mujahedeen
leader advance notice of the upcoming operation.) Masoud wrote:

> I received your warning. The bombings which followed it and
> those crimes which your people committed in Salang and Jabal
> os-Saraj will change nothing ... this forces us to believe that you
> want to impose a dying regime on our Muslim people. This is
> impossible and illogical. We hope that the new Soviet leader-
> ship and its responsible representatives in Afghanistan will act
> in accordance with their own convictions and acquire the cour-
> age to realize reality and act in accordance with it. Respectfully,
> Ahmad Shah Masoud.[79]

As the Soviet withdrawal progressed, the CIA played a secret role in
tactical crisis-management, in parallel with the delays in restocking
the Mujahedeen's arms reserves – as Yousaf had hinted (see above). In
August 1988 a Soviet SU-25 fighter was shot down near the border
with Pakistan. The ISI, as always seeking financial gain, informed the
CIA cell, offering to sell it. Eventually, it was discovered that the nose-
cone, containing advanced electronics, had survived in good condition,
and the CIA authorised the bartering of the cone for six pick-up trucks
and some rockets. After the conclusion of the deal, the Pakistanis
informed the cell that the Russian pilot had also survived, but had
been captured by the Mujahedeen. Bearden urged them not to exe-
cute him, and thereby shake Moscow's confidence in a peaceful withdrawal, and offered to provide more trucks in return for his life. The
rebels accepted, and Bearden tried zealously to convince the pilot to
defect; the latter remained adamant, however, and Bearden contacted

his KGB counterparts to hand him over, which they happily accepted. (This pilot, Colonel Alexander Rutskoi, was to be the leader of a failed coup against President Boris Yeltsin a few years later.)[80]

In December 1988 the CIA was again taken by surprise, the perceptiveness of its prior analysis offered to the White House being called into question: Gorbachev announced at the UN that he intended to cut Soviet military forces by 500,000 troops. Congress rushed to query the CIA, which the following week Doug MacEachin, the chief Sovietologist at the Directorate of Intelligence, tried to defend. Even if the agency had discovered Gorbachev's intentions, 'We never would have been able to publish it, quite frankly … [H]ad we done so, people would have been calling for my head.'[81] Indeed, intentions always remain secret, and bad news and pessimistic estimates always sell better than good news.

The pattern of analysis of the Soviet economy and reform was based on fragmented Soviet official statements that claimed the economy was growing, while in fact it was rapidly collapsing. Mark Palmer, a key Kremlinologist under the administration of George Bush Sr, later admitted that the CIA:

> used to simply take what the Soviets officially announced, discounted it a percent and put it out. And it was just wrong, and anybody who had spent time in the Soviet Union, in the villages and towns and could look around and see that this was just crazy.[82]

Post–Cold War recriminations followed. Admiral William J. Crowe, the JCS chairman, blamed the CIA: 'They talked about the Soviet Union as if they weren't reading the newspapers, much less developed clandestine intelligence.'[83] But the DIA, throughout the 1980s, also followed a pessimistic analysis of Soviet intentions and capabilities; the Pentagon could not evade some of the blame.

On 15 February 1989, the last Soviet troops crossed the Friendship Bridge linking Uzbekistan with Afghanistan. KGB officers and advisers remained in the country, but in a symbolic move General Boris Gromov, commanding the 40th Army, crossed the bridge on foot, the 'last man' to leave Afghanistan. While he and his troops enjoyed the welcome of their families, however, no Kremlin officials were in attendance to receive them. The Soviet chairman made it clear that full television coverage of the withdrawal would do nothing to boost his country's prestige – it should not look like Saigon in April 1975, with panicked refugees and helicopters hovering overhead. Allegedly, he remarked: 'We must not appear before the world in our underwear or even without any ... A defeatist position is not possible.'[84] (One of the ironies of history is that Gromov, who became governor of the Moscow region, and Dmitry Rogozin, the Russian ambassador to NATO, though bitter at the defeat by the CIA in Afghanistan, wrote in 2010 that NATO and the United States must succeed in their counter-insurgency, otherwise a serious threat to Russian security would grow from the Taleban: 'A more challenging issue is to understand the political ramifications for NATO, Western security and the future of Central Asia. It is imperative for all three that NATO keep to its commitment in Afghanistan.')[85]

In February 1989, back in Washington, George Bush – who had just taken the oath as president, renewed the authorisation for CIA covert action in Afghanistan; but there was an amendment: covert action would henceforth focus on the 'self-determination' of the Afghans.[86]

AFTERMATH

CONTINUING COVERT ACTION

With the Soviets out, the Afghan warlords and the regime of Najibullah were left to fight among themselves. The CIA continued to back the Mujahedeen, while giving Masoud modest support, and the ISI channelled more money and resources to Hekmatyar. The post-occupation phase had not been considered by the CIA, as Bearden, the CIA station chief in Islamabad later admitted. Indeed, for US intelligence Afghanistan was yet another Cold War battlefield – not a country to liberate, occupy and help to stand on its own feet, as Germany, Japan and Italy had been after the Second World War. Covert action was put on auto-pilot until Washington had reviewed its Afghan policy. Meanwhile, President Bush, preoccupied with the invasion of Panama, Iraq's attack on Kuwait and the demise of communism in Russia and eastern Europe, appeared less than well-informed about developments in Afghanistan. In 1991, Bearden had a short conversation with the president, who surprised him by asking if the civil war in Afghanistan was still in progress.[1]

Congress's appropriations for covert action were considerably reduced from 1989 onwards, but Moscow continued to supply Najibullah with whatever he requested, save troops and pilots. The CIA tried to find ways of signalling to the Soviets that they should stop doing so. Soon a Shiite Mujahedeen leader was approached – a man who had made a reputation for bomb attacks (which could justly be called a form of terrorism) in Afghan cities. The CIA supplied him with Stingers, and instructions to shoot down a Soviet transport aircraft over Kabul, so as to frighten the Kremlin into de-escalating their aid to Najibullah; the rebels complied, but missed their target. Another CIA-supported operation had boron carbide sludge poured into vehicles' petrol tanks. Again, no positive results were reported, and the aid to Najibullah continued.[2]

The State Department was sceptical about the utility of backing religious extremists (in fact all Afghan warlords were fundamentalists; some called themselves moderates simply to secure politico-military support from foreign governments; no secular royalist existed, and King Zahir Shah remained isolated in Rome throughout the decade, uninterested in Afghan affairs.) Angry debates between diplomats and intelligence officers led to a policy review which, once concluded in 1990, outlined a two-track policy. The State Department would work with the Soviet Union, Prime Minister Benazir Bhutto of Pakistan and the exiled King Zahir Shah on a political settlement, sidelining not only the regime of Najibullah but also extremist leaders like Hekmatyar and Sayyaf. Meanwhile, the CIA would cooperate with the ISI in confronting the Kabul regime, while in parallel it would further develop channels with other leaders like Masoud, Abdul Haq and Ismail Khan, providing them with both money and arms. The calling of one Afghan commanders' *shura* (council) could lead, it was thought, to the formation of a new interim government.[3]

The two-track policy, however, remained only on paper. Efforts to find and boost royalists (if there were any) soon proved unsuccessful. The CIA developed a secret funding channel to Masoud – in one month (May 1989) his brother received $900,000 on his behalf, in addition to the warlord's monthly stipend of $200,000.[4] But Masoud was also an ardent Islamist who was receiving support from Abdullah Azzam and his Arab fighters in Panjir. Azzam was the mentor of Osama Bin Laden, who leaned towards Hekmatyar, whom in turn the CIA-backed ISI was arming.[5] The agency was trapped in a complex web of covert action and of its surrogates' own aspirations, in its bid to overthrow Najibullah. During 1989, the State Department began urging the CIA to abandon Hekmatyar and back the coalition government in exile (composed of the seven ISI-backed warlords). British intelligence sided with this option, but the CIA–ISI–Saudi connection maintained its momentum. In all this, Bhutto concurred in an operation, supported by the ISI, that backed the Mujahedeen in their objective of seizing Jalalabad and proclaiming their own government. The CIA as well as the ISI were optimistic that Najibullah would fall within six to twelve months of the Soviet withdrawal. Even the Chinese agreed, considering the days of the Kabul regime to be numbered. A Chinese government magazine proclaimed that the PDPA was 'unable to recover the momentum' and 'marking time until defeat'.[6]

The offensive commenced in March 1989, but soon failed: despite materiel support from the ISI and CIA, the rebels failed to make ground, lacking coordination and good tactical intelligence as well as adequate arms.[7] It was a victory for Najibullah that damaged the ISI-backed rebels' morale.

In early 1990, the CIA refused a State Department request to cease supporting ISI and Hekmatyar; Pakistani staff officers had visited Washington and informed the agency of plans for a new rebel offensive that could succeed.[8] Masoud and Hekmatyar were now competing for power; in July 1989 the latter killed eight of Masoud's senior commanders in an ambush, and Masoud, who had intercepted Hekmatyar's communications with a British-donated frequency scanner, promptly retaliated.[9]

On 7 March 1990, Defence Minister Shahnawaz Tanai, secretly in partnership with Hekmatyar and the ISI, launched a coup against Najibullah. After brief fighting in Kabul the attempt failed, and Tanai escaped to Pakistan.[10]

In October, the CIA discovered that Hekmatyar was moving 700 trucks mounted with rockets to start an indiscriminate bombardment of Kabul. Fears of mass civilian casualties compelled the CIA to act, and only very strong pressure on Islamabad led the ISI to call off its surrogate's attack. This was a case of using good tactical intelligence, fast policy formation and influence over the Pakistanis.[11] The, ISI of course, was less than happy at this outcome.

A week or so later, a Mujahedeen commanders' *shura* was convened in Chintral, Pakistan, with Masoud in attendance; the ISI tried to show that it sought to bring Masoud onto its own side, but essentially it supported only Hekmatyar.[12] Meanwhile, Najibullah's regime persisted. After the end of the Gulf War the CIA secretly transferred captured Iraqi T-55 and T-72 tanks from Pakistan, to be turned over to the Mujahedeen of Hekmatyar, Jalaluddin Haqqanni and other warlords (but excluding Masoud). This increase in conventional capabilities, however, failed to bring the rebels any nearer to victory. Already the CIA had reported that the country was turning into a training centre for Islamist guerrillas to be dispatched by the ISI to fight India in Kashmir; the agency also issued a secret warning to the Indians on the danger of US-made long-range sniper rifles, supplied earlier to the Mujahedeen, being turned against them.[13]

Back in Moscow, after the failed coup against Gorbachev on 19 August 1991, the Russian leader decided to suspend all aid to Najibullah; the Americans reciprocated. On 13 September, Secretary of State James Baker and his Soviet counterpart, Boris Pankin, agreed to cut off aid by the end of 1991. The legal authority of the CIA to conduct covert action in Afghanistan expired with the dissolution of the Soviet Union, on 1 January 1992, but the CIA station in Islamabad maintained its secret sources. Some spies were also assigned to the covert operation to buy back Stinger missiles.[14] Effectively, the clandestine confrontation was over for the Americans and the British. The CIA's Afghan Operating Directive was altered: the collection of intelligence on Masoud's, Hekmatyar's and others' intentions and capabilities was to cease. Spies could be recruited as long as they reported only on drugs, terrorism and the Stingers.[15] The US human-intelligence capability was 'weak to non-existent' in Afghanistan, according to Ambassador Peter Tomsen (who resided in Washington since the embassy in Kabul could not be re-opened due to the security situation there).[16]

The civil war in Afghanistan dragged on; the regime was collapsing. On 16 April 1992, Najibullah was forced by his own party to resign, and sought refuge in the UN compound in Kabul, where he stayed for the next four years. Masoud outmanoeuvred Hekmatyar and reached Kabul, setting up a loose government with him as defence minister. Initially Sibghatullah Mojaddedi, the head of the interim government (one of the seven warlords receiving aid from the ISI) was named president, only to be replaced after two months by Burhanuddin Rabbani (an Islamist scholar and leader of Masoud's political party; he was killed by the Taleban in September 2011). Hekmatyar laid siege to Kabul, but despite the devastation and massive civilian casualties he caused, the new government did not crumble.

By 1994 the Taleban, a youth militia led by veterans of the war against the Soviet Union, gained influence over the Pashtun population and, backed by the ISI, achieved surprising military victories against competing warlords.[17] Their movement had been structured in late 1988 by the ISI's Quetta office, which formed and armed the Argestan *shura* to be led by ultra-conservative Pakistani and Afghan mullahs, also veterans of the war against the Soviets. After the latter had pulled out, the office directed the *shura* to confront the secular Durrani tribal aristocracy seeking to restore their position in Kandahar (their high status in the region having lasted for almost two centuries, after Ahmad Shah Durrani in alliance with Persian King Nadir Shah had defeated the Mirwais Hotak dynasty, expelling them from Kandahar). The ISI took advantage of the ancient vendetta between the Durranis and the Ghilzais Hotaks (of which Mullah Omar was a member). The latter tribal group was composed of Ghilzai Pashtuns with only a poor religious education who sought revenge against the Durrani clan and other ethnic communities; more importantly, the leadership of the Taleban movement was drawn from among its members.[18]

The US embassy in Islamabad maintained a secret source it considered both reliable and well-informed, who disclosed in April 1994 that the ISI, with Pakistani officers, was helping the Taleban in their attack against Spin Boldak, to the extent that Pakistani artillery from Frontier Corps bases was providing covering fire.[19] US diplomats who met with a delegation of middle-ranking Taleban in February 1995 concluded:

> The meeting with the Taleban representatives was more significant for what was omitted than for what was said. Some of the Taleban responses appeared coached and the overall impression was one of disingenuity and a degree of deception.[20]

Later the same month, a profile of Mullah Omar was provided by an ostensibly more reliable individual, who declared him to be close to the Taleban but not a fighter who accompanied them in battle. US diplomats and intelligence, anxious to discover the identities of the Taleban leaders, took this source seriously. He claimed that there was no foreign support being provided to the movement, and that its leading personalities prohibited contacts with foreigners so as to safeguard their reputation. Nonetheless, 'since the United States was an important and unbiased friend', he had decided to talk to a US diplomat.[21] He disclosed that Mullah Omar, the leader, was receiving financial and materiel support from Haji Bashar, one of Hekmatyar's Hizb-I-Islami commanders during the war against the Soviets. Omar belonged to the Hotak clan of the 'Mirwais Hotak who briefly ruled Afghanistan before Ahmed Shah Durrani. He had built a reputation as a brave and honest Islamist, but his religious education had been 'on a small scale', barely achieving the level of *mawlavi* (the graduate of a madrassa).[22] The source stated that the Taleban received support and recruits from 'the madrassa network' in Pakistan. Sophisticated weaponry such as fixed-wing aircraft, helicopters and tanks were operated by former Afghan military officers 'who were being paid twice the usual salary of 20,000 Afghanis a month', while all Taleban were volunteers supported by the population of the country.[23] The movement's leadership structure was composed of two bodies: the 'high council' of eight (with Mullah Omar at the top) and a 22-member *shura* assigned to administrative matters. The Taleban leader's immediate aim was to establish an Islamic state under Sharia law,[24] and he tried to deceive the Americans into believing that his movement would respect the Shiites in Afghanistan, as well as other ethnicities.[25] In any case, no clear picture of the Taleban could emerge. The Hotaks' factor, and their vendetta against the Durranis that the ISI had taken advantage of, could not be understood and properly assessed by either the CIA or the State Department.

The covert support of Russia, India and Iran for the Masoud camp commenced at this juncture, Moscow fearing Islamist insurgencies in the Central Asian states of what had now become the Commonwealth of Independent States (CIS). The revolt in Chechnya in 1995–96 pointed the way to a rising threat – the international fundamentalist movement was receiving support from the Taleban and from Afghan warlords. China was also nervous at the rise of the Taleban. In 1998 Masoud had a secret meeting with Chinese delegates, and in July 2000 the Chinese foreign minister asked Pakistan to put pressure on the Taleban not to support Uyghur fighters trained in Afghan terrorist camps.[26]

Abandoning Hekmatyar, Pakistan and Saudi Arabia now backed the Taleban, who went on to seize Kabul, and on 27 September 1996 killed Najibullah, installing their own regime and sidelining both Masoud and Hekmatyar, who fled to the north. The new rulers proclaimed the Emirate of Afghanistan. At that time the prevailing (but mistaken) assessment in Washington was that 'The Taleban does not practise the anti-US style of fundamentalism practised by Iran. It is closer to the Saudi model.'[27]

The US administration showed some interest in engaging the Taleban diplomatically in a bid to obtain permission for a US oil company to set up a pipeline. In early 1997, there was an effort to convince the Taleban to sell the CIA the Stingers they held. The Taleban argued that they would need them in their fight against Iran; the CIA operative sent to negotiate the return of the missiles failed in his mission.[28] Soon it became evident that the Taleban were not willing to develop full diplomatic relations with the Americans, who abstained from covert action but focused on operations against Bin Laden, who was living in Afghanistan. A plan for a kidnap operation by CIA surrogates, though drafted, was not forwarded to the White House; George Tenet, the CIA director, feared civilian casualties. Eventually, after the attacks on the US embassies in Kenya and Tanzania in August 1998, cruise missiles were launched against Islamist bases in Afghanistan. Nonetheless, the White House had no intention of toppling the Taleban; covert action focused on the hunt for Bin Laden, and Masoud had now realised that Washington viewed him simply as a tactical intelligence asset in that operation. Russia's own covert action, meanwhile, aimed to help Masoud's United Front/Northern Alliance to defeat the Islamist regime.[29] Clearly Masoud and his allies took their secret partnership with Russia more seriously.

Two days after the American missile attack, Mullah Omar talked directly (through an interpreter) on the telephone with Michael Malinowksi, director of the Southeast Asia/Pakistan/Afghanistan/ Bangladesh Bureau of the State Department. The initiative took Washington by surprise – it was the first time the Taleban leader had sought to communicate directly with the Americans. He claimed to doubt that Bin Laden had been implicated in the terrorist attacks in Kenya and Tanzania, and reproduced the usual anti-American rhetoric, warning that strikes against Afghanistan would be 'counterproductive'. It was reported that Omar had 'conducted himself in a careful and controlled manner. At no time did he bluster or threaten.' In any case,

> Omar's contact with a [US Government] official is rather remarkable, given his past reclusive nature and his past avoidance of contact with all things American. It is indicative of the seriousness of how the Taleban view the US strikes and our anger over Bin Laden. The Taleban, despite implying that we should initiate the contact, are interested in a dialogue with us on Bin Laden and other issues. This is a long way, however, from the Taleban doing the right thing on Bin Laden.[30]

In the meantime, espionage operations had a rare success: in 1999 secret intelligence acquired by the French and Americans revealed two death lists compiled by the Taleban regime. Abdul Ahad Karzai, the father of today's Afghan president, had already been murdered, and his son's name also appeared in a 'priority assassination list' signed by Mullah Omar.[31]

Russian aid to Masoud increased, with more armour and ammunition, as well as infrastructure construction (also, according to a Russian defector, a former intelligence officer, Russian intelligence personnel were assigned to the training of Masoud's forces).[32] US imagery intelligence revealed that Russian engineers were building a new bridge across the Amu Darya, in order to facilitate supplying the warlord, and had already upgraded the airport at Taloquan to accommodate more flights to Bagram (before the latter was captured by the Taleban) to support Masoud's forces. Moscow also submitted a request to Tajikistan to allow the airbase at Kolyob, in the south of that country, to be used as a logistics facility and airfield for Masoud's bombers; the request was granted. In early 2001, Masoud met with Igor Sergeyev, the Russian defence minister, in Dushanbe, the capital of Tajikistan, and the warlord was granted more armour and war materiel. Along with financial aid, India dispatched aircraft technicians as early as 1996 to support Masoud's small air force; Indian military advisers were sent to discuss with Masoud and his allies, the Northern Alliance, possible operations against the Taleban.[33]

Chinese security services noted the presence of Uyghur fighters receiving training and fighting alongside the Taleban. Later, when some of them returned to Xuar, they were implicated in terrorist attacks and training of Islamists. In addition, Beijing was worried by radical Islamism's potential spread to Uzbekistan and Kyrgyzstan. Intelligence liaison with Moscow and other CIS members was upgraded in December 1999, with the signing of a Memorandum on the Organisation of Practical Cooperation between the heads of the intelligence and law-enforcement agencies of China, Russia, Kazakhstan, Kyrgyzstan and Tajikistan. Another agreement, a Convention on the Fight against Terrorism, was signed by all of the above plus Uzbekistan; the signatories established the Shanghai Cooperation Organisation in June 2001.[34]

Meanwhile, the CIA was suffering from a lack of both secret sources and specialists. In 2001, a former CIA officer admitted that the Directorate of Operations 'never developed a team of Afghan experts'. Intelligence officers stationed in Islamabad could not speak Afghan dialects, and stayed in the country for only two to three years[35] – too short a time to develop high-grade secret sources. The agency provided Masoud with modest funding and with communications equipment as part of the overall project to locate Bin Laden. The State Department and the White House were in no mood to boost Masoud's capabilities to topple the Taleban. In his turn, in 2000 and 2001 he declined a US–French proposal to deploy troops in the areas under his control – ostensibly special-forces teams to cooperate in a raid against Bin Laden.[36]

The United States declared its neutrality towards the factions in the Afghan civil war. To the State Department, the Taleban were nationalists rather than radical Islamists fomenting terrorist attacks all over the world.[37] Nonetheless, in private the Americans acknowledged and did not object to the secret arming of Masoud and his allies by Russia, Iran and India.[38] In any event, Washington disregarded intelligence to the effect that Pakistan was conducting a 'creeping invasion' committing more than 10,000 military personnel, arms and logistics to support the Taleban against the United Front.[39]

Eventually, the covertly supplied arms aid saved the Northern Alliance from annihilation, but failed to turn the tables on the battlefield. The fall of the Taleban was only brought about by the US/UK invasion of 2001, following the 9/11 terrorist attacks on New York and Washington. Two days before the attacks, Masoud was assassinated by al-Qaeda, but until May 2011 Osama Bin Laden escaped US intelligence. Mullah Omar is still at large; unconfirmed stories of his murder by the ISI – or of ISI support for him – are circulating, and the Taleban continue to pose a direct threat to the government of Afghanistan.

Reflections without hindsight

Doves as well as hawks are liable to flinch in the face of both the enemy and the ally. In January 1980, Carter and Brzezinski, who initiated US covert action in Afghanistan, forgot that China, Pakistan and Saudi Arabia, as key long-term contenders with Soviet influence, ideology and policy in the region, would certainly have given unilateral financial and military support to the Mujahedeen. Indeed, in early January 1980, the Saudis had already announced the formation of committees to raise funds for the rebels. Besides, the CIA had secret intelligence from April 1979 that the Chinese were considering embarking on a policy of support for the Mujahedeen; Beijing intended to proceed with covert action, while Pakistan's strategy under Zia was to interfere in Afghan affairs. Had the White House refused to pay for the Afghan resistance (providing Pakistan only with humanitarian aid for the refugees), Islamabad would have had no other option but to arm the Mujahedeen out of their own resources; but Carter and Vance flinched again, easing the pressure on Pakistan over its nuclear programme. (Eventually, in February 1989, President George Bush Sr decided to exert strong pressure himself, suspending military aid to Pakistan from 1990 onwards; but it was too late – the Chinese had provided Islamabad with vast amounts of military hardware, and the Pakistanis had nearly completed their nuclear weapon.) Reagan and Casey had also blinked, by increasing aid to Pakistan and the Mujahedeen, and had wrongly assumed that Zia acted in good faith when he had reassured them that his country was not developing a nuclear weapon. Proliferation of weapons of mass destruction put US national security in jeopardy, while Afghanistan became yet another tactical battlefield in the Cold War. In essence, the militarily weak Pakistan took advantage of the superpower's eagerness to come to its aid. From 1980 onwards, US intelligence had reassured the White House that Pakistan was under no threat of a Soviet invasion, and thus that there was no compelling reason for Reagan to step up collaboration with Islamabad. In the meantime, Reagan and Casey blinked when dealing with the Iranians, assuming that a secret arms deal could liberate hostages held by Hezbollah; the Iran–Contra scandal exploded at the same time that the Mujahedeen received their first Stingers, the delivery of which showed that the CIA under Casey was uninterested in maintaining deniability. This was understood by Zia, who realised that he could keep up pressure on the Americans to serve his policy agenda on Afghanistan. In the meantime, he could evade any real pressure from Washington to abandon his nuclear programme.

Britain also blinked, in the sense that London rushed to Pakistan's aid without asking questions. Nonetheless, there was no intention in the first place to invest large amounts of money in Afghan covert action. Thatcher readily accepted sending MI6 and SAS missions, though only for intelligence-gathering and some training, and cleared the sale to the CIA of $44 million worth of Blowpipe missiles.[40] The British commitment was very modest and thus, save for the Blowpipes, deniable. Besides, during the mid-1980s, top civil servants in Whitehall and the intelligence community struggled with limited budgets; an attempt to develop Zircon, a signals-intelligence satellite, a project that was about to consume immense amounts of money, was eventually dropped.[41] The Soviet Union, rather than Afghanistan, was Britain's key intelligence target, meriting considerable investment of resources. Meanwhile, yet another challenge was to ascertain Chinese intentions in the negotiations over Hong Kong.

Intentions always remain secret. Official statements, negotiating positions, dinner table remarks and propaganda might constitute means to probe the opponent's plans; all these might be indicators of intentions – but not confirmation. From 1981 onwards, the Kremlin managed to keep secret its evolving policy on withdrawal from Afghanistan. A year after Gorbachev came to power, he tried (hesitantly) to signal his intention to withdraw the Soviet troops, but the CIA analysis was stalled in suspicion, claiming that he had been endeavouring to mount a public-relations strategy to gain time, and failing to relate Gorbachev's possible options to Nixon's earlier strategy of withdrawal from Vietnam. It is evident that a combination of factors – including the absence of high-grade spies like Gordievsky (a number of key secret sources were betrayed by Ames from 1985 onwards), and a trend analysis of official Soviet statements and propaganda – inhibited an understanding of Gorbachev's evolving intentions until early 1988, when he courageously announced that he would start to pull back the Soviet troops from 15 May provided an agreement was reached in Geneva. Shevardnadze had been reassuring Shultz that there was a clear intention to withdraw, but the CIA did not take the possibility of such an outcome seriously.

What if the CIA, in agreement with the State Department, had planned for an Afghan policy well before the Soviet withdrawal, promoting a national coalition government to replace Najibullah? It is a virtual-history question, and one that invites justified criticism. In any case, we have to take into account the pervasive role of Pakistan, and particularly the ISI, in Afghan affairs. The ISI made possible the CIA's arming of the Mujahedeen – via the seven warlords Islamabad had hand-picked. The massive covert arming was not solely a CIA operation, however, and the agency's officers, as well as their MI6 counterparts remained in Pakistan, making only occasional journeys to Afghanistan. Their presence was simply too sparse to create secret-service momentum and to influence events – for example, a momentum similar to that of the OSS and SOE deployments and their cooperation with the resistance movements in Europe and Asia during the Second World War. Intelligence officers of the 1980s might have reflected on the lessons of secret-service operations from that conflict and from the early Cold War, among them the failure of covert paramilitary pro-grammes in Vietnam to aid tribes fighting against the Vietcong.

In the meantime, the ISI spied all over the world – and especially in the United States – to acquire nuclear technology useful to the Pakistani programme. Washington could not compete with the ISI on regional policy: the Americans enjoyed key satellite and signals-intelligence technology, but lacked boots on the ground accustomed to dealing with warlords, tribes and ethnic groups and their constantly changing relations. The Pakistanis were determined to help whoever they saw fit to support their interests in Afghanistan: Hekmatyar and (from 1994 onwards) the Taleban. Certainly, they could not be per-suaded to support a national government with the participation of Masoud, a Tajik. The Saudis, the benefactors of the Mujahedeen, could not be persuaded to stop their support either, since by backing the Islamists they had found a convenient way to rid themselves of the waves of religious fanatics posing a direct threat to the House of Saud. In any case, despite their world-power status and their eventual victory in the Cold War, Washington and London could not exert leverage over Pakistan and the warlords fighting each other. Even if the ISI had the same policy objectives as Washington, this would not have meant that their policy would have been blindly accepted by the warlords; they were too well-armed and too independent-minded, with their own personal aspirations and strong fundamentalist faith, to change course. In addition, the involvement of Russia, Iran and India in the arming of the Northern Alliance put into the equation their own hid-den intentions and interests in Afghanistan.

In Afghanistan itself, there was a permanent state of 'war of all against all' (from the times of Daoud and Taraki to that of the

Taleban), as Thomas Hobbes would have remarked. Anglo-American and Russian intelligence, despite their resources (and even when their accurate estimates had some impact on the development of foreign policy) had only a marginal influence on events and on the control of leading personalities, absorbed as the latter were by their feuds, seeking always to secure outside aid to help them win the battle at hand.

NOTES

Chapter 1. Afghan Feuds and Secret Intelligence

1. Vasili Mitrokhin, *The KGB in Afghanistan* (Washington, DC: Cold War International History Project, 2009), Working Paper No. 40, pp. 17–18.
2. Ibid., p. 22.
3. Douglas MacEachin, *Predicting the Soviet Invasion of Afghanistan: The Intelligence Community's Record* (Washington, DC: CIA, 2002), available at <http://www.cia.gov/library/center-for-the-study-of-intelligence/csi-publications/books-and-monographs/predicting-the-soviet-invasion-of-afghanistan-the-intelligence-communitys-record.html>, accessed 1 September 2010.
4. Mitrokhin, *The KGB in Afghanistan*, p. 23.
5. US Embassy (Kabul) to Department of State, 17 July 1973, available at <http://history.state.gov/historicaldocuments/frus1969-76ve08/media/pdf/d4.pdf>, accessed 1 November 2010.
6. US Embassy (Kabul) to Department of State, 17 September 1973, available at <http://history.state.gov/historicaldocuments/frus1969-76ve08/media/pdf/d8.pdf>, accessed 2 November 2010.
7. Ibid.
8. 'Demonstrations against the Daud government in Afghanistan', CIA Intelligence Information Report, August 1973, available at <http://www.foia.cia.gov/docs/DOC_0000200631/DOC_0000200631.pdf>, accessed 10 April 2011.
9. Intelligence Information Cable, 'Political ramifications in Afghanistan of the death of former Prime Minister Maiwandwal', 2 October 1973, available at <http://www.foia.cia.gov/docs/DOC_0000200633/DOC_0000200633.pdf>, accessed 14 March 2011; Intelligence Information Cable; 'Death of former Prime Minister Mohammad Hashim Maiwandwal', 16 October 1973, available at <http://www.foia.cia.gov/docs/DOC_0000200632/DOC_0000200632.pdf>, accessed 14 March 2011.

10. MacEachin, *Predicting the Soviet Invasion of Afghanistan*.

11. 'CC CPSU Information for the Leaders of the Progressive Afghan Political Organisations "Parcham" and "Khalq" concerning the results of the visit of Mohammad Daoud to the USSR', 21 June 1974, Cold War International History Project, Virtual Archive, available at <http:// legacy.wilsoncenter.org/va2/index.cfm?topic_id=1409&fuseaction=home. document&identifier=5034D649-96B6-175C-9E98082C2D1E6186& sort=collection&item=Soviet%20Invasion%20of%20Afghanistan>, accessed 10 June 2011.

12. CC CPSU to KGB Resident in Kabul, 2 June 1974, Cold War International History Project, Virtual Archive, available at <http://www. wilsoncenter.org/index.cfm?topic_id=1409&fuseaction=va2.document &identifier=5034D63A-96B6-175C-93188791687AA8A3& sort=Collection &item=Soviet%20Invasion%20of%20Afghanistan>, accessed 10 June 2011.

13. Memorandum of conversation (Kissinger, Naim et al.), 1 November 1974, available at <http://history.state.gov/historicaldocuments/frus1969-76ve08/ d15>, accessed 2 November 2010.

14. MacEachin, *Predicting the Soviet Invasion of Afghanistan*.

15. Mitrokhin, *The KGB in Afghanistan*, chronology for May 1978.

16. A comment made by Stansfield Turner, cited in Alexander Antonovich Liakhovskii, *Inside the Soviet Invasion of Afghanistan and the Seizure of Kabul, December 1979* (Washington, DC: Cold War International History Project, 2007), Working Paper No. 51, p. 5.

17. MacEachin, *Predicting the Soviet Invasion of Afghanistan*.

18. Memorandum of conversation (Kissinger, Naim et al.), 30 June 1976, available at <http://history.state.gov/historicaldocuments/frus1969-76ve08/d24 >, accessed 2 November 2010.

19. Memorandum of conversation (Ford, Kissinger, Naim et al.), 1 July 1976, available at <http://history.state.gov/historicaldocuments/frus1969-76ve08/ d26>, accessed 2 November 2010.

20. Memorandum of conversation (Daoud, Kissinger et al.), 8 August 1976, available at <http://history.state.gov/historicaldocuments/frus1969-76ve08/ d27>, accessed 2 November 2010.

21. MacEachin, *Predicting the Soviet Invasion of Afghanistan*.

22. Ibid.

23. Liakhovskii, *Inside the Soviet Invasion of Afghanistan*, p. 5.

24. MacEachin, *Predicting the Soviet Invasion of Afghanistan*.

25. Thomson to FCO, 27 April 1978, PREM 16/1930, The National Archives (Kew, Surrey) hereafter 'TNA'.

26. Crook to FCO, 28 April 1978, PREM 16/1930 TNA.

27. Gregory Feifer, *The Great Gamble: The Soviet War in Afghanistan* (New York: Harper Collins, 2008), p. 23.
28. Mitrokhin, *The KGB in Afghanistan*, p. 26.
29. Ibid., p. 28.
30. Ibid., p. 29.
31. Feifer, *The Great Gamble*, p. 24.
32. Crook to FCO, 30 April 1978, PREM 16/1930 TNA.
33. Ibid.
34. Ewans to FCO, 2 May 1978, PREM 16/1930 TNA.
35. Fearn to FCO, 3 May 1978, PREM 16/1930 TNA.
36. Parsons to FCO, 8 May 1978, PREM 16/1930 TNA.
37. BGC to Prendergast, 9 May 1978, PREM 16/1930 TNA.
38. Crook to FCO, 9 May 1978, PREM 16/1930 TNA.
39. Mitrokhin, *The KGB in Afghanistan*, p. 38.
40. MacEachin, *Predicting the Soviet Invasion of Afghanistan*.
41. Ibid.
42. Ibid.
43. Mitrokhin, *The KGB in Afghanistan*, pp. 150–1.
44. MacEachin, *Predicting the Soviet Invasion of Afghanistan*.
45. Communist Policy and Tactics, January 1979; 'Soviet-Afghan Friendship Treaty', FCO 37/2134 TNA.
46. Crook to Murray, 12 February 1979, p. 2, FCO 37/2133 TNA.
47. Crook to FCO, 10 April 1979, PREM 16/1930 TNA.
48. Thatcher to Lord Avebury, House of Lords, August 1979 (no precise date available), FCO 37/2133 TNA.
49. Zbigniew Brzezinski, *Power and Principle: Memoirs of the National Security Adviser, 1977–1981* (New York: Farrar Straus & Giroux, 1983), p. 427.
50. Jimmy Carter, *Keeping Faith: Memoirs of a President* (New York: Bantam Books, 1982), p. 264.
51. MacEachin, *Predicting the Soviet Invasion of Afghanistan*.
52. 'The CIA's Intervention in Afghanistan: Interview with Zbigniew Brzezinski *Le Nouvel Observateur*, 15–21 January 1998, available at <http://www.global-research.ca/articles/BRZ110A.html>, accessed 10 August 2010.
53. Peter Tomsen, *The Wars of Afghanistan: Messianic Terrorism, Tribal Conflicts, and the Failures of Great Powers* (New York: Public Affairs, 2011), p. 741 note 69.
54. Lawrence Freedman, *A Choice of Enemies: America Confronts the Middle East* (London: Phoenix, 2009), p. 99.
55. Ibid.

56. MacEachin, *Predicting the Soviet Invasion of Afghanistan*.

57. Feifer, *The Great Gamble*, p. 18.

58. MacEachin, *Predicting the Soviet Invasion of Afghanistan*.

59. Ibid.

60. Ibid.

61. Ibid.

62. Ibid.

63. Tomsen, *The Wars of Afghanistan*, pp. 99, 135.

64. CPSU Memorandum; The Position of the PRC on Afghanistan, 12 May 1982, trans. from Russian by David Wolff, 'New evidence on the war in Afghanistan', *Cold War International History Project Bulletin*, No. 14/15, p. 246.

65. Robert Gates, *From the Shadows: The Ultimate Insider's Story of Five Presidents and How They Won the Cold War* (New York: Shimon & Schuster 1996), p. 146.

Chapter 2. Wrong Estimates and the Invasion

1. Mitrokhin, *The KGB in Afghanistan*, p. 50.

2. Ibid., p. 47.

3. Odd Arne Westad, 'Concerning the situation in "A": new Russian evidence on the Soviet intervention in Afghanistan', *Cold War International History Bulletin*, Nos 8–9 (Winter 1996–97), p. 130.

4. Mitrokhin, *The KGB in Afghanistan*, p. 30.

5. Keeble to FCO, 11 September 1979 (tel. no. 597), FCO 28/3878 TNA; Keeble to FCO, 18 September 1979 (tel. no. 617), FCO 28/3878 TNA.

6. MacEachin, *Predicting the Soviet Invasion of Afghanistan*.

7. Thornton to Brzezinski, 17 September 1979, pp. 1–2 in Christian F. Ostermann, and Mircea Munteanu (eds), *Towards an International History of the War in Afghanistan, 1979–1989; Documents Reader*, Vol. 1, *US Documents* (Washington, DC: Woodrow Wilson International Center for Scholars, 2002).

8. MacEachin, *Predicting the Soviet Invasion of Afghanistan*.

9. Ibid.

10. Howell to FCO, 1 October 1979, FCO 37/2133 TNA.

11. White to Cortazzi, 21 September 1979, FCO 28/3878 TNA.

12. Rose to FCO, 25 September 1979 (tel. no. 193), FCO 28/3878 TNA.

13. Afghanistan and the 'Brezhnev Doctrine', May 1980, p. 2, FO 973/92 TNA.

14. Keeble to FCO, 25 December 1979, pp. 1–2, FCO 28/3878 TNA.
15. Carrington to Keeble, October 1979, pp. 1–2, FCO 27/2135 TNA.
16. Ibid., pp. 4–5.
17. Ibid., p. 10.
18. Ibid., p. 12.
19. Ibid., p. 11.
20. MacEachin, *Predicting the Soviet Invasion of Afghanistan*.
21. Spiers to Vance, 1 October 1979, in Ostermann and Munteanu (eds), *Towards an International History*, p. 106.
22. Mallaby to White, 8 November 1979, FCO 28/3878 TNA.
23. White to Mallaby, 23 November 1979, FCO 28/3878 TNA.
24. Archer to White, 23 November 1979, pp. 1–2, FCO 28/3878 TNA.
25. Ibid.
26. MacEachin, *Predicting the Soviet Invasion of Afghanistan*.
27. Ibid.
28. Liakhovskii, *Inside the Soviet Invasion of Afghanistan*, p. 15.
29. MacEachin, *Predicting the Soviet Invasion of Afghanistan*.
30. Ibid.
31. Secretary of State (Washington) to US Embassy in Kabul, 17 December, FCO 37/2132 TNA.
32. Barker to FCO, 'National Organisation for the Defence of the Revolution', 11 December 1979, p. 2, FCO 37/2126 TNA.
33. Lavers to Barker, 11 December 1979, FCO 37/2126 TNA.
34. Barker to Lavers, 18 December 1979, FCO 37/2132 TNA.
35. MacEachin, *Predicting the Soviet Invasion of Afghanistan*.
36. Henderson to FCO, 13 December 1979, FCO 37/2132 TNA.
37. Henderson to FCO, 18 December 1979, FCO 37/2132 TNA.
38. Minutes, Special Coordination Committee Meeting (Mondale, Christopher, Brown, Jones, Turner et al.), 17 December 1979, in Ostermann and Munteanu, *Towards an International History*, p. 2.
39. Minutes, Special Coordination Committee Meeting, pp. 3–4; MacEachin, *Predicting the Soviet Invasion of Afghanistan*.
40. Barker to FCO, 19 December 1979, FCO 37/2126 TNA.
41. Alexander to Walden, 'Prime Minister's visit to the United States', 19 December 1979, pp. 3–4, FCO 37/2132 TNA.
42. Ibid.
43. UK Embassy (Moscow) to FCO, 19 December 1979, FCO 37/2132 TNA.
44. MacEachin, *Predicting the Soviet Invasion of Afghanistan*.
45. Hillier-Fry to FCO, 20 December 1979, pp. 1–2, FCO 37/2132 TNA.
46. White to Lavers, 'Afghanistan: Soviet reinforcements', 21 December 1979, pp. 1–2, FCO 37/2132 TNA.

47. MacEachin, *Predicting the Soviet Invasion of Afghanistan*.
48. Ibid.
49. Ibid.
50. Ibid.
51. Parsons to FCO, 26 December 1979, FCO 37/2132 TNA.
52. MacEachin, *Predicting the Soviet Invasion of Afghanistan*.
53. UK Embassy (Washington) to FCO, 26 December 1979, pp. 1–2, FCO 37/2132 TNA.
54. Ibid.
55. Henderson to FCO, 26 December 1979, FCO 37/2135 TNA.
56. Hillier-Fry to FCO, 27 December 1979, FCO 37/2135 TNA.
57. Hillier-Fry to FCO, 27 December 1979 (tel. no. 286), FCO 37/2135 TNA.
58. Hillier-Fry to FCO, 27 December 1979 (tel. no. 287), FCO 37/2135 TNA.
59. MacEachin, *Predicting the Soviet Invasion of Afghanistan*.
60. Private Secretary to Lever, 28 December 179, FCO 37/2135 TNA.
61. FCO to UK Embassy (Moscow), 29 December 1979, FCO 37/2135 TNA.
62. Hillier-Fry to FCO, 30 December 1979, FCO 37/2135 TNA.
63. Report, FCO, 'Afghanistan: Soviet Occupation', February 1980, p. 2, FO 973/80 TNA.
64. Christopher Andrew and Vasili Mitrokhin, *The KGB in the World: The Mitrokhin Archive II* (London: Penguin, 2006), p. 401.
65. 'Afghanistan: Soviet Occupation', p. 2.
66. Ibid.
67. Ibid., p. 3.
68. Ibid.
69. Hillier-Fry to FCO, 28 December 1979, FCO 37/2126 TNA.
70. FCO, 'Afghanistan: Soviet Occupation', p. 3.
71. Ibid., p. 4.
72. Freedman, *A Choice of Enemies*, pp. 95–6.
73. Parsons to FCO, 30 December 1979, p. 2, FCO 37/2135 TNA.
74. Liakhovskii, *Inside the Soviet Invasion of Afghanistan*, p. 5.
75. Feifer, *The Great Gamble*, p. 30.
76. Meeting of the Politburo of the Central Committee, 17 March 1979, pp. 142–9.
77. Ibid., p. 137.
78. Ibid., 18 March 1979, p. 141.
79. Ibid.
80. Ibid., 19 March 1979, p. 143.
81. Ibid., pp. 144–5.
82. Telephone conversation, Kosygin-Taraki (transcript), 17 or 18 March 1979, ibid., p. 146.

83. Record of meeting (Kosygin, Gromyko, Ustinov, Ponomarev, Taraki), 20 March 1979, ibid., p. 147.
84. Ibid., pp. 148–9.
85. Session of Politburo (transcript), 22 March 1979, ibid., p. 151.
86. Instruction to Soviet Ambassador, 24 May 1979, ibid., p. 152.
87. Report to Central Committee (Gromyko, Andropov, Ustinov, Ponomarev), 28 June 1979, ibid., pp. 152–3.
88. Record of conversation, Puzanov-Taraki, 10 July 1979, ibid., p. 153.
89. Reports, Ponomarevs, 19–20 July 1979, ibid.
90. Feifer, *The Great Gamble*, pp. 35–6.
91. Tomsen, *The Wars of Afghanistan*, p. 129.
92. Record of conversation, Puzanov-Amin, Meeting of the Politburo of the Central Committee, 21 July 1979, p. 153.
93. Record, Pavlovskii, 25 August 1979, ibid., p. 154.
94. Andrew and Mitrokhin, *The KGB in the World*, p. 399.
95. Feifer, *The Great Gamble*, p. 43.
96. Artemy M. Kalinovsky, *A Long Goodbye: The Soviet Withdrawal from Afghanistan* (Cambridge MA: Harvard University Press, 2011), p. 95.
97. Feifer, *The Great Gamble*, p. 41.
98. Ibid., p. 43.
99. Mitrokhin, *The KGB in Afghanistan*, p. 51.
100. Ibid., p. 52.
101. Ibid., pp. 53–5.
102. Ibid., p. 62.
103. Central Committee Decision, 13 September 1979, *Cold War International History Bulletin*, Nos 8–9 (Winter 1996–97), p. 154.
104. Feifer, *The Great Gamble*, pp. 47–8.
105. Ibid., p. 48.
106. Mitrokhin, *The KGB in Afghanistan*, pp. 53–5.
107. Politburo Decision, 15 September 1979, *Cold War International History Bulletin*, Nos 8–9 (Winter 1996–97), p. 155.
108. Mitrokhin, *The KGB in Afghanistan*, p. 65.
109. Excerpt from transcript, Politburo meeting, 20 September 1979, *Cold War International History Bulletin*, Nos 8–9 (Winter 1996–7), p. 156.
110. Brezhnev-Honecker summit (transcript), 4 October 1979, ibid., p. 157.
111. Liakhovskii, *Inside the Soviet Invasion of Afghanistan*, p. 3.
112. Ibid., p. 5.
113. Andrew and Mitrokhin, *The KGB in the World*, p. 396.
114. Liakhovskii, *Inside the Soviet Invasion of Afghanistan*, p. 17.

115. Report to Central Committee (Gromyko, Ustinov, Andropov, Ponomarev), 29 October 1979, *Cold War International History Bulletin*, Nos. 8–9 (Winter 1996–97), pp. 158–9.
116. Ibid.
117. Mitrokhin, *The KGB in Afghanistan*, p. 83.
118. Ibid.
119. Ibid., pp. 85–6, 92.
120. Ibid., p. 85.
121. 'The 3 A.M. Phone Call: False Warnings of Soviet Missile Attacks during 1979–80 Led to Alert Actions for U.S. Strategic Forces', available at <http://www.gwu.edu/~nsarchiv/nukevault/ebb371/index.htm>, accessed 27 March 2012.
122. Personal memorandum, Andropov to Brezhnev, early December 1979, *Cold War International History Bulletin*, Nos 8–9 (Winter 1996–97), p. 159.
123. Mitrokhin, *The KGB in Afghanistan*, pp. 12, 93.
124. Liakhovskii, *Inside the Soviet Invasion of Afghanistan*, p. 12.
125. Westad, 'Concerning the situation in "A"', p. 131.
126. Liakhovskii, *Inside the Soviet Invasion of Afghanistan*, p. 17.
127. KGB report from Kabul, 17 December 1979, in A. A. Liakhovskii, *Tragediya I Doblest Afghana* ('Tragedy and Valour of the Afghanistan veteran), (Moscow: Iskon, 1995), transl. Gary Goldberg, Cold War International History Project, in Ostermann (ed.), *Towards an International History of the War in Afghanistan, 1979–1989: Document Reader*, Vol. 2, *Russian and East European Documents* (Washington, DC: Woodrow Wilson International Center for Scholars, 2002).
128. Tomsen, *The Wars of Afghanistan*, p. 169.
129. Feifer, *The Great Gamble*, pp. 58–9.
130. Mitrokhin, *The KGB in Afghanistan*, p. 95.
131. Feifer, *The Great Gamble*, p. 62.
132. Lester W. Grau, 'The take-down of Kabul: an effective coup de main', in W. G. Robertson and L. A. Yates, (eds), *Block by Block: The Challenges of Urban Operations* (Fort Leavenworth, KS: US Army Command and General Staff Press, 2003), p. 298.
133. Feifer, *The Great Gamble*, p. 63.
134. Tomsen, *The Wars of Afghanistan*, p. 170.
135. Feifer, *The Great Gamble*, p. 70.
136. Ibid., pp. 70–1.
137. Grau, 'The take-down of Kabul', p. 302.
138. Ibid., p. 303.

139. Feifer, *The Great Gamble*, p. 67.

140. Ibid., p. 71.

141. Ibid., p. 77.

142. Ibid.

143. Ibid., p. 78.

144. Grau, 'The take-down of Kabul', p. 311.

145. Ibid., p. 308; Mitrokhin, *The KGB in Afghanistan*, pp. 12–13, 95–6, 102.

146. Ibid., p. 106.

147. 'The Soviet invasion of Afghanistan: implications for warning', October 1980, p. 38, available at <http://www.foia.cia.gov/docs/DOC_0000278538/DOC_0000278538.pdf>, accessed 19 May 2011.

148. Ibid., p. 65.

149. Ibid., p. 72.

150. Ibid., p. 65.

151. Richard Aldrich, *GCHQ: The Uncensored Story of Britain's Most Secret Intelligence Agency* (London: Harper Press, 2011), p. 387.

152. 'The Soviet invasion of Afghanistan: implications for warning', p. 71.

153. Ibid., pp. 70, 72.

Chapter 3. International Reactions

1. Minutes, SCC meeting (Vance, Christopher, Turner, Brown, Brzezinski et al), 26 December 1979, p. 2, in Ostermann and Munteanu, *Towards an International History*, Vol. 1.

2. Ibid.

3. Henderson to FCO, 27 December 1979 (tel. no. 4364), FCO 37/2135 TNA.

4. Henderson to FCO, 27 December 1979 (tel. no. 4377), FCO 37/2135 TNA.

5. Ibid.

6. FCO to UK Embassy (Moscow), 28 December 1979 (tel. no. 796), ibid.

7. Brzezinski to Carter, 'Reflections on Soviet Intervention in Afghanistan', 26 December 1979, pp. 1–2, in Ostermann and Munteanu, *Towards an International History*, Vol. 1.

8. Minutes, Presidential Review Committee meeting (Mondale, Vance, Christopher, Turner, Brown, Brzezinski et al), 27 December 1979, in ibid.

9. Private Secretary to Lever, 28 December 1979, FCO 37/2135 TNA.

10. John O. Koehler, *Stasi: The Untold Story of the East German Secret Police* (Boulder, CO: Westview, 1999), p. 261.

11. Carrington to UK Mission (UN), 28 December 1979 (tel. no. 1010), FCO 37/2135 TNA.

12. FCO to UK Embassy (Moscow), 29 December 1979 (tel. no. 800), FCO 37/2135 TNA.

13. H. A. H. Cortazzi to Private Secretary, 29 December 1979, pp. 1–2, FCO 37/2135 TNA

14. 'In what way might the allies best respond?' Action with Iran', undated (possibly 31 December 1979), pp. 22, FCO 37/21 TNA.

15. 'Effects of the Soviet Invasion in the Rest of the World: Iran', 30 December 1979, p. 1, FCO 37/21 TNA.

16. UN Security Council Resolution 461, 31 December 1979, available at <http://daccess-dds-ny.un.org/doc/RESOLUTION/GEN/NR0/370/75/IMG/NR037075.pdf?OpenElement>, accessed 12 September 2010.

17. Lever to Miers, 28 December 1989, pp. 1–2, FCO 37/2135 TNA.

18. FCO to UK Embassy (Kabul), 28 December 1979 (tel. no. 210), FCO 37/2135 TNA

19. Carrington to UK Embassy (Kabul), 31 December 1979 (tel. no. 216), FCO 37/2135 TNA.

20. Background brief, 'Recognition', undated (possibly 31 December 1979), pp. 1–2, FCO 37/2135 TNA.

21. Hibbert to FCO, 28 December 1979 (tel. no. 1023), FCO 37/2135 TNA.

22. Hibbert to FCO, 31 December 1979 (tel. no. 1035), FCO 37/2135 TNA.

23. Bonn (EEC representative) to all EEC Member States, 28 December 1979, FCO 37/2135 TNA.

24. Warburton to FCO, 28 December 1979 (tel. no. 318), FCO 37/2135 TNA.

25. Dublin to all EEC members, 28 December 1979, FCO 37/2135 TNA.

26. Ford to FCO, 28 December 1979 (tel. no. 655), FCO 37/2135 TNA.

27. Henderson to FCO, 29 December 1979 (tel. no. 4394), FCO 37/2135 TNA.

28. Henderson to FCO, 28 December 1979 (tel. no. 4396), FCO 37/2135 TNA.

29. Private Secretary to Lever, 28 December 1979, FCO 37/2135 TNA.

30. Henderson to FCO, 28 December 1979 (tel. no. 4395), FCO 37/2135 TNA.

31. Parsons to FCO, 28 December 1979 (tel. no. 1971), FCO 37/2135 TNA.

32. Howells to FCO, 29 December 1979 (tel. no. 358), FCO 37/2135 TNA.

33. Howells to FCO, 29 December 1979 (tel. no. 359), FCO 37/2135 TNA.

34. Carter, *Keeping Faith*, p. 472; Brzezinski, *Power and Principle*, p. 429.

35. Ibid; Carter, *Keeping Faith*, p. 472.

36. Henderson to FCO, 29 December 1979 (tel. no. 4401), FCO 37/2135 TNA.

37. Parsons to FCO, 29 December 1979 (tel. no. 1974), FCO 37/2135 TNA

38. Hillier-Fry to FCO, 30 December 1979 (tel. no.292), FCO 37/2135 TNA.

39. Donovan to Carter, 2 January 1980, p.1, in Ostermann and Munteanu, *Towards an International History*, Vol. 1.

40. Interview with Brzezinski on Iran and Afghanistan, 30 December 1979, FCO 37/2135 TNA.

41. Ibid., p. 2; Henderson to FCO, 30 December 1979 (tel. no. 4404), pp. 1–2, FCO 37/2135 TNA.

42. Interview with Brzezinski, p. 6.
43. Ibid.
44. Henderson to FCO, 30 December 1979 (tel. no. 4404), p. 3, FCO 37/2135 TNA.
45. Cyrus Vance, *Hard Choices: Critical Years in America's Foreign Policy* (New York: Simon & Schuster, 1983), p. 391.
46. Secretary of Defense, Report to Congress, 29 January 1980 (Washington, DC: USGPO, 1980), p. 52.
47. Henderson to FCO, 30 December 1979 (tel. no. 4407), pp. 1–3, FCO 37/2135 TNA.
48. Henderson to FCO, 30 December 1979 (tel. no. 1979), p. 2, FCO 37/2135 TNA.
49. Record of discussions held on 31 December 1979, 1 January 1980, pp. 2, 7, 9, FCO 28/3878 TNA.
50. Ibid., p. 3.
51. Ibid., p. 6.
52. Ibid., p. 5.
53. Ibid., p. 4.
54. Ibid., pp. 5, 12.
55. Ibid., p. 6.
56. Ibid., pp. 5–6.
57. Ibid., p. 9.
58. Hurd to Carrington, 31 December 1979, pp. 1–2, FCO 37/2135 TNA.
59. Ibid., pp. 1–2, FCO 37/2135 TNA.
60. Record of conversation, Minister of State/Marshall Brement, 31 December 1979, pp. 1–2, FCO 37/2135 TNA.
61. Hillier-Fry to FCO, 31 December 1979 (tel. no. 295), FCO 37/2135 TNA.
62. 'Impact of the Soviet intervention in Afghanistan on détente, China, disarmament and arms control', December 1979, p. 1, FCO 37/2135 TNA.
63. 'Western Strategy in the Wake of the Soviet Invasion of Afghanistan', January 1980, p. 18, PREM 19/136 TNA.
64. 'Impact of the Soviet intervention', pp. 2–3.
65. 'What are the current foreign policy objectives of the Soviet Union?', 31 December 1979, pp. 1–2, ibid.
66. Minutes, NSC meeting (Carter, Brzezinski, Vance, Brown et al.), 2 January 1980, p. 6, in Ostermann and Munteanu, *Towards an International History*, Vol. 1.
67. Ibid., p. 7.
68. Ibid.
69. Ibid., p. 4.
70. Ibid., p. 10.
71. Ibid., p. 18.
72. Ibid.

73. Ibid., p. 22.
74. Ibid., p. 23.
75. Carrington to Thatcher; 'Soviet Intervention in Afghanistan', 8 January 1980, p. 1, AIR 8/2811 TNA.
76. Ibid.
77. Keeble to FCO, 30 December 1979, p. 2, FCO 37/2135 TNA.
78. Brzezinski, *Power and Principle*, p. 431.
79. Mitrokhin, *The KGB in Afghanistan*, p. 110, n. 112.
80. Robert L. Paarlberg, 'Lessons of the grain embargo', *Foreign Affairs*, Vol. 59, No. 1 (Fall 1980).
81. Memorandum, R. T. Jackling, 'Afghanistan and the Western Response', 10 January 1980, p. 1, AIR 8/2811 TNA.
82. Ibid., p. 2.
83. Ibid.
84. Ibid.
85. 'Secretary of State's visit to Oman', 13 January 1980, FCO 37/2135 TNA.
86. Agenda Item D: 'In what may might the allies best respond? Action with Pakistan', undated (possibly 32 December 1979), p. 24, FCO 37/2135 TNA.
87. Ibid.
88. European Political Cooperation, Asia Working Group, 'Pakistan nuclear', 12–13 December 1979, p. 2, FCO 37/2126 TNA.
89. 'Afghanistan: further responses to Soviet intervention', March 1980, p. 7, FCO 973/83 TNA.
90. 'Action at the United Nations; Uniting for Peace Procedure', undated (possibly 31 December 1979), pp. 1–2, FCO 37/2135 TNA.
91. Ibid., p. 7, FCO 973/83 TNA.
92. Statement, Government of the People's Republic of China, 30 December 1979, FCO 37/2135 TNA.
93. 'Afghanistan: further responses', p. 7.
94. Cradock to FCO, 31 December 1979 (tel. no. 1089), pp. 1–3, FCO 37/2135 TNA.
95. Brzezinski, *Power and Principle*, p. 424.
96. Westad, 'Concerning the situation in "A", p. 132.
97. Elizabeth Wishnick, *Mending Fences: The Evolution of Moscow's China Policy from Brezhnev to Yeltsin* (Seattle, WA: Washington University Press, 2001), pp. 73–4.
98. 'Afghanistan: Response to Soviet Intervention', January 1980, pp. 1–2, FCO 973/75 TNA.
99. Ibid., pp. 1, 5.

100. Ibid., p. 2; Forster to FCO, 30 December 1979 (tel. no. 859), FCO 37/2135 TNA.

101. Forster to FCO, 30 December 1979 (tel. no. 861), FCO 37/2135 TNA.

102. Ibid.

103. 'In what way might the allies best respond?', p. 22.

104. 'Afghanistan: further responses', p. 2.

105. Ibid., p. 3.

106. Forster to FCO, 31 December 1979, FCO 37/2135 TNA.

107. Thomson to FCO, 31 December 1979 (tel. no. 210), pp. 2–3, FCO 37/2135 TNA.

108. Thomson to FCO, 31 December 1979 (tel. no. 1097), pp. 1–2, FCO 37/2135 TNA.

109. Thomson to FCO, 31 December 1979 (tel. no. 1098), FCO 37/2135 TNA

110. 'Afghanistan: Response to Soviet Intervention', p. 3.

111. Graham to FCO, 31 December 1979 (tel. no. 1415), p. 103, FCO 37/2135 TNA.

112. 'Afghanistan: further responses', p. 2.

113. Stirling to FCO, 31 December 1979 (tel. no. 531), ibid.

114. 'Afghanistan: Response to Soviet Intervention', p. 3.

115. 'Afghanistan: further responses', p. 2.

116. Craig to FCO, 30 December 1979 (tel. no. 743), FCO 37/2135 TNA.

117. 'Afghanistan: Response to Soviet Intervention', p. 3.

118. 'Afghanistan: further responses', p. 3.

119. Cambridge to FCO, 30 December 1979 (tel. no. 563), FCO 37/2135 TNA.

120. Cambridge to FCO, 31 December 1979 (tel. no. 565), FCO 37/2135 TNA.

121. Walker to FCO, 31 December 1979 (tel. no. 283), FCO 37/2135 TNA.

122. Brant to FCO, 31 December 1979 (tel. no. 287), pp. 1–2, FCO 37/2135 TNA.

123. Haskell to FCO, 31 December 1979 (tel. no. 236), FCO 37/2135 TNA.

124. Weir to FCO, 28 December 1979 (tel. no. 944), FCO 37/2135 TNA.

125. 'Afghanistan: Response to Soviet Intervention', p. 3.

126. Dodson to FCO, 31 December 1970 (tel. no.739), FCO 37/2135 TNA.

127. Sutherland to FCO, 31 December 1979 (tel. no. 430), pp. 1–2, FCO 37/2135 TNA.

128. 'Afghanistan: Response to Soviet Intervention', p. 3.

129. Faber to FCO, 30 December 1979 (tel. no. 284), FCO 37/2135 TNA.

130. Wilford to FCO, 31 December 1979 (tel. no. 772), FCO 37/2135 TNA.

131. 'Afghanistan: further responses', p. 6.

132. 'Afghanistan: Response to Soviet Intervention', p. 3.

133. Ibid., p.4.

134. Ibid.

135. Farquharson to FCO, 31 December 1979 (tel. no. 179), FCO 37/2135 TNA.

136. Farquharson to FCO, 31 December 1979 (tel. no. 247), FCO 37/2135 TNA.
137. 'Afghanistan: Response to Soviet Intervention', p. 5.
138. 'Afghanistan: further responses', p. 4.
139. Carrington to Thatcher, 'Afghanistan', 19 January 1980, p. 1, PREM 19/135 TNA.
140. Ibid.
141. Ibid., p. 2.
142. Ibid., p. 3.
143. Walden to Alexander, 'Soviet Foreign Policy after Afghanistan', 31 January 1980, p. 5, PREM 19/135 TNA.
144. Carrington to Thatcher, 'Afghanistan', 19 January 1980, p. 4, PREM 19/135 TNA.
145. 'Western Strategy in the Wake of the Soviet Invasion', p. 25.
146. Armstrong to Alexander, 18 January 1980, annex to minutes of 15 January 1980 meeting, p. 2, PREM 19/135 TNA.
147. Ibid.
148. Partial record of meeting between Prime Minister and Chancellor Schmidt, 25 February 1980, p. 5, PREM 19/136 TNA.
149. Ibid., p. 3.
150. Armstrong to Alexander, 18 January 1980, p. 13.
151. Walden to Alexander, 'Soviet Policy after Afghanistan', 1 February 1980, p. 5, PREM 19/136 TNA.
152. Meeting of the Central Committee, CPSU Politburo, 17 January 1980, 'The Issue of Afghanistan', pp. 1–4, Archive of the President of the Russian Federation, Fond. No. 3, Opis No. 120, File No. 44, pp. 31, 42–4, available at <http://www.gwu.edu/~nsarchiv/NSAEBB/NSAEBB57/r12.pdf>, accessed 1 October 2010; CPSU CC Politburo Decision, 28 January 1980, with report by Gromyko, Andropov, Ustinov and Ponomarev, 27 January 1980, available at <http://www.gwu.edu/~nsarchiv/NSAEBB/NSAEBB57/r13.pdf>, accessed 1 October 2010.
153. Mitrokhin, *The KGB in Afghanistan*, pp. 156, 159
154. Ibid., p. 157.
155. Ibid., pp. 157–8.
156. Meeting of the Central Committee, 'The Issue of Afghanistan', pp. 1–4.
157. Ibid.
158. John Lewis Gaddis, *The Cold War* (London: Penguin, 2007), p. 211.
159. Schecter to Brzezinski, 'SCC Working Group on Iran and Afghanistan: Public Posture', 14 January 1980, p. 1, in Ostermann and Munteanu, *Towards an International History*, Vol. 1.
160. SCC meeting (Brzezinski, Newsom, Jones et al.), 14 January 1980, p. 1, in ibid.

161. Ibid., p. 2.
162. Ibid., p. 3.
163. Ibid., p. 5.
164. Ibid.
165. Ibid., p. 6.
166. Minutes, SCC meeting (Brzezinski, Vance, Brown, Jones et al.), 17 January 1980, p. 6, ibid.
167. Ibid., p. 8.
168. Brzezinski to Wade-Gery, 4 February 1980, PREM 19/136 TNA.
169. Tomsen, *The Wars of Afghanistan*, p. 205.
170. Ibid., p. 206.

Chapter 4. Assessing the Kremlin's Intentions, and Its Fears

1. Brzezinski, *Power and Principle*, p. 429.
2. Ibid., p. 426.
3. Ibid., p. 430.
4. Ibid., p. 431.
5. Vance, *Hard Choices*, p. 388.
6. Ibid.
7. Carter, *Keeping Faith*, p. 265.
8. Ibid., p. 473.
9. Memorandum, Chief of Defence Staff, 'Implications of recent events for defence strategy', 30 January 1980, p. 1, DEFE 25/350 TNA.
10. Ibid.
11. Ibid., p. 2.
12. Ibid.
13. Ibid.
14. Ibid.
15. Ibid.
16. Ibid.
17. Ibid., p. 4.
18. Ibid.
19. Ibid.
20. Ibid., p. 5.
21. Ibid.
22. Ibid.
23. Remarks by General Rogers on the crisis in Afghanistan, 30 January 1980, p. 1, ibid.
24. Ibid., p. 2.
25. Ibid., pp. 2–3.

26. Goulden to Scott, 'US Paper on Strategic Implications of Afghanistan', 27 February 1980, pp. 1–2, ibid.
27. Ibid., p. 2.
28. Ibid.
29. Ibid.
30. Ibid.
31. Ibid., p. 3.
32. Ibid.
33. Ibid.
34. Vance, *Hard Choices*, p. 392.
35. Ibid., p. 393.
36. Ibid.
37. Clive to FCO, 25 March 1980, DEFE 25/350 TNA.
38. UK delegation, NATO, to Logan, 26 March 1980, DEFE 25/350 TNA.
39. The Afghan Crisis: Summing-up of Consultations in the Senior Political Committee, 21 March 1980, p. 21, DEFE 25/350 TNA.
40. Ibid., p. 22.
41. Thatcher to Carter, 2 April 1980, DEFE 25/350 TNA.
42. Vance, *Hard Choices*, p. 394.
43. Ibid., p. 395.
44. Ibid.
45 'Nation: Muskie's Maiden Mission', *Time* magazine, 19 May 1980, available at <http://www.time.com/time/magazine/article/0,9171,924096,00.html>, accessed 1 August 2010.
46. Henderson to FCO, 'Muskie's Meeting with Gromyko in Vienna: US/Soviet Relations', 19 May 1980, p. 1, AIR 8/2812 TNA.
47. Ibid.
48. Ibid.
49. Ibid.
50. Ibid.
51. Ibid.
52. Ibid.
53. Ibid.
54. Ibid.
55. Ibid.
56. Ibid.
57. Henderson to FCO, 'Muskie/Gromyko Talks: Iran', 19 May 1980, AIR 8/2812 TNA.
58. Henderson to FCO, 'Muskie's Meeting with Gromyko in Vienna: US/Soviet Relations', 19 May 1980, p. 2, AIR 8/2812 TNA.
59. Ibid., p. 3.

60. Ibid.

61. Memorandum of information given by Ambassador Abrassimov to Erich Honecker, 27 May 1980, in Christian-Friedrich Ostermann, 'New evidence on the war in Afghanistan', *CWIHP Bulletin*, Nos 14/15, p. 244.

62. Ibid.

63. Memorandum, R. T. Jackling, 'US/Soviet relations: Afghanistan and Iran', 21 May 1980, AIR 8/2812 TNA.

64. Turner to FCO, 19 May 1980, AIR 8/2812 TNA.

65. Quoted in Kalinovky, *A Long Goodbye*, p. 62.

66. Record of meeting between the Prime Minister and the US Secretary of Defense, 2 June 1980, p. 1, DEFE 25/350 TNA.

67. Ibid., p. 2.

68. Ibid.

69. Ibid., p. 3.

70. Ibid.

71. Ibid., p. 4.

72. Ibid., p. 5.

73. CC CPSU Politburo transcript, 7 February 1980 (excerpt), 'US–Soviet relations and the turn toward confrontation, 1977–1980: new Russian and East German documents', *CWIHP Bulletin*, Issues 8–9, Winter 1996/97, p. 165.

74. Ibid., p. 166.

75. Memorandum, CC CPSU, 10 March 1980, in ibid., p. 168.

76. Memorandum, CC CPSU, 7 April 1980, in ibid., p. 171.

77. Information for Erich Honecker, CC CPSU, 18 July 1980, in ibid., p. 176.

78. CPSU CC Directive to Soviet Ambassadors in Communist countries, 4 March 1980, in Elizabeth Wishnick, 'Sino-Soviet tensions, 1980: two Russian documents', *Cold War International History Project*, Winter 1995/96, p. 202.

79. Ibid.

80. CPSU CC Politburo Directive to Soviet ambassadors and representatives, 2 October 1980, in ibid., p. 203.

81. Ibid., p. 204.

82. Ibid.

83. Ibid., pp. 204–5.

84. Ibid., p. 205.

85. 'Defense Modernization in China: An Intelligence Assessment', October 1980, p. iv, available at <http://www.foia.cia.gov/docs/DOC_0000278538/DOC_0000278538.pdf>, accessed 10 May 2011.

86. Ibid., p. 2.

87. Ibid.

88. US Department of Commerce, 'US–China relations', August 1995, released by court action no. 398CV716, quoted in Mahmud S. Ali, *US–China Cold War Collaboration, 1971–1989* (London: Routledge, 2005), pp. 251–2, n. 70.

89. Research report, 'The Sino-Vietnamese problem in 1981: a new baseline for military action', 25 March 1981, p. 3, available at <http://www.foia.cia.gov/docs/DOC_0000789477/DOC_0000789477.pdf> accessed 12 May 2011.

90. Ibid., p. 3.

91. Ibid., p. 4.

92. Ibid., p. 5.

93. Richard V. Allen, 'The Day Reagan Was Shot', available at <http://www.hoover.org/publications/hoover-digest/article/6281>, accessed 26 May 2011.

94. Koehler, *Stasi,* pp. 261–2.

95. Mitrokhin, *The KGB and the World,* pp. 131–2.

96. David E. Hoffman, *The Dead Hand: Reagan, Gorbachev and the Untold Story of the Cold War Arms Race* (London: Icon Books, 2011), p. 145.

97. Ibid., p. 40.

98. Mitrokhin, *The KGB and the World,* pp. 131–2.

99. Possible Soviet Responses to the US Strategic Defense Initiative, 12 September 1983, pp. 1–2, available at <http://www.foia.cia.gov/docs/DOC_0000268224/DOC_0000268224.pdf>, accessed 16 May 2011.

100. Anatoly Dobrynin, *In Confidence: Moscow's Ambassador to America's Six Cold War Presidents, 1962–1986* (New York: Random House, 1995), p. 528.

101 See Benjamin B. Fischer, *A Cold War Conundrum: The 1983 Soviet War Scare* (Washington, DC: Centre for the Study of Intelligence), available at <https://www.cia.gov/library/center-for-the-study-of-intelligence/csi-publications/books-and-monographs/a-cold-war-conundrum/source.htm>, accessed 31 May 2011; Mitrokhin, *The KGB and the World,* p. 131.

102. Hoffman, *The Dead Hand,* p. 82.

103. Ibid., p. 93

104. Ibid., p. 55

105. Ibid., p. 95.

106. Ronald Reagan, *An American Life* (New York: Simon & Schuster, 1990), pp. 588–9.

107. Entry for 18 November 1983 in Ronald Reagan, *The Reagan Diaries* (New York: HarperCollins, 2007) p. 199.

108. Hoffman, *The Dead Hand,* p. 97.

109. Ibid., 217–19.

110. Mitrokhin, *The KGB and the World,* p. 133.

111. Hoffman, *The Dead Hand*, pp. 160–1.
112. Ibid., p. 154.
113. Ibid., pp. 64–71.
114. Ibid., p. 99.
115. SINE 11-9-84, 'Soviet Policy toward the United States in 1984', 14 August 1984, p. 10, available at <http://www.foia.cia.gov/docs/DOC_0000518055/DOC_0000518055.pdf>, accessed 1 June 2011.
116. SNIE 11/30-83, 'Soviet Policy in the Middle East and South Asia under Andropov', p. 14, available at <http://www.foia.cia.gov/docs/DOC_0000273238/DOC_0000273238.pdf>, accessed 26 May 2011.
117. Ibid., p. 5.
118. Ibid., p. 8.
119. Ibid., pp. 8, 13.
120. NIE 11-9-83, 'Andropov's approach to key US-Soviet issues', 9 August 1983, p. 22, available at <http://www.foia.cia.gov/docs/DOC_0000518054/DOC_0000518054.pdf>, accessed 26 May 2011.
121. Kalinovsky, *A Long Goodbye*, p. 67.
122. Ibid., pp. 70–1.
123. Ibid., p. 69.
124. Referring to the memoirs of Kornienko, in ibid., pp. 61–2, 65.
125. Ibid., p. 67.
126. Ibid., p. 68.
127. Session of the CC CPSU Politburo, 10 March 1983, in 'US–Soviet Relations and the turn toward confrontation, 1977–1980', transl. D. Rozas, *CWIHP Bulletin*, Issues 8–9, Winter 1996/97, p. 177.
128. SNIE 11/30-83, 'Soviet policy in the Middle East and South Asia under Andropov', p. 8.
129. Ibid., p.12.
130. Ibid.
131. Kalinovsky, *A Long Goodbye*, p. 57.
132. Rundown of visitor's comments on 19/20 September 1986, p. 2, in Ostermann and Munteanu, *Toward an International History*, Vol. 1.

Chapter 5. Espionage and Clandestine Arming

1. Tim Weiner, *Legacy of Ashes: The History of the CIA* (London: Penguin, 2008), p. 367.
2. George Crile, *Charlie Wilson's War: The Extraordinary Story of the Covert Operation that Changed the History of Our Times* (London: Atlantic Books, 2007), p. 167.

3. Lester W. Grau, (ed.), *The Bear Went Over the Mountain: Soviet Tactics in Afghanistan* (London: Routledge, 2010), p. xix.

4. Gates, *From the Shadows*, p. 224.

5. Thatcher to Carter, 26 January 1980, p. 3, PREM 19/136 TNA.

6. Nigel West, *The Third Secret: The CIA, Solidarity and the KGB's Plot to Kill the Pope* (London: HarperCollins, 2001), p. 150; Gordon Corera, *The Art of Betrayal: Life and Death in the British Secret Service* (London: Weidenfeld & Nicolson, 2011), pp. 298, 302.

7. Report by 'representatives of military intelligence', September 1981, in Alexander A. Liakhovskii, *Plamya Afghana* ('Flame of the Afghanistan Veteran') (Moscow: Ikson, 1999), transl. Gary Goldberg for the Cold War International History Project, pp. 275–6. Included in Ostermann and Munteanu, *Towards an International History*, Vol. II.

8. Paul Kengor, *The Crusader: Ronald Reagan and the Fall of Communism* (New York: HarperCollins, 2006), p. 258.

9. Mark Urban, *UK Eyes Alpha: The Inside Story of British Intelligence* (London: Faber & Faber, 1997), pp. 35–6.

10. Crile, *Charlie Wilson's War*, p. 115.

11. Ibid., p. 104.

12. Report, Gromyko, Andropov, Ustinov, Ponomarev, 'CPSU CC Politburo decision', 28 January 1980, available at <http://www.gwu.edu/~nsarchiv/NSAEBB/NSAEBB57/r13.pdf>, accessed 1 October 2010.

13. Crile, *Charlie Wilson's War*, p. 103.

14. Ibid., p. 102.

15. Mohammad Yousaf, and Mark Adkin, *Afghanistan: The Bear Trap: The Defeat of a Superpower* (London: Pen & Sword, 1992), p. 183.

16. Andrew and Mitrokhin, *The KGB and the World*, p. 356.

17. Ibid., p. 357.

18. Ibid.

19. Ibid., p. 360.

20. Ibid., p. 361.

21. Ibid., p. 363.

22. Ibid., p. 365.

23. Ibid.

24. Christopher Andrew, *For the President's Eyes Only: Secret Intelligence and the American Presidency from Washington to Bush* (London: HarperCollins, 1996), p. 459.

25. Crile, *Charlie Wilson's War*, pp. 15–16.

26. Minutes, Special Coordination Committee Meeting (Brzezinski, Vance, Brown, Jones et al.), 17 January 1980, p. 8 in Ostermann and Munteanu, *Towards an International History*, Vol. 1.

27. Andrew, *For the President's Eyes Only*, p. 448.
28. Crile, *Charlie Wilson's War*, p. 75.
29. SNIE 11/50/37-82, 'The use of toxins and other lethal chemicals in Southeast Asia and Afghanistan', Vol. II, 'Supporting Analysis', 2 February 1982, p. 24, available at <http://www.foia.cia.gov/docs/DOC_0000284014/DOC_0000284014.pdf>, accessed 26 May 2011.
30. Ibid., p. 23.
31. Ibid., pp. 23–4.
32. Ibid., p. 23.
33. Ibid., pp. 23–4.
34. Ibid., p. 24.
35. Ibid., p. 28.
36. Ibid., p. 30.
37. Ibid.
38. Ibid.
39. Ibid.
40. Ibid.
41. Ibid.
42. Ibid., p. 35.
43. Ibid.
44. Report, Soviet Defence Minister Ustinov to the CPSU CC, 'Foreign Interference in Afghanistan', 2 October 1980, in *US–Soviet Relations and the Turn toward Confrontation, 1977–1980*, New Russian and East German Documents, Cold War International History Project, pp. 176–7.
45. Ibid.
46. Ibid.
47. Cabinet, conclusions of meeting, 18 September 1980, p. 2, CAB 128/68/10 TNA.
48. Ibid.
49. Crile, *Charlie Wilson's War*, pp. 158–9.
50. Coll, *Ghost Wars*, p. 66.
51. Andrew, *For the President's Eyes Only*, p. 459.
52. Coll, *Ghost Wars*, p. 96.
53. For Casey's attitudes, see Gates, *From the Shadows*, pp. 198–225.
54. Coll, *Ghost Wars*, pp. 96–7.
55. Two contemporary accounts include Joseph E. Persico, *Casey: The Lives and Secrets of William J. Casey: From the OSS to the CIA* (New York: Viking, 1990); and Bob Woodward, *Veil: The Secret Wars of the CIA, 1981–1987* (New York: Simon & Schuster, 1987).
56. US Defense Attaché to DIA, 21 June 1980, in Ostermann and Munteanu, *Towards an International History*, Vol. 1.

57. Mahmud S. Ali, *US–China Cold War Collaboration, 1971–1989* (London: Routledge, 2005), p. 177.
58. CPSU memorandum, 'The Position of the PRC on Afghanistan', 12 May 1982, transl. from Russian by David Wolff, in 'New evidence on the war in Afghanistan', *CWIHP Bulletin*, Nos. 14/15, p. 246.
59. Information Office of the PRC State Council, '"East Turkestan" Terrorist Forces cannot get away with their offences', 1 January 2002; Yitzhak Shichor, 'Fact and fiction: a Chinese documentary on Eastern Turkestan terrorism', *China and Eurasia Forum Quarterly*, Vol. 4, No. 2 (2006), pp. 89–108.
60. Andrew and Mitrokhin, *The KGB and the World*, pp. 278–9.
61. Ibid., p. 415.
62. Crile, *Charlie Wilson's War*, p. 134.
63. Ibid., p. 165.
64. 'USSR: domestic fallout from Afghan war', February 1988, p. 12, available at <http://www.foia.cia.gov/docs/DOC_0000500659/DOC_0000500659.pdf>, accessed 28 May 2011.
65. Ibid.
66. Kalinovsky, *A Long Goodbye*, pp. 49–52.
67. Crile, *Charlie Wilson's War*, p. 128.
68. Ibid., p. 161.
69. Yousaf and Adkin, *Afghanistan*, p. 50.
70. Coll, *Ghost Wars*, p. 86.
71. Feifer, *The Great Gamble*, pp. 169–70.
72. Coll, *Ghost Wars*, p. 90.
73. Tomsen, *The Wars of Afghanistan*, p. 221.
74. 'Iranian support to the Afghan resistance', 15 July 1985, available <http://www.gwu.edu/~nsarchiv/NSAEBB/NSAEBB57/us6.pdf>, accessed 20 October 2010.
75. 'Soviet–Iranian relations after Khomeini', 23 June 1989, p. 4, available at <http://www.foia.cia.gov/docs/DOC_0000602666/DOC_0000602666.pdf>, accessed 2 July 2011.
76. 'Afghanistan situation report', 26 October 1982, p. 2, available at <http://www.foia.cia.gov/docs/DOC_0001486830/DOC_0001486830.pdf>, accessed 20 May 2011.
77. Feifer, *The Great Gamble*, pp. 157–8, 172; Coll, *Ghost Wars*, pp. 118–19.
78. Ibid., pp. 121, 175.
79. Report, USSR Ministry of Defence Operations Group headed by Marshal of the Soviet Union S. L. Sokolov, about the results of operations so far that year, June 1984, in Liakhovskii, *Plamya Afghana*, pp. 284–5.
80. Kalinovsky, *A Long Goodbye*, p. 35.
81. Crile, *Charlie Wilson's War*, p. 198.
82. Ibid., p. 199.

83. Ibid., p. 201.
84. Ibid., p. 213.
85. Coll, *Ghost Wars*, p. 100.
86. Ibid., p. 208.
87. Ibid., p. 215.
88. Ibid., pp. 217, 219.
89. Ibid., p. 229.
90. Yousaf and Adkin, *Afghanistan*, p. 93.
91. Coll, *Ghost Wars*, pp. 242, 246.
92. 'USSR: Domestic fallout from Afghan war', p. 19.
93. Ibid.
94. Crile, *Charlie Wilson's War*, pp. 257, 259.
95. Ibid., p. 258.
96. Ibid., p. 263.
97. Ibid., pp. 277, 303.
98. Yousaf and Adkin, *Afghanistan*, p. 88.
99. Crile, *Charlie Wilson's War*, pp. 305, 319.
100. Ibid., p. 269.
101. Tomsen, *The Wars of Afghanistan*, p. 267.
102. Yousaf and Adkin, *Afghanistan*, p. 106.
103. Ibid., p. 102.
104. Crile, *Charlie Wilson's War*, pp. 463–4.
105. Ibid., p. 305.
106. Ibid., p. 333.
107. Ibid., p. 339.
108. Ibid., p. 342.
109. 'The Soviet invasion of Afghanistan: five years after', information as of 19 April 1985, p. 3, available at <http://www.gwu.edu/~nsarchiv/NSAEBB/NSAEBB57/us5.pdf>, accessed 2 October 2010.
110. Grau, *The Bear Went Over the Mountain*, p. xix.
111. 'The Soviet invasion of Afghanistan: five years after', p. 3.
112. Ibid., p. 10.
113. Andrew and Mitrokhin, *The KGB and the World*, p. 409.
114. Ibid., p. 410.
115. Yousaf and Adkin, *Afghanistan*, p. 105.
116. Peter L. Bergen, *Holy War Inc.: Inside the Secret World of Osama Bin Laden* (New York: Free Press, 2001), pp. 68–9.
117. Ibid., p. 69.
118. Quoted in Liakhovskii, *Plamya Afghana*, p. 282.
119. Crile, *Charlie Wilson's War*, p. 351.

120. Ibid., p. 353.
121. Ibid., pp. 354–5.
122. Ibid., p. 356; Coll, *Ghost Wars*, p. 127.
123. Crile, *Charlie Wilson's War*, p. 405.
124. Ibid., p. 409.
125. Ibid., pp. 414, 419.
126. Ibid., p. 421.
127. Rundown of visitors' comments on 19/20 September 1986, p. 3 in *Towards an International History of the War in Afghanistan*, Vol. 1.
128. Urban, *UK Eyes Alpha*, p. 69.
129. Rundown of visitors' comments on 19/20 September 1986, p. 3.
130. Lester W. Grau, and Ahmad Ali Jalali, 'Forbidden cross-border vendetta: Spetsnaz strike into Pakistan during the Soviet–Afghan War', *Journal of Slavic Military Studies*, Vol. 18, No. 4 (2005), pp. 661–72.
131. Lester Grau, 'The battle for Hill 3234: last ditch defense in the mountains of Afghanistan', *Journal of Slavic Military Studies*, Vol. 24, No. 2 (2011), pp. 217–31.
132. Milton Bearden, and James Risen, *The Main Enemy: The CIA's Battle with the Soviet Union* (London: Century, 2003), p. 258.
133. Alan J. Kuperman, 'The Stinger missile and US intervention in Afghanistan', *Political Science Quarterly*, Vol. 114, No. 2 (Summer 1999), p. 231.
134. Ibid., p. 232.
135. Kengor, *The Crusader*, pp. 259–60.
136. Kuperman, 'The Stinger missile', p. 243.
137. Ibid., p. 438.
138. West, *The Third Secret*, pp. 155–6.
139. Andrew and Mitrokhin, *The KGB and the World*, p. 416.
140. Ibid., p. 579, n. 47.
141. Coll, *Ghost Wars*, p. 122.
142. Yousaf and Adkin, *Afghanistan*, p. 187.
143. Kuperman, 'The Stinger missile', p. 248.
144. Crile, *Charlie Wilson's War*, pp. 477–8.
145. Bearden and Risen, *The Main Enemy*, p. 350.
146. Coll, *Ghost Wars*, pp. 128–9.
147. Ibid., p. 137.
148. Yousaf and Adkin, *Afghanistan*, p. 202.
149. Ibid., p. 195.
150. Ibid., pp. 197–8.
151. Ibid., p. 198.

152. Ibid.
153. Ibid., p. 199.
154. Ibid., p. 200.
155. CPSU CC Politburo transcript (excerpt), 13 November 1986, *CWIHP Bulletin*, Nos 8–9 (Winter 1996–97), p. 180.
156. Coll, *Ghost Wars*, p. 161; Yousaf and Adkin, *Afghanistan*, pp. 200, 202–6.
157. Coll, *Ghost Wars*, p. 162.
158. Ibid., p. 162.
159. Ibid., p. 130
160. Ibid., pp. 151–2.
161. Ibid., pp. 152–3.
162. Ibid., p. 155.
163. Bergen, *Holy War Inc.*, p. 74.
164. Kuperman, 'The Stinger missile', p. 255.
165. Coll, *Ghost Wars*, p. 337.
166. Bergen, *Holy War Inc.*, p. 74.
167. West, *The Third Secret*, p. 160.
168. Bergen, *Holy War Inc.*, p. 75.
169. Kuperman, 'The Stinger missile', p. 250.

Chapter 6. Discovering Chinese Intentions

1. Chen Jian, 'China and the Cold War after Mao', in Melvyn P. Leffler, and Odd Arne Westad, (eds), *Cambridge History of the Cold War*, Vol. 3 (Cambridge: Cambridge University Press, 2010), pp. 187–8, 191.
2. 'US–China Relations', 15 April 1983, pp. 1–2, available at <http://www.foia.cia.gov/docs/DOC_0000242636/DOC_0000242636.pdf>, accessed 21 May 2011.
3. Ibid., p. 2.
4. Ibid.
5. SNIE, 13-9-83, 'China's Policies Toward the United States and the USSR: Short-term Prospects', 14 January 1983, pp. 1–2, available at <http://www.foia.cia.gov/docs/DOC_0001113431/DOC_0001113431.pdf>, accessed 20 May 2011.
6. Ibid., p. 3.
7. Ibid., p. 4.
8. Ibid.
9. Ibid., p. 5.
10. Ibid.
11. Ibid.
12. Ibid., p. 6.

13. Ibid.

14. Ibid., p. 7.

15. Ibid.

16. Ibid., p. 8.

17. Ibid.

18. Ibid., p. 9.

19. Wishnick, *Mending Fences*, pp. 75–6.

20. Ibid.; Peter Vamos, "'Only a handshake, but no embrace': Sino-Soviet normalization in the 1980s', in Thomas P. Bernstein, and Li Hua-yu (eds), *China Learns from the Soviet Union, 1949–Present* (New York: Lexington Books, 2010), p. 87.

21. Wishnick, *Mending Fences*, p. 77.

22. Ali, *US–China Cold War Collaboration*, p. 153; White House, 'Peaceful Nuclear Cooperation with China', NSDD76, 18 January 1983, available at <http://www.fas.org/irp/offdocs/nsdd/nsdd-76.pdf>, accessed 14 October 2012.

23. Quoted in Wishnick, *Mending Fences*, p. 78.

24. Ibid., p. 79.

25. Ibid., p. 81.

26. Ibid., p. 84.

27. SNIE 13-4-83, 'China's Security Policy: Political Implications of Growing Capabilities for Nuclear Conflict', 29 July 1983, p. 17, available at <http://www.foia.cia.gov/docs/DOC_0001113433/DOC_0001113433.pdf>, accessed 21 May 2011.

28. Ibid., p. 10.

29. Ibid., p. 19.

30. Ibid., p. 12.

31. Ibid., p. 4.

32. Ibid., p. 15.

33. Ibid.

34. Ibid., p. 12.

35. Ibid., p. 14.

36. Wishnick, *Mending Fences*, p. 87.

37. Andrew and Mitrokhin, *The KGB and the World*, p. 292

38. Ibid., pp. 292–3.

39. Ibid., p. 293.

40. Ibid.

41. NIE 13/11-84, 'The Changing Sino-Soviet Relationship', 14 June 1985, p. 13, available at <http://www.foia.ucia.gov/docs/DOC_0000261349/DOC_0000261349.pdf>, accessed 31 May 2011.

42. Wishnick, *Mending Fences*, p. 82.
43. Chen Jian, 'China and the Cold War after Mao', p. 193.
44. NIE 13/11-84, p. 14.
45. Ibid., p. 15.
46. Cable, Hungarian Ambassador Laszlo Ivan, 6 June 1985, included in Vamos, 'Only a handshake, but no embrace', p. 90.
47. Ibid., p. 92.
48. NIE 13/11-84, p. 3.
49. Ibid., p. 8.
50. Ibid., p. 7.
51. Ibid.
52. Ibid., p.8.
53. Ibid.
54. Ibid.
55. Ibid., p. 10.
56. Ibid., p. 11.
57. NIE 13-7-86, 'China's Second Revolution', May 1986, p. 1, available at <http://www.foia.cia.gov/docs/DOC_0001097741/DOC_0001097741.pdf>, accessed 10 May 2011.
58. Ibid., p. 14.
59. Ibid., p. 3.
60. Ibid., p. 4.
61. Ibid.
62. Ibid., p. 5.
63. Ibid., p. 6.
64. Wishnick, *Mending Fences*, p. 100.
65. Ibid., p. 102.
66. NIE 13/11-22-88, 'The Prospect for Change in Sino-Soviet Relations', August 1988, pp. 4–5, available at <http://www.foia.cia.gov/docs/DOC_0001353863/DOC_0001353863.pdf>, accessed 1 June 2011.
67. Ibid., p. 9
68. NIE 11-14/40-81, 'Soviet Military Forces in the Far East', October 1985, p. 4, available at <http://www.foia.cia.gov/docs/DOC_0000261289/DOC_0000261289.pdf>, accessed 1 June 2011.
69. Gates, *From the Shadows*, p. 122.
70. 11-14/40-81, p. 5.
71. Ibid.
72. NIE 13/11-22-88, p. 9.
73. Vamos, 'Only a handshake, but no embrace', p. 92.
74. NIE 13/11-22-88, p. 18.
75. Ibid., p. 16.

76. Wishnick, *Mending Fences*, pp. 81, 110.
77. Ibid., p. 253, n. 13.
78. Ibid., p. 111.
79. Ibid.
80. 'Gorbachev's Foreign Policy', February 1989, p. 17, available at <http://www.foia.cia.gov/docs/DOC_0000499113/DOC_0000499113.pdf>, accessed 16 June 2011.
81. Wishnick, *Mending Fences*, pp. 104–5
82. National Intelligence Daily, 'Striving for a Successful Summit', 15 May 1989, p. 3, available at <http://www.foia.cia.gov/docs/DOC_0000444697/DOC_0000444697.pdf>, accessed 12 June 2011.
83. Ibid.
84. Ibid.
85. National Intelligence Estimate, 'Deng–Gorbachev Summit', 10 May 1989, p. 12, available at <http://www.foia.cia.gov/docs/DOC_0000444696/DOC_0000444696.pdf>, accessed 16 June 2011.
86. 'Sino-Soviet Relations: The Summit and Beyond', 9 May 1989, p. 7, available at <http://www.foia.cia.gov/docs/DOC_0000444694/DOC_0000444694.pdf>, accessed 17 June 2011.
87. National Intelligence Daily, 15 May 1989, p. 7.
88. Urban, *UK Eyes Alpha*, p. 111.
89. Wishnick, *Mending Fences*, p. 115.
90. Ibid., p. 116.
91. Ibid.
92. 'Sino-Soviet Relations: The Summit and Beyond', 9 May 1989, p. 5.
93. 'Chinese and Soviet views on Border Demarcation', in ibid.
94. 'China: Tilting the Balance in Its Approach to Post-Cold War South Asia', Appendix, 27 October 1992, p. 9, available at <http://www.foia.gov/docs/DOC_0001233766/DOC_0001233766>, accessed 15 June 2011.
95. 'China and the Indian–Pakistani Nuclear Issue', 11 January 1990, p. 1, available at <www.foia.cia.gov/docs/DOC_0001233767/DOC_0001233767.pdf>, accessed 15 June 2011.

Chapter 7. The CIA and Gorbachev

1. Gates, *From the Shadows*, p. 327.
2. 'Gorbachev, Mikhail (Sergeyevich), CIA current biography', August 1985, p. 21, available at <http://www.foia.cia.gov/docs/DOC_0001088022/DOC_0001088022.pdf>, accessed 10 May 2011.
3. Corera, *The Art of Betrayal*, p. 272.

4. Professor Archie Brown attended a meeting with the prime minister on 14 December 1984, when the latter actually voiced criticism of Reagan's SDI initiative. Archie Brown, *The Gorbachev Factor* (Oxford: Oxford University Press, 1996), p. 371, n. 96.

5. 'Gorbachev . . . CIA current biography', p. 22.

6. Gates, *From the Shadows*, p. 329.

7. Ibid., p. 334.

8. Hoffman, *Dead Hand*, pp. 190–1.

9. Ibid., pp. 211–12.

10. Coll, *Ghost Wars*, p. 159.

11. Kalinovsky, *A Long Goodbye*, p. 88.

12. Bearden and Risen, *The Main Enemy*, p. 226.

13. SNIE 11/37-2-85L, 'Soviet problems, prospects, and options in Afghanistan in the next year', March 1985, p. 2, available at <http://www.foia.cia.gov/docs/DOC_0000518057/DOC_0000518057.pdf>, accessed 1 June 2011.

14. Ibid.

15. Ibid., p. 3.

16. Ibid.

17. Coll, *Ghost Wars*, p. 606, n. 18.

18. 'Soviets offer apology in killing of US Major', Associated Press, 15 June 1988.

19. Andrew and Mitrokhin, *The Mitrokhin Archive*, p. 280.

20. 'USSR: domestic fallout from Afghan War', February 1988, p. 17, available at <http://www.foia.cia.gov/docs/DOC_0000500659/DOC_0000500659.pdf>, accessed 28 May 2011.

21. Andrew and Mitrokhin, *The Mitrokhin Archive*, p. 287.

22. See Ronald Kessler, *Moscow Station: How the KGB Penetrated the American Embassy* (New York: Scribner's, 1989).

23. 'The Soviet invasion of Afghanistan: five years after', May 1985, p. v., available at <http://www.foia.cia.gov/docs/DOC_0000496704/DOC_0000496704.pdf>, accessed 1 June 2011.

24. Ibid., p. 7.

25. Ibid., p. 9.

26. Andrei Grachev, *Gorbachev's Gamble: Soviet Foreign Policy and the End of the Cold War* (London: Polity, 2008), p. 102.

27. Dobrynin, *In Confidence*, p. 447.

28. *Chernayev Diary*, entry for 17 October 1985, pp. 142–3.

29. Kalinovsky, *A Long Goodbye*, p. 88.

30. 'GRU dossier on Najibullah', *CWIHP Bulletin*, Nos. 14/15, p. 250.

31. 'Regional issues at the November meeting: Gorbachev's options', 6 November 1985, p. 3, available at <http://www.foia.cia.gov/docs/DOC_0000587621/DOC_0000587621.pdf >, accessed 1 June 2011.

32. 'Soviet interest in bilateral discussion of regional conflicts', 14 August 1986, p. 4, available at <http://www.foia.cia.gov/docs/DOC_0000515561/DOC_0000515561.pdf>, accessed 1 June 2011.

33. Ibid., p. 2.

34. Ibid., p. 4.

35. SNIE 11-9-86, 'Gorbachev's policy toward the United States, 1986–88', September 1986, pp. 3–5, available at <http://www.foia.cia.gov/docs/DOC_0000519265/DOC_0000519265.pdf>, accessed 1 June 2011.

36. Hoffman, The Dead Hand, pp. 263–9.

37. CPSU CC Politburo transcript, 13 November 1986, in 'US–Soviet relations and the turn toward confrontation', CWIHP Bulletin, Nos 8/9, pp. 179–81.

38. Ibid., p. 181.

39. 'Record of conversation, M. S. Gorbachev with Italian Minister of Foreign Affairs Giulio Andreotti', 27 February 1987, CWIHP Bulletin, Nos. 14/15, p. 147.

40. 'Gorbachev's new foreign policy apparatus', August 1987, pp. ii–iv, available at <http://www.foia.cia.gov/docs/DOC_0000498796/DOC_0000498796.pdf >, accessed 1 June 2011.

41. 'Moscow's Afghan quagmire: no end in sight after eight years', 20 September 1987, p. 5, available at <http://www.foia.cia.gov/docs/DOC_0001482036/DOC_0001482036.pdf>, accessed 3 June 2011.

42. Ibid., pp. 6–7.

43. Ibid., p. 9.

44. Ibid., p. 10.

45. 'Soviet strategy on Afghanistan: playing for time', 15 October 1987, pp. 2, 5, available at <http://www.foia.cia.gov/docs/DOC_0001481855/DOC_0001481855.pdf>, accessed 1 June 2011.

46. Hoffman, The Dead Hand, pp. 294–5.

47. Ibid.

48. Ibid., p. 332–6.

49. Bearden and Risen, The Main Enemy, p. 331.

50. Kalinovsky, A Long Goodbye, p. 126.

51. Bearden and Risen, The Main Enemy, pp. 331–2.

52. Robert Gates, From the Shadows: The Ultimate Insider's Story of Five Presidents and How They Won the Cold War (New York: Touchstone, 1997), p. 425.

53. Kalinovsky, *A Long Goodbye*, pp. 134–8.

54. SNIE 11/37-88, 'USSR withdrawal from Afghanistan', March 1988, pp. 1–2, available at <http://www.gwu.edu/~nsarchiv/NSAEBB/NSAEBB57/us9.pdf>, accessed 1 June 2011.

55. Ibid.

56. Ibid., p. 2.

57. Annex I, 'Bilateral agreement between the Republic of Afghanistan and the Islamic Republic of Pakistan on the principles of mutual relations, in particular on non-interference and non-intervention' available at <http://www.institute-for-afghan-studies.org/Accords%20Treaties/geneva_accords_1988_pakistan_afghanistan.htm>, accessed 23 June 2011.

58. Annex III, 'Statement by the United States', available at ibid.

59. Kalinovsky, *A Long Goodbye*, p. 141.

60. Michael R. Gordon, 'US officials link Pakistan blast to Kabul regime', *New York Times*, 17 April 1988.

61. Yousaf and Adkin, *The Bear Trap*, p. 223.

62. Ibid., p. 230.

63. 'Gorbachev's growing confrontation with the KGB: a coming showdown?', June 1988, p. 1, available at <http://www.foia.cia.gov/docs/DOC_0000500661/DOC_0000500661.pdf>, accessed 6 June 2011.

64. Ibid., p. 2.

65. Ibid., p. 3.

66. Ibid.

67. Ibid., p. 6.

68. Ibid., p. 7.

69. Ibid.

70. Ibid., p. 9.

71. Ibid., p. 10.

72. Ibid., p. 12.

73. Ibid., p. 14.

74. Artemy Kalinovsky, 'Decision-making and the Soviet war in Afghanistan: from intervention to withdrawal', *Journal of Cold War Studies*, Vol. 11, No. 4 (Autumn 2009), pp. 66–8.

75. Minutes of Politburo meeting, 18 September 1988, held at the Gorbachev Foundation, quoted in ibid., p. 68

76. Urban, *UK Eyes Alpha*, p. 83.

77. Ibid., pp. 74–5.

78. Lester W. Grau, 'Breaking contact without leaving chaos: the Soviet withdrawal from Afghanistan', *Journal of Slavic Military Studies*, Vol. 20, No. 2 (April 2007), pp. 235–61.

79. Masoud to Vorontsov, 26 January 1989, in Lyakhovski, *Plamya Afghana*, included in *Toward and International History of the War in Afghanistan*, Vol. II.
80. Coll, *Ghost Wars*, pp. 177–8.
81. Weiner, *Legacy of Ashes*, p. 429.
82. Ibid., pp. 429–30.
83. Ibid., p. 430.
84. Minutes of Politburo meeting, 24 January 1989, quoted in Dmitri Volkogonov, *Autopsy for Empire: The Seven Leaders Who Built the Soviet Regime* (New York: Simon & Schuster, 1998), p. 464.
85. Boris Gromov, and Dmitry Rogozin, 'Russian advice on Afghanistan', *New York Times*, 12 January 2010, available at <http://www.nytimes.com/2010/01/12/opinion/12iht-edrogozin.html>, accessed 3 July 2011.
86. Coll, *Ghost Wars*, p. 195.

Aftermath: Continuing Covert Action

1. Coll, *Ghost Wars*, p. 228.
2. Ibid., p. 194.
3. Ibid., pp. 208–9.
4. Ibid., p. 198.
5. Ibid., pp. 202–3.
6. Tomsen, *The Wars of Afghanistan*, p. 268.
7. Coll, *Ghost Wars*, p. 210.
8. Ibid.
9. Ibid., p. 202; Tomsen, *The Wars of Afghanistan*, p. 325.
10. Coll, *Ghost Wars*, p. 212–13.
11. Ibid., p. 219.
12. Ibid., p. 220.
13. Ibid., p. 227.
14. Ibid., p. 233.
15. Ibid., pp. 315–16.
16. Tomsen, *The Wars of Afghanistan*, p. 523.
17. Ahmed Rashid, *Taliban: Militant Islam, Oil and Fundamentalism in Central Asia* (New Haven, CT: Yale University Press, 2001), pp. 18–54.
18. Tomsen, *The Wars of Afghanistan*, pp. 532–3.
19. US Embassy (Islamabad) to Department of State, 6 December 1994, 'Secret', pp. 1–3, available at <http://www.gwu.edu/~nsarchiv/NSAEBB/NSAEBB97/tal5.pdf>, accessed 23 October 2011.
20. Ibid., 15 February 1995, pp. 1–7, available at <http://www.gwu.edu/~nsarchiv/NSAEBB/NSAEBB97/tal7.pdf>, accessed 23 October 2011.

21. Ibid., 20 February 1995, p. 3, available at <http://www.gwu.edu/~nsarchiv/NSAEBB/NSAEBB97/tal8.pdf>, accessed 23 October 2011.

22. Ibid., p. 4.

23. Ibid., p. 7.

24. Ibid., p. 9.

25. Ibid., p. 11.

26. James Risen, 'Russians are back in Afghanistan', *New York Times*, 27 July 1998; Tomsen, *The Wars of Afghanistan*, pp. 542, 546–7.

27. Coll, *Ghost Wars*, p. 339.

28. Ibid., p. 340.

29. Ibid., p. 395.

30. Cable, Department of State to US Embassy (Islamabad), 23 August 1998, pp. 3–4, available at <http://www.gwu.edu/~nsarchiv/NSAEBB/NSAEBB134/Doc%202.pdf>, accessed 23 October 2011.

31. Tomsen, *The Wars of Afghanistan*, p. 459.

32. Risen, 'Russians are back'.

33. Thomas Withington, 'The early anti-Taliban team', *Bulletin of the Atomic Scientists*, November/December 2001, pp. 13–15; Risen, 'Russians are back'.

34. Vladimir Paramonov and Oleg Stolpovski, *Chinese Security Interests in Central Asia* (Wiltshire: Advanced Research Assessment Group, Defence Academy of the UK, 2008), pp. 6–7.

35. Tomsen, *The Wars of Afghanistan*, p. 553.

36. Ibid., p. 796.

37. Ibid., p. 561.

38. Coll, *Ghost Wars*, pp. 463–6.

39. Tomsen, *The Wars of Afghanistan*, p. 559.

40. Crile, *Charlie Wilson's War*, p. 277.

41. Urban, *UK Eyes Alpha*, pp. 62–3.

BIBLIOGRAPHY

Archives

Unpublished

The National Archives, Kew, Surrey, United Kingdom

Published Collections

Foreign Relations of the United States (FRUS)1973-1976, Vol.E8, *Documents on South Asia, 1973–1976* (Washington DC: Department of State, 2007).

Freedom of Information Act CIA Collection available at <http://www.foia.cia.gov>.

Cold War International History Project Virtual Archive available at <http://www.wilsoncenter.org/program/cold-war-international-history-project>

Cold War International History Project Bulletin, Nos 8/9; 14/15.

Ostermann, Christian F. and Munteanu, Mircea, eds, *Towards an International History of the War in Afghanistan, 1979–1989; Documents Reader,* Vols 1, 2 (Washington, DC: Woodrow Wilson International Center for Scholars, 2002).

Federation of American Scientists: National Security Decision Directive 76, available at <http://www.fas.org/irp/offdocs/nsdd/nsdd-76.pdf>.

Books/Articles

Allen, Richard V., 'The Day Reagan Was Shot', available at <http://www.hoover.org/publications/hoover-digest/article/6281>, accessed 26 May 2011.

Aldrich, Richard, *GCHQ: The Uncensored Story of Britain's Most Secret Intelligence Agency* (London: Harper Press, 2011).

Ali, Mahmud S., *US. China Cold War Collaboration, 1971–1989* (London: Routledge, 2005).

Andrew, Christopher, and Mitrokhin, Vasili, *The KGB in the World: The Mitrokhin Archive II* (London: Penguin, 2006).

—— *For the President's Eyes Only: Secret Intelligence and the American Presidency from Washington to Bush* (London: Harper Collins, 1996).

—— and Mitrokhin, Vasili, *The Mitrokhin Archive: The KGB in Europe and the West* (London: Allen Lane, 1999).

Bearden, Milton, and Risen, James, *The Main Enemy: The CIA's Battle with the Soviet Union* (London: Century, 2003).

Bergen, Peter L., *Holy War Inc.: Inside the Secret World of Osama Bin Laden* (New York: The Free Press, 2001).

Bernstein, Thomas P., and Li, Hua-Yu, eds, *China Learns from the Soviet Union, 1949–Present* (New York: Lexington Books, 2010).

Braithwaite, Rodric, *Afgantsy: The Russians in Afghanistan, 1979-1989* (Oxford: Oxford University Press, 2011).

Brzezinski, Zbigniew, *Power and Principle: Memoirs of the National Security Adviser, 1977–1981* (New York: Farrar, Straus & Giroux, 1983).

Carter, Jimmy, *Keeping Faith: Memoirs of a President* (New York: Bantam Books, 1982).

Coll, Steve, *Ghost Wars: The Secret History of the CIA, Afghanistan and Bin Laden, from the Soviet Invasion to September 10, 2001* (London: Penguin, 2004).

Corera, Gordon, *The Art of Betrayal: Life and Death in the British Secret Service* (London: Weidenfeld & Nicolson, 2011).

Crile, George, *Charlie Wilson's War: The Extraordinary Story of the Covert Operation that Changed the History of Our Times* (London: Atlantic Books, 2007).

Dobrynin, Anatoly, *In Confidence: Moscow's Ambassador to America's Six Cold War Presidents, 1962-1986* (New York: Random House, 1995),

Feifer, Gregory, *The Great Gamble: The Soviet War in Afghanistan* (New York: HarperCollins, 2008).

Fischer, Benjamin B., *A Cold War Conundrum: The 1983 Soviet War Scare* (Washington, DC: Centre for the Study of Intelligence, 2007).

Freedman, Lawrence, *A Choice of Enemies: America Confronts the Middle East* (London: Phoenix, 2009).

Gaddis, John Lewis, *The Cold War: The Deals. The Spies. The Lies. The Truth* (London: Penguin, 2007).

Gates, Robert, *From the Shadows: The Ultimate Insider's Story of Five Presidents and How They Won the Cold War* (New York: Shimon & Schuster, 1996).

Gordon, Michael R., 'U.S. Officials Link Pakistan Blast to Kabul Regime', *New York Times*, 17 April 1988.

Grachev, Andrei, *Gorbachev's Gamble: Soviet Foreign Policy and the End of the Cold War* (London: Polity, 2008).

Grau, Lester W., ed., *The Bear Went Over the Mountain: Soviet Tactics in Afghanistan* (London: Routledge, 2005).

——'The Battle for Hill 3234: Last Ditch Defense in the Mountains of Afghanistan' *Journal of Slavic Military Studies*, Vol. 24, 2011.

——'Breaking Contact without leaving Chaos: The Soviet withdrawal from Afghanistan' *Journal of Slavic Military Studies*, Vol. 20, No. 2 (2007).

——and Jalali, Ahmad Ali, 'Forbidden Cross-border Vendetta: Spetsnaz strike into Pakistan during the Soviet-Afghan War', *Journal of Slavic Military Studies*, Vol. 18, Issue 4 (2005).

Gress, Michael A., and Lester W. Grau, eds, *Russian General Staff: The Soviet–Afghan War: How a Superpower Fought and Lost* (Lawrence, KA: University Press of Kansas, 2002).

Gromov, Boris, and Rogozin, Dmitry, 'Russian Advice on Afghanistan' *New York Times*, 12 January 2010.

Harper, Lamberton John, *The Cold War* (Oxford: Oxford University Press, 2011).

Haslam, Jonathan, *Russia's Cold War: From the October Revolution to the Fall of the Wall* (New Haven: Yale University Press, 2011).

Hoffman, David E., *The Dead Hand: Reagan, Gorbachev and the Untold Story of the Cold War Arms Race* (London: Icon Books, 2011).

Kalinovsky, Artemy M., *A Long Goodbye: The Soviet Withdrawal from Afghanistan* (Cambridge, MA: Harvard University Press, 2011).

Kengor, Paul, *The Crusader: Ronald Reagan and the Fall of Communism* (New York: HarperCollins, 2006).

Kessler, Ronald, *Moscow Station: How the KGB Penetrated the American Embassy* (New York: Scribner's, 1989).

Koehler, John O., *Stasi: The Untold Story of the East German Secret Police* (Boulder: Westview, 1999).

Kuperman, Alan J., 'The Stinger Missile and US Intervention in Afghanistan', *Political Science Quarterly*, Vol. 114, No. 2 (Summer 1999).

Leffler, Melvyn P., and Westad, Odd Arne, eds, *The Cambridge History of the Cold War*, Vol. 3 (Cambridge: Cambridge University Press, 2010).

Liakhovskii, Alexander Antonovich, *Inside the Soviet Invasion of Afghanistan and the Seizure of Kabul, December 1979* (Washington, DC: Cold War International History Project, 2007), Working Paper No. 51.

Mitrokhin, Vasili, *The KGB in Afghanistan* (Washington, DC: Cold War International History Project, 2009), Working Paper No. 40.

MacEachin, Douglas, *Predicting the Soviet Invasion of Afghanistan: The Intelligence Community's Record* (Washington, DC: CIA, 2002).

Paarlberg, Robert L., 'Lessons of the grain embargo', *Foreign Affairs*, Vol. 59, No. 1 (Fall 1980).

Paramonov, Vladimir, and Stolpovski, Oleg, *Chinese Security Interests in Central Asia* (Defence Academy of the UK: Advanced Research Assessment Group, 2008).

Persico, Joseph E., *Casey: The Lives and Secrets of William J. Casey: From the OSS to the CIA* (New York: Viking, 1990).

Rashid, Ahmed, *Taliban: Militant Islam, Oil and Fundamentalism in Central Asia* (New Haven: Yale University Press, 2001).

Reagan, Ronald, *An American Life* (New York: Simon & Schuster, 1990).

—— *The Reagan Diaries* (New York: Harper Collins, 2007).

Risen, James, 'Russians Are Back In Afghanistan' *New York Times*, 27 July 1998.

Robertson, W. G., and Yates, L. A., (eds), *Block by Block: The Challenges of Urban Operations* (Fort Leavenworth, KA: US Army Command and General Staff Press, 2003).

Rubin, Barnett R., *The Fragmentation of Afghanistan* (New Haven: Yale University Press, 2002).

Shichor, Yitzhak, 'Fact and Fiction: A Chinese Documentary on Eastern Turkestan Terrorism', *China and Eurasia Forum Quarterly*, Vol. 4, No. 2 (2006).

Steele, Jonathan, *Ghosts of Afghanistan: The Haunted Battleground* (London: Portobello Books, 2011).

Tanner, Stephen, *Afghanistan: A Military History from Alexander the Great to the Fall of the Taliban* (Cambridge, MA: Da Capo Press, 2002).

Thatcher, Margaret, *The Downing Street Years* (London: HarperCollins, 1993).

'The CIA's Intervention in Afghanistan: Interview with Zbigniew Brzezinski', *Le Nouvel Observateur*, 15–21 January 1998, available at <http://www.globalresearch.ca/articles/BRZ110A.html>.

'The 3 A.M. Phone Call: False Warnings of Soviet Missile Attacks during 1979–80 Led to Alert Actions for U.S. Strategic Forces', 1 March 2012, available at <http://www.gwu.edu/~nsarchiv/nukevault/ebb371/index.htm>.

Tomsen, Peter, *The Wars of Afghanistan: Messianic Terrorism, Tribal Conflicts, and the Failures of Great Powers* (New York: Public Affairs, 2011).

Urban, Mark, *UK Eyes Alpha: The Inside Story of British Intelligence* (London: Faber & Faber, 1997).

Vance, Cyrus, *Hard Choices: Critical Years in America's Foreign Policy* (New York: Simon & Schuster, 1983).

Volkogonov, Dmitri, *Autopsy for an Empire: The Seven Leaders Who Built the Soviet Regime* (New York: Shimon & Schuster, 1998).

Weiner, Tim, *Legacy of Ashes: The History of the CIA* (London: Penguin, 2008).

West, Nigel, *The Third Secret: The CIA, Solidarity and the KGB's Plot to Kill the Pope* (London: HarperCollins, 2001).

Westad, Odd Arne, 'Concerning the situation in "A": new Russian evidence on the Soviet intervention in Afghanistan', *Cold War International History Bulletin*, Nos 8–9 (Winter 1996–97).

Wishnick, Elizabeth, *Mending Fences: The Evolution of Moscow's China Policy from Brezhnev to Yeltsin* (Seattle, WA: Washington University Press, 2001).

——'Sino-Soviet Tensions, 1980: Two Russian Documents', *Cold War International History Project Bulletin*, Nos 6–7, (Winter 1995/1996).

Withington, Thomas, 'The early anti-Taliban team', *Bulletin of the Atomic Scientists*, November/December 2001.

Woodward, Bob, *Veil: The Secret Wars of the CIA, 1981–1987* (New York: Simon & Schuster, 1987).

Yousaf, Mohammad, and Adkin, Mark, *Afghanistan: The Bear Trap: The Defeat of a Superpower* (London: Pen & Sword, 1992).

INDEX

CPSIA information can be obtained
at www.ICGtesting.com
Printed in the USA
LVHW080326260623
750773LV00008B/315